THE IDEA OF THE NOVEL IN EUROPE, 1600–1800

THE GOTHAM LIBRARY
OF THE NEW YORK UNIVERSITY PRESS

The Gotham Library is a series of original works and critical studies published in paperback primarily for student use. The Gotham hardcover edition is primarily for use by libraries and the general reader. Devoted to significant works and major authors and to literary topics of enduring importance, Gotham Library texts offer the best in literature and criticism.

Comparative and Foreign Language Literature:
Robert J. Clements, Editor
Comparative and English Language Literature:
James W. Tuttleton, Editor

The Idea of the Novel in Europe, 1600–1800

IOAN WILLIAMS

New York · New York University Press · 1979

Library of Congress Catalog Card Number: 78-78112

Williams, Ioan
   The idea of the novel in Europe, 1600–1800.
   1. Fiction—17th century—History and criticism
   2. Fiction—18th century—History and criticism
   I. Title
   809.3'3   PN3491

   ISBN 0-8147-9187-5 Cloth
         0-8147-9188-3 Paper

Printed in Great Britain

I Rieni Heledd

Contents

Preface

The Idea of the Novel is neither history nor polemic though it shares some of the qualities of both. It is designed to add to, and partly to correct, existing views of the novel's development during the period from 1600 to 1800, by demonstration rather than by argument. There are strong tendencies in historical accounts of the novel either to expand the concept beyond any usefulness as a critical term or to define it too narrowly, linking its appearance too closely to specific social and cultural contexts. It is often assumed that the novel developed first in eighteenth-century England, that its rise was linked to the process by which distinctively middle-class attitudes and circumstances developed and that one of its essential qualities is the realistic or critical spirit associated with them. It is often spoken of as an anti-romantic form, historically later than romance, which embodies the attitudes of previously dominant, aristocratic, classes. To some extent, of course, this view has sound historical basis, nowhere more convincingly presented than in Ian Watt's justly celebrated *Rise of the Novel* (1958), but it seems to me distorted and a serious danger in so far as it is often made the basis or the excuse for critical judgements of individual novels and pronouncements about the future of the form.

Of course the novel did go through a revolutionary phase of development during the eighteenth century, particularly in England, a development which prepared for and even anticipated what happened in the following century, when it became the dominant literary form throughout Europe. What happened was essentially a change of focus, which brought the novel closer to the texture of individual and social experience and widened its range to include new areas of both. I want to suggest, however, that this change did not amount to the development of a new literary form but rather the evolution of an existing one, and that the development of the novel through the previous two hundred years in Europe as a whole may be seen as continuous though irregular.

In effect, though it is not part of my primary purpose to do so, my thesis challenges conventional assumptions about the connection between the rise of the middle classes and the rise of the novel. This is not because I doubt the existence of a causal relationship, or series of relationships, but rather because I feel that the whole business is a great deal more complex than it is often assumed to be. The key to understanding this aspect of history seems to me to lie with Lucien Goldman rather than Ian Watt. What we need to understand is the relationship between the framework of values and experiences embodied in individual literary works and the multifarious, overlapping systems and structures of value and experience in contemporary life. Class, as Goldman has demonstrated beyond dispute, is at all times the most fundamentally important of these structures and perhaps he is right in maintaining the traditional Marxist viewpoint that it is to class and its underlying economic basis that we will have final resort in our attempt to understand literature. But in the first instance, in so far as we are interested in the particular dimension of literature, we must start with the context in which social and cultural values are transformed, reflected, or distorted, in individual novels. One of the major factors which affects this process is the group of ideas, techniques and standards associated with particular genres. This group, different in its constituents from time to time, or from place to place, is yet sufficiently clear in its central principles to be identifiable as such, and it is this which I refer to when I use the phrase 'The Idea of the Novel'. In itself it comprises an important structure within which social and moral values undergo transformation to become the constituent parts of literary works. Like any other group of ideas, or any other 'structure', of course, it lacks material embodiment except that which it finds in individual novels. To study it, and so to understand the way in which these individual novels have historically been related and remain so, we must move to and fro between them and from them to the circumstances in which they acquired their particular being. It is perhaps not unreasonable to describe this process as imitating the dialectic which Marxist critics discover in the process by which all human activity takes place.

This is why, although the book rests on certain assumptions as to the nature of the novel as a literary form, I have chosen not to argue them out in the text. It seems to me that an objective definition of the novel is impossible, except in the simplest and most general terms. On the other hand, of course, my own particular idea of the novel has dictated the method of study and the selection of texts, so it is perhaps necessary to say that I regard the novel as a distinctively modern, that is, a post-Renaissance form, which came into being at the point when consciousness of the individual as an end in himself and not merely as part of a larger social, political or metaphysical entity, introduced a new element into European thought. From that point on it became possible for fiction to be used in a new way—that is, in order to provide a dimension in which the relations between individual and social interests could be explored and adjusted *directly* and in concrete detail.

At this point Cervantes published *Don Quixote* and the history of the novel began. Its subsequent development depended on particular social and cultural conditions. The fact that it was possible to think of the individual life as an end in itself, requiring interpretation in its own terms, did not necessarily mean that society as a whole in any Western European country proceeded to do it. On the contrary, although the period 1600–1800 reflects a constantly increasing awareness of individual experience as such, it also records the fact that for a long time European society, for varying social and intellectual reasons, refused to adjust its social and intellectual structures to match that increasing pressure. The novel, if it is to flourish in the hands of many rather than few, and come close to the centre of cultural activity, demands certain conditions. Above all it requires that there be a certain consonance between the moral and social values that writers of a given society wish to project within it and the actual forms of life in that society. This consonance is particularly marked in the nineteenth century, when the values embodied in literary culture in France and England especially were capable of being presented as social or psychological realities. This of course we may attribute to the dominance of a group of classes committed to the idea of reconciling personal experience with social experience. Individual writers may well have argued that a given society was corrupt because that reconciliation could not take place, but it remained conceivable in artistic and psychological terms. The novelist continued to live himself in a world fundamentally similar to that of the novel!

The enormous success of the novel in the nineteenth century has been the primary factor which has distorted our view of its history during the whole period from 1600, making it difficult not to accept the application of crude evolutionary terms. The explosive development of ideas in what we call the Romantic period, which preceded and prepared for the achievement of the nineteenth-century novelists, represents a sudden increase in the speed by which ideas and combinations of ideas present throughout the post-Renaissance period were brought together and developed, but this is in no sense a culmination. In a very real sense we still live in the shadow of the Renaissance, and it is interesting to see that the position of the novel is now much closer to that which it occupied in the middle years of the eighteenth century than the middle years of the nineteenth. Though it would take me too far from my subject even to suggest it, it could be that the middle of the present century shows characteristics similar to those of the period between 1600 and 1800. The most important consideration during those years was that although the novel remained constantly a possibility and was constantly realising itself in the hands of individual writers, conditions as a whole were unfavourable to its consistent development. In many different ways, which it is the business of the book to suggest, circumstances made it difficult for writers to project a criticism of the world in which they lived primarily by representing actual forms of experience. Consequently there was no consistently strong pressure which urged towards the choice of the novel as a literary form, and when it did present itself to the individual there was a strong likelihood that the encounter would not be successful.

The method of *The Idea of the Novel* has been dictated by the way in which these conditions differ from place to place at various times during the period. In the beginning the emphasis falls on Cervantes as an isolated figure, then moves to the background of the novel in France, to literary theory, then to individual works in relation to each other in the years from 1715 to 1760, and eventually to the synoptic approach of the last chapters, which attempt to relate development and lack of develop-ment in the transitional period from 1760 to 1800. The area is vast and the approach necessarily selective. I have tried to focus on individual novels, the source and embodiment of any 'Idea'. As in a previous book, *The Realist Novel in England*, I have tried to give a sketch rather than a definition, and one which I hope will be confirmed in its outlines by subsequent studies.

Throughout the book I have tried to present a readable text, though I have not ventured to modernise or otherwise change the spelling, punctuation or presentation of the texts I have used. Major quotations from languages other than English are followed in the text by a translation, which perhaps tends to err on the side of the literal rendering: minor quotations are translated in the text but the originals are given in footnotes. Quotations from German authors are given only in English translation because that is how I have read them myself. In each case a full reference to the edition used is given on the first occasion and thereafter in abbreviation.

I would like to mention my gratitude to the University of Warwick, whose generosity in the matter of sabbatical leave made it easier for me to write this book, and to the University College of Aberystwyth, which gave me refuge while I finished it.

A final point: the book is written in English rather than in Welsh partly because it reflects a debate which takes place between all the countries to whose literature it refers and because English is in some measure its common medium, but largely because English is at present the only language of the majority of my countrymen. Nevertheless I think of it primarily as a contribution to Welsh criticism. *The Idea of the Novel* attempts to combine respect for the particularity of times, places and literary works with a recognition of the shaping forces at work in distinctive cultural environments and linguistic contexts. It seems to me that such an attempt, disregarding the degree of its competence, relates very directly to the cultural condition of my own country and in large measure reflects its influence.

Lledrod, 1950   IOAN WILLIAMS

1 The Novel as Romance: Cervantes' *Don Quixote*

Historians of the novel tend to relate the appearance of the two separate volumes of *Don Quixote* (1605 and 1615) to the development in Spain and in Europe as a whole of the picaresque tale. Chronologically this is tempting. The anonymous *Lazarillo de Tormes* appeared as early as 1554 but was followed by Mateo Alemán's *Guzmán de Alfarache* (1599–1604) in the years immediately before the appearance of *Don Quixote I* and by Quevedo's *La Vida del Buscón* in 1626. In so far as there was a picaresque movement, Cervantes must have been affected by it, and its influence is certainly clear in those of his *Novelas Ejemplares* (1613) which depict events in the lower levels of society. The relationship, however, is no closer than this. In the first place it is important to remember that Cervantes drew much of the inspiration for his own realism, in common with the picaresque authors, from medieval sources, and especially from works like the *Tragicomedia de Calixto y Melibea* (1499–1502). Secondly, it is important to remember that Cervantes became a novelist not because he shared the reductive realism of the picaresque writers or the medieval moralists, but because he was an idealist. In his case awareness of material reality and of the elements which reduce human aspirations and human dignity made up a secondary element in his sensibility. Without that secondary element Cervantes could never have become a novelist, but the primary impulse which shaped his *Don Quixote* came from elsewhere.

Around 1600 the cruder, sharper, rationalism of Quevedo was more modern that the humanistic attitude of Cervantes. But Cervantes' conservatism was an important factor in his ability to transform older forms of prose fiction into the novel without taking the further step towards modernism which would have impoverished his work. For other writers of the period modern ways of thinking meant the abandonment of the whole system of idealism centred around the neo-Platonic ideas of love as enshrined in Renaissance romance and pastoral, just at the moment when they had reached their fullest development. Cervantes was able to belong to both worlds and as a result he came to create a world of his own. In *Don Quixote* he works within the same framework of sensibility as in his pastoral *Galatea* (1585) and his Heliodoran romance *Persiles y Sigismunda* (1617). This framework is fundamentally similar to that shared by his contemporaries in France and England, Honoré d'Urfé and Sir Philip Sidney. For all three, in whose hands romance takes on new forms, the central factor in the human situation is love, the mainspring of all things, 'the movement which bears all finite things towards God',[1] and an idealist mode of literature the only means of expressing truth directly. But of course, both d'Urfé and Sidney were social and cultural aristocrats.[2] Cervantes shared with Shakespeare a breadth of vision, a sense of the nation as a whole and enough of the modern spirit to bring about a shift in his whole perspective. Behind *Don Quixote* there are several shadowy figures — the knights of *Amadis* and *Tirante lo Blanc*, the impoverished hidalgo from *Lazarillo de Tormes*, the peasant hero of medieval folklore and the nameless villeins who make up the mobs and armies of chronicle and romance. But in the forefront of the novel are two characters who are uniquely alive because they can react to one another and to circumstances, overflowing the categories which produced them and through this very flexibility reinforcing the central statement of the whole novel.

What transformed the author of *Galatea* into the creator of Don Quixote and Sancho Panza was the practical sense that he shared with Shakespeare. As it grew stronger in his later years it obliged him to question the relationship between the concepts of romance and the human content which they might be supposed to have. And this questioning led him not to the realism of the picaresque writers but rather to a reinforced awareness of the reality of concepts. From then on his major work focused on the constant interchange which takes place in experience between conceptual factors and the demands and impulses arising from human nature. The basic tension between Don

[1] '. . . le mouvement qui porte tout le fini vers Dieu.' A. Adam, *Histoire de la Littérature Française au xviiᵉ Siècle*, I (1962), p. 7.

[2] Honoré d'Urfé (1567–1625), related to the Ducal house of Savoy. Soldier, dramatist and moralist, his pastoral romance, *L'Astrée*, appeared in parts between 1607 and 1627. Sir Philip Sidney (1554–86), like d'Urfé, a soldier, and like him too, killed in action, was nephew to the Earl of Leicester. His *Arcadia* appeared in different versions in 1590 and 1598.

Quixote and Sancho derives from the fact that they represent different attitudes to human experience. One is an idealist, the other a realist, one stressing the importance of the conceptual as the only reality, the other preoccupied with physical appetites. But of course they demonstrate in their relationship, and even in their own characters, the central fact that conceptual and material elements exist only in terms of one another. And their relationship is the frame through which we are introduced to a whole network of narrative and characterisation, a complex analysis of human nature within the terms of Renaissance romance literature.

It is often assumed that it was from the conflict between these attitudes to life, and particularly from the imposition of a questioning, reductive, anti-idealist, spirit on older, romance or idealist standards, that the novel arose, and consequently, that the supremacy of the reductive element is an essential quality of the novel as a literary form. It is certainly true that the reductive spirit is the most common agent in the process by which a story becomes a novel, but the other, shaping, conceptual, factor which gives meaning to experience and form to fiction, the spirit more exclusively developed in romance, is at least equally essential. And farther than this, it is historically precedent over the realist element. What happened in Cervantes' fiction was not the imposition of a realist impulse on romance material, leading to the development of a new mode. Rather the realist impulse, not historically new in itself but inherited from earlier literature, came together for the first time with a spirit recently developed in isolation—the ambitiously humanistic impulse of Renaissance romance and pastoral. Without *this*, *Don Quixote* was simply inconceivable. The impulse to write the book in the first place, to satirise the chivalric romance, came not in the form of a simple anti-romantic, anti-idealist impulse, but rather in the form of a desire to impose on the shapeless body of chivalric romance the criteria, consistency and form of Renaissance fiction. The satiric and reductive impulse for Cervantes always remains within a framework which is conceptual and idealist.

This is nowhere more apparent than in the *Novelas Ejemplares* (1613), where realist and idealist elements are kept in conscious and elaborate balance throughout, and this important volume of tales makes the best possible introduction to *Don Quixote* itself. One tale in particular, however, makes Cervantes' position particularly clear, partly because it treats a theme which is commonly the means of asserting a reductive view of human character, and partly because it exists in more than one version.

This is the seventh in his series of thirteen tales, 'El Celoso Ex-tremeñno', the central situation of which Cervantes treated first in the early *entrémes* (one-act farce) entitled *El Viejo Celoso*. Here we have the standard treatment of the old man married to a young girl who succeeds in cuckolding him in spite of all his precautions. It ends with her throwing water in his face while her lover escapes and with the neighbours brought in to witness her exculpation. As it took shape in the exemplary novel, for which we have a manuscript version dating from around 1606,[3] the story is completely different in tone and emphasis. Not surprisingly, in the prose fiction the emphasis is shifted from action to character. Cervantes presents the story in the first place through the character of the husband, and we come to the central situation, his imprisoning a young wife in a house with double doors and no windows, guarded by a eunuch porter, only after we have learnt his background and character, the outline of his life and reasons for his marriage. The central character of the wife is lightly sketched. The third protagonist, the would-be lover, is given more detailed treatment, as the primary actor in the whole narrative. The central action predict-ably concerns the process by which the young man obtains an entrance, persuading the negro porter that he can teach him to play the guitar, introducing a soporific ointment into the house which the women are encouraged to use on the husband so as to enable them to take pleasure in his singing undisturbed. An important factor is the lust of the duenna who hopes to make the seduction of the mistress of the house a means of satisfying herself. The catastrophe occurs when the husband wakes unexpectedly, comes across the young man and his wife asleep in each other's arms, retires to his bed and dies of grief, forgiving his wife and urging her in his will to marry the young man. In comic versions of this theme the standard reaction to the assertion of nature against restraint is anger and reconciliation. Here instead we have shock and grief, an attempt on the part of the husband at acceptance which his own nature is unable to sustain. The wife's response is to refuse to marry her lover and to go into a nunnery. So, rather than leaving us with a sense of the essential healthiness and reasonableness of the basic impulses of human nature, Cervantes' story is problematic. It leaves us instead with a sense that the ultimate importance of concepts in human character is at least as great as the jealousy in the mind of the husband. Carrizales, the jealous husband, is capable of a relationship with his wife only within the framework of his own ideas—even though he accepts her adultery intellectually, he is quite incapable of adjusting to

[3] See A. Castro, *Hacia Cervantes*, 3rd ed. (Madrid, 1967).

it emotionally.

This point is made far more forcibly in the published version of the story which appeared in 1613. Here Cervantes introduced one substantial change which greatly developed the complexity of the tale. That is, he omitted the adultery, leaving Leonora victorious over her lover:

> Pero, con todo esto, el valor de Leonora fué tal, que en el tiempo que más le convenía, le mostró contra las fuerzas villanas de su astuto engañador, pues no fueron bastantes a vencerla, y él se cansó en balde, y ella quedó vencedora, y entrambos dormidos.

> But with all this, the fortitude of Leonora was such that in the time when it was most needed it showed itself against the villainous efforts of her astute deceiver since they were not sufficient to defeat her; and he tired himself in vain, and she remained victorious, and both slept.

> *Novelas Ejemplares*, Clásicos Castellanos II (1969), p. 158

In this case, what should we make of the husband's grief and consequent death? In the first version we attribute it to the shock of discovering the reality of the situation, that nature asserts itself against restraints. But in this case, nature has not so asserted itself. Leonora actually is chaste, in spite of temptation, and consequently Carrizales' death is not the result of a realisation of reality, but rather a failure to allow for the ability of the conceptual element in her character to prevail against the instinctive, sexual motivation. The alteration has considerable effect in strengthening our awareness of Cervantes' own faith in this element, but more important than this, it throws the power of the concept which works on Carrizales' mind into high relief. The total effect of the whole story is closely related to that of 'El Curioso Impertinente' in *Don Quixote*, and indeed to that whole novel. That is, it forces us to revise our crude idea of the relationship between conflicting elements in human nature. Most important, however, it goes beyond comedy and posits a question about the nature of reality itself as an interrelationship between those different elements.

Don Quixote does this, of course, much more thoroughly than any single story could have done, not only because of its greater length and complexity but also because it is designed to work out much more insistently issues which are held in suspension in the exemplary novels as a whole. In both works Cervantes' thought moves in the same direction. From the crude physical confrontation between ideal and reality which begins *Don Quixote* and persists throughout it, Cervantes moves towards complexity in the first instance through the introduction of Sancho Panza. Then he introduces and gradually gives more and more prominence to the intrigue regarding Cardenio, Dorotea, Fernando and Luscinda, a love-intrigue borrowed from Montemayor's *Diana* (1559) and strikingly close to the situation Shakespeare develops from the same source in *A Midsummer-Night's Dream*. The interweaving of these two sources of action—the journey of the two heroes and the love-intrigue—is central to *Don Quixote*, having the effect of moving the action back into a romance world whose values and meanings are clear. At the same time the texture of the novel introduces a third factor. The structural frame of the journey and the intrigue does not account for the great number of conversations, encounters, inserted stories and narratives which make up the stuff of Cervantes' narrative. The principle of organisation of the book is as arbitrary as that of any Renaissance romance. In fact *Don Quixote is* a romance, to all intents and purposes, putting forward by means of fiction and discourse an elaborate analysis of life as a whole in terms common to romantic fictions of the day. It is also a novel though, because the arbitrary analysis of romance is dramatised in an unprecedented way. It is an analysis of life as a whole, made in its own terms. This is achieved in two ways. Firstly, through his skilful manipulation of the narrative process and our awareness of it, Cervantes fixes the debate concerning the nature of experience within our own present consciousness. Secondly, by allowing his characterisation of Don Quixote and Sancho to swell to the proportions of humour, giving them independence and instability, making them a law to themselves, Cervantes creates a frame within which the conceptualisation which his other narrative material demands is subject to continual modification and questioning.

This, of course, is primarily a description of his method in *Don Quixote I*, published in 1605. Tone and technique, and even subject matter, are different in *Don Quixote II* (1615). In the later volume Cervantes was answering a challenge from the modern spirit, in the person of Avellaneda, but his answer took the form of a reassertion of his basic principles, so that in a very important way the two separately published novels make up a unity. By 1615 the lightness, ease and plentiful elaboration have given way to a more rational, consistent mode of organisation, and the romance techniques are muted. But of course, Don Quixote and Sancho remain as humorous as ever and Cervantes' narrative mode is unchanged, itself an essential part of his sensibility and the primary factor which made it possible for him to initiate the development of the novel as a form of narrative art.

EL INGENIOSO HIDALGO . . . (1605)

As originally published, the first part of *Don Quixote* was divided into four books, containing respectively Chapters 1–8, 9–14, 15–27, and 28–52. The first book includes the first sally of Don Quixote alone, his knighting by the innkeeper, his saving the boy Andrés from a beating, confrontation with the merchants, carrying home, the scrutiny of the library, his second sally with Sancho, the episode with the windmills. It ends half-way through the conflict with the irascible Biscayan.

In fact this book gives a thorough treatment of the satiric, anti-chivalric theme, and it is no coincidence that it is through one of the incidents related here—the encounter with the windmills—that *Don Quixote* is most widely remembered. Already at this point, however, Cervantes develops the narrative so as to introduce elements which are quite incapable of being contained within a simplistic, satiric interpretation, or even the subtler reading in terms of 'illusion and reality'. The central incident here is the scrutiny and destruction of Don Quixote's library, which should act as a warning to the reader. The episode is ambiguous. The priest, the barber and the housekeeper are supposed to be scrutinising the books with a view to their destruction on the basis of the fact that they have turned Don Quixote's head. The only one of the three who is wholehearted in this approach, however, is the house-keeper, whose ignorant zeal makes all books appear equally pernicious, whether they touch on chivalry or not. The priest and the barber condemn some and save others according to whether they are good or not. So *Tirante lo Blanc* is approved because it is realistic, others are destroyed because they lack verisimilitude. This is ironic because the very fact that they are good is likely to have made them more dangerous to Don Quixote. A second source of irony, of course, lies in the fact that when they are destroyed and the library blocked up this circumstance is turned by Don Quixote into new food for his imaginings. In fact the whole book-burning incident is turned into a scrutiny of recent litera-ture, a means of awarding praise or blame according to certain princi-ples of consistency and verisimilitude which are of great importance in the novel and which Cervantes introduces here as a primary means of modifying our assessment of the hero's crazy attempt to turn himself into a knight errant. Don Quixote's madness, in fact, does not consist in the fact that he tries to realise a concept in his own person but rather in a lack of proportion in his attitude to the concept. This in turn stems from the absence of the qualities of consistency and order which are essential parts of all good literature, and of life. But not only Don Quixote and the authors of chivalrous romances are at fault in this particular. The housekeeper herself is not beyond reproach, and characters like the Biscayan are every bit as bad as the Don himself.

The episode of the windmills, Don Quixote and Sancho's first mutual adventure, defines their positions and begins to develop the rivalry between them. This incident, so well known, even among those who have never come closer to the novel itself than a souvenir shop, symbolises the Quixotic attack on reality which is condemned to failure before it begins. But in the episode which follows, which includes the encounter with the irascible Biscayan who challenges Don Quixote, the narrative develops in an unexpected direction. The behaviour of the Biscayan is the first indication that the world of Don Quixote is not so far isolated from the world in which other people live. The anger, pride and ignorance of the Biscayan not only break through the restraints provided by common sense, but they also break through the chivalric code and anger Don Quixote. The result is a mock-heroic combat which is actually very serious and also shocking to the reader who has already settled the hero within a private world of madness, failing to appreciate the fact that there is a large dimension of madness to which he has access in common with the sane.

At this point Cervantes breaks off the first book and introduces his pseudo-author, Cide Hamete Benengeli, claiming that the history of Don Quixote is actually the reaction by him of an account provided by the sages of La Mancha. Presumably, however, he did not expect us to forget that in the discussion of Don Quixote's library the priest and the barber had been discussing books published as recently as 1587, eighteen years before the date of publication of Cide Hamete's history. Bearing this in mind, we must know that his claims regarding the historicity of the fiction cannot be strictly true and that we are being deliberately mystified regarding its composition at three removes. Cervantes' intention in this, of course, is to direct our attention to our own situation as readers and so to comment indirectly on the issues raised by the priest and the barber's literary discussion. Not only is what he is claiming at this point untrue; it is impossible. But we are actually uninterested in the question of truthfulness. We still want to continue, careless of exactitude, to find out what is going to happen to Don Quixote. And when we do find out we are again surprised, our confidence in externally applied criteria severely shaken. It is not the weak and mentally unstable old man who loses, but the strong and angry Biscayan. Reality has not impinged on Don Quixote's dream as we expected it to; and indeed, as we are reading, increasingly dependent on event rather than preconception, reality itself has begun to change.

In Book II as a whole the relationship between Don Quixote and Sancho is considerably developed through the discussion of the theory of knight errantry and their comments on what happens to them. A good deal of narrative material is now introduced, however, which has its own focus and which begins to create a new background for their adventures. First of all we encounter the goatherds and hear Don Quixote's discourse on the Golden Age, then hear Vivaldo's attack on knight errantry, Crysostomo's poetry and Marcela's vindication of her own conduct. The order and the substance of these incidents are important. Don Quixote's discourse is a regular Renaissance set-piece which is entirely consistent in itself and reminds us that literature may have its own values independent of any relationship with historical reality. The goatherds decide after hearing it that Don Quixote is insane but partly as a result of their reaction we see that it does function as a reasonable reaction to the circumstances, though they fail to recognise it as a reasonable description. This is not Arcadia, perhaps, but here is a knight errant receiving charity and hospitality, including entertainment and simple food, from shepherds!

Crysostomo's story is very important because it is the first introduction of love into the action of the novel, except in so far as it is contained in Don Quixote's relationship with his Dulcinea. Inset into Crysostomo's story is the debate between Vivaldo and Don Quixote about knight errantry, which raises the question of the relationship between intellectual conceptualisation and reality. Vivaldo's argument is a sophisticated and reasonable assertion of the principle underlying Sancho's viewpoint. Don Quixote finds this surprisingly easy to avoid in terms of their dignified and logical discussion. The discussion as a whole throws light directly on to the action regarding the relationship between Crysostomo and Marcela, which in turn illuminates the debate.

In the first instance the mere fact that Crysostomo has died from unrequited love gives a shock to the reader's prejudices and greatly strengthens his understanding of the role of conceptualisation in human life. This is developed by means of the debate about love. Crysostomo has died accusing Marcela of cruelty. Her defence brings to light a basic difficulty in Renaissance theories of love. The lover is drawn in spite of himself to love the beautiful object because of the aspiration of his whole nature towards good, of which beauty is one form. But if the lover is so attracted, must the attraction be mutual? And if it is not, does not love, the creator of harmony, thereby become the creator of disharmony? Marcela puts her case energetically and carries conviction:

> Yo conozco, con el natural entendimiento que Dios me he dado, que todo lo hermoso es amable; mas no alcanzo que, por razón de ser amado, esté obligado lo que es amado por hermoso a amar a quien le ama. Y más, que podría acontecer que el amador de lo hermoso fuese feo, y siendo lo feo digno de ser aborrecido, cae muy mal el decir: 'Quiérote por hermosa; hasme de amar aunque sea feo.' Pero, puesto caso que corran igualmente las hermosuras, no por eso han de correr iguales los deseos, que no todas las hermosuras enamoran; que algunas alegran la vista y no rinden la voluntad . . .

> I know, by the understanding which God has given me, that whatever is beautiful is amiable; but it does not follow that the object beloved for its beauty is obliged to return love for love. Besides, it may happen that the lover is ugly, and as the ugly is worthy of being hated it ill befits him to say: 'I love you because you are beautiful, love me although I am ugly.' But supposing beauty to be equal, it does not follow that inclinations should be equal; for all beauty does not inspire love; some please the sight without capturing the will . . .
>
> *Don Quixote* I, xiv; ed. M. de Riquer (1968), p. 130

We can see that Marcela would have been a very difficult person to dispute with, and when she has finished speaking we have a good deal more sympathy with the soft-hearted Crysostomo, who seems to have taken the only course open to him after falling in love with her. It is interesting that in their case the male and female principles seem to have become confused. Her idea of sylvan chastity is positively heroic in its ferocity; his despair implies a feminine tenderness of nature. Their history tells us a good deal about love, but something more about character, and more still about the way in which human reaction and motivation combine factors deriving from the intellect with impulses arising from within the personality. Crysostomo and Marcela are both, in their different ways, after all, rather more than a little mad, without losing control of their ability to write poetry or present reasoned discourse. Both play literary games with quite shocking seriousness, with a degree of fixed passionateness which reminds us quite how gentle is Don Quixote's military delusion.

Book III develops a complex skein of action while still following out the confrontation between Don Quixote's view of reality and Sancho Panza's, though there is an increasing tendency for these views to merge. There are three central events which are all climactic in different ways. These are the capture of Mambrino's helmet, the freeing of the galley slaves and the confrontation with Cardenio in the Sierra Morena. The book opens, however, with an incident which has the dual purpose of humiliating the two heroes and of further modifying our ideas about love as they had been developed in the previous book. The problem arises through the introduction of sex when Rocinante pays attention to the mares of the Yanguesan carriers and ends with a beating for Don Quixote and Sancho. This theme is further developed during Don Quixote's confrontation with Maritornes, at the inn which he mistakes for a castle. Once again here he suffers as a result of someone else's sexual desires. A fitting punishment for someone who so coyly flirts with powerful sexual impulses; and an appropriate comment on the action of a character whose motivation is wholly conceptual, lacking the passionate, instinctive element we had seen in the episode with Crysostomo and Marcela.

Two further incidents involving the balsam of Fierabras and Sancho's blanket-tossing fix us firmly in confident knowledge of what reality is, in spite of Don Quixote's appeal to enchantment to explain his own impotence. But then the incident of Mambrino's helmet, stolen from a barber in the form of a brass basin, comes to introduce a further element of complexity. Mambrino's helmet seems of less importance at this stage than it is, of course, because we are not yet aware that the confusion over identity and function is capable of spreading quite so disastrously as it later does at the inn. The freeing of the galley slaves is much more obviously climactic because it brings closer the confrontation with the powers of the State which we have been expecting all along. The introduction of the Holy Brotherhood at the inn, directly resulting from this incident, actually does initiate the process which brings the novel to an end, though nothing happens immediately. Even then, however, the effect of what we had feared was a final commitment to madness is very muted, and here our attention is drawn away from the physical dimension of the situation by Cervantes' re-introduction of aesthetic debate. This is indirect, coming as a result of Sancho's incoherent story during the night which precedes the discovery of the fulling-mills. Basically the same point is made here as emerged when Cervantes stopped his narrative during the fight between Don Quixote and the Biscayan. Sancho's story is absurd and incoherent, but it is also compelling. To get to the end we would have to suffer the interminable process of ferrying three hundred goats one by one and though this may be too much for our patience, as it is for Don Quixote himself, we are still involved in the narrative. The question is, what light does our involvement with this story throw on the one that we are reading? Questions like this are brought to our attention yet again during the episode with the galley slaves when Cervantes reflects on the popularity of picaresque tales by making the notorious Ginés de Passamonte talk about writing his own autobiography.

At this point we are almost exactly mid-way through the novel, in Chapter 22, and are introduced to new material which takes up the greater part of the second half. Don Quixote decides to go mad in the Sierra Morena, in imitation of predecessors like Amadis of Gaul and Orlando. This is another absurd exercise in conceptualisation which directs our attention onto the nature of action and motivation again. Amadis went mad because he was so deeply affected by Oriana's unfairness; Orlando had a more substantial motive in jealousy because Angelica was unfaithful with a Moorish page. Don Quixote is mad in going mad whereas they were sane in going mad because they had adequate motivation within their own terms, whereas he has none except the desire to imitate literary reality. At this point, with the introduction of Cardenio into the story, we come into contact with someone who has gone mad through jealousy, disappointment and frustrated love, combined with grief and exposure. Interestingly, Cardenio does all the things his literary forbears did and which Don Quixote is also busy doing. His madness, in fact, differs from Don Quixote's only in that it is motivated by passion, though as later events teach us, this passion is to be studied against a very similar background as that provided in the debate between Crysostomo and Marcela.

Shortly after the introduction of Cardenio, while we are being entertained with Don Quixote's solemn antics and the foolish slyness of Sancho during his embassy to Dulcinea, we come into contact again with the priest and the barber, who are seeking Don Quixote, and in their company meet Dorotea, who has been deserted by her husband Fernando for Cardenio's Luscinda. These four concoct the story of the Princess Micomicona to lure Don Quixote back home, Sancho following in the hope of an earldom or an island. Cardenio, by contrast with Don Quixote, has been restored to sanity by the relief of his despair which comes through meeting Dorotea and hearing that she is actually married to Fernando. Together they arrive at the inn.

This is to be the scene of the greater part of the novel's remaining action, a scene of astonishing confrontations, coincidental meetings, explications and confusions which is bound to heighten our awareness of the book's pure fictionality. To begin with, previous debates about the relationship between fiction and reality and the nature of the reading process are picked up again when the innkeeper and his family display their own attitudes to books. Then the narrative stream is broken into by the inset story of 'El Curioso Impertinente', which gives very precise indications as to the way in which we should be reading Cervantes' account of the adventures of his knight and squire. We need to bear in mind that this is not a part of the narrative, that it represents a different fictional mode which is intended as a more direct representation of reality than Don Quixote's story. For the attractiveness of romance the *nouvelle* as Cervantes produces it here substitutes the simplicity and directness of truth. The hero, without showing any sign of mental instability, is one who reveals himself to be effectively mad because he allows an obsession with the relationship between concept and reality to destroy his whole life. Happily married to a chaste wife, enjoying the benefits of a close and loyal friendship, he instigates his friend to test his wife's chastity. Our response to this must surely be impatient and angry because Anselmo has no justification for querying whether his wife is actually chaste or merely seems chaste. This reaction changes, however, when we find that Camila and Lotario actually fall in love and begin an adulterous relationship. We must now ask the question which tormented Anselmo. How real was the chastity of Camila, and for that matter the loyalty of Lotario? Of course we feel that they were chaste and loyal and that their virtue has been undermined by the unreasonable behaviour of Anselmo, but the question still remains, especially when we notice, firstly, that the whole character of Camila changes with her decline into adultery, and secondly, that the discovery of the relationship leads directly to the death of the husband and the wife and indirectly to that of the lover-friend as well. What the story suggests is the central statement of *Don Quixote* as a novel, concerning the interpenetration of conceptual and affective elements in the human character and the necessity of one as a frame for the other.

The ending of 'El Curioso Impertinente' is followed by the arrival of Fernando and Luscinda, very much a romance event, which ends with the reconciliation of the lovers. The confrontation and debate which precede this relate back directly to the story of Crysostomo and

Marcela. At the centre here is Fernando, whose inconstancy has motivated the whole action. He is brought back to Dorotea not by any simple factor or combination of factors, but by a sort of dialectic interplay of conceptual elements, social considerations and moral reflections. Particularly important is the combination of beauty and modesty in his wife, which works on the misguided passion which has carried him away from decency and honour. The priest urges him:

> que pusiese los ojos ansimesmo en la beldad de Dorotea, y vería que pocas o ninguna se le podían igualar, cuanto más hacerle ventaja, y que juntase a su hermosura su humildad y el estremo del amor que le tenía, y, sobre todo, advirtiese que si se preciaba de caballero y de cristiano, que no podía hacer otra cosa que cumplille la palabra dada; y que, cumpliéndosela, cumpliría con Dios y satisfaría a las gentes discretas, las cuales saben y conocen que es prerrogativa de la hermosura, aunque esté en sujeto humilde, como se acompañe con la honestidad, poder levantarse e igualarse a cualquiera alteza . . . ; y cuando se cumplen las fuertes leyes del gusto, como en ello no intervenga pecado, no debe de ser culpado el que las sigue.

> that he should likewise direct his eyes to the beauty of Dorotea and would see that few or none could equal her, much less excel her, and that he should join to her beauty her humility and the extreme love which she bore him, and, above all, he should take note that if he valued himself as a gentleman and a christian, he could do nothing else than accomplish his word when given; and that, accomplishing this, he would set himself right with God and would satisfy discreet people, who know and recognise that it is the prerogative of beauty, even though in a humble subject, when it is accompanied by honesty, to be able to raise itself and equal itself with any height . . . ; and when the strong laws of appetite are satisfied, so long as no sin occurs, he who follows them ought not to be blamed.
>
> *Don Quixote* I, xxxvi, p. 378

These and other similar reasons, Cervantes tell us, acted on the gentle nature of Fernando so as to soften his temper and bring him to recognise truth. Consequently he returns to Dorotea and allows Luscinda to go back to Cardenio, thus resolving the whole situation which might well, as in the case of Crysostomo and Marcela, have ended in disaster for everyone concerned.

The next major contribution to this debate concerning the nature of love and human motivation in general comes through the Captive's story, which has a special place in the novel in so far as it is based on truth. We are prepared for this account by Don Quixote's discourse on arms and letters, which corresponds to his earlier discussion of the Golden Age. Like the earlier one, this discourse is a literary set-piece, a notable piece of sanity which displays attitudes which Cervantes himself elsewhere in his work puts forward with great seriousness. Don Quixote's central point, in fact, concerning the nobility of the soldier's profession, is borne out quite strangely by the story of the Captive. This is at once firmly anchored in contemporary reality, not least by its references to Cervantes' own adventures in Algeria, and demonstrates the truth of central Renaissance ideals. In Zoraida, the Moorish girl who leaves her home and her father to follow the Captive to Spain and a Christian life, we see the power of truth when sown like a seed in the mind, and the ability of the pure soul to recognise truth and goodness in other people. Seeing in the Captive's soldierly bearing signs of inner rectitude and true manliness, Zoraida abandons her father and trusts herself to him. Two small details make the contrast between this story and Shakespeare's *The Merchant of Venice* sharper than it would otherwise have been. Zoraida's father, though bitterly hurt by his daughter's behaviour, reacts in a way which makes us see her actions primarily as the result of spiritual aspiration; and on their way home they are robbed of the riches they bring with them, arriving poor but honest beyond reproach.

This extraordinary story is followed by events which are also surprising, though by this time the reader is quite prepared to accept the unusual as the usual, the ideal for the real. The captive is reunited with his own brother and the history of his family completed for us. Entangled with this incident is the story of Don Luis and Doña Clara, which is a story of noble and innocent love in conflict with social circumstance and parental authority. Here a contemporary social setting is the background for a confrontation which may well prove tragic unless the reason and experience of Doña Clara's father can bring it to a happier solution.

Further hectic adventures at the inn reinforce the novel's comic dimension and remind us of the fact that delusion, ignorance, selfishness or lust can all reduce the character and bring him within the forces which express themselves through physical affront and violent humiliation. The adventures at the inn, however, are finally resolved with the reassertion of social order, the harmonious settling of disputes and the reconciliation of the powers of law. So Don Quixote is subjected to a real enchantment and carried away in a cage. Once again Cervantes holds up his narrative here to continue literary discussion. In the discourse between his priest and a canon met on the road he reviews the aesthetic criteria on which his own work was based. Here rationalist, Aristotelian criteria are made to blend with an interest in variety and surprising effects and idealist elements in much the same way as they do throughout *Don Quixote*.

Two episodes remain after the canon and the priest have closed their discourse, which has given Don Quixote one final opportunity to rise to the heights of rational discourse in defence of the anti-rational. The novel's central themes continue through both to the very end of the action. The goatherd whom the party meet as they are dining in the country is just such a one as Crysostomo, on a lower level of society and passionate involvement. His story about Leandra, who abandons honourable lovers and her home for the sake of a soldier and is by him robbed and abandoned in the mountains, is a reductive parallel to the story of Zoraida. This is concluded by a conflict between the goatherd and Don Quixote, the former showing a degree of active aggression in this context which throws an ironic light on his passivity as a lover, and shows again how closely ignorance and anger can be allied to madness. Then follows the final episode in which sturdy country sense, in defence of its own safety, lays the false hero low and makes good its escape. After this final assertion of reality no further action is appropriate. The anti-climactic ending is part of the novel's whole conception. It is precisely what the canon said that a romance might be—a web of various and beautiful texture which would equally delight and instruct—a web, furthermore, through which various reductive and conceptual elements are allowed to identify themselves, to combine, separate and recombine so as to embody dramatically Cervantes' statement regarding the nature of life itself.

LA SEGUNDA PARTE . . . (1615)

Cervantes might never have written a continuation of *Don Quixote*, after waiting as long as ten years, but in 1614 there appeared the pseudonymously published 'Life and Exploits' of Don Quixote attributed to one Avellaneda, which, for one reason or another, seems to have stimulated Cervantes to bring out his own Second Part. In itself this was not unusual; any writer failing to follow up his own success was likely to find others only too willing to make up the deficiency. So there were several continuations to the anonymous *Lazarillo*, and Alemán's *Guzmán* was also followed by an inferior work whose hero Alemán neatly disposed of in his own continuation by making him run mad and fall overboard at sea. What is different in the case of Avellaneda and Cervantes is firstly that they seem to have been personally known to each other and on very bad terms, and that secondly they were consciously critical of the cultural and intellectual position embodied in each other's work.

Avellaneda was very much a modern and responded to Cervantes' *Don Quixote I* with a version implicitly critical of the older writer's secular, humanistic attitude. Avellaneda, a rationalist, is also moved by the spirit of the Counter-Reformation. He is implicitly hostile to the idea of fiction unless it is explicitly justified by religious or moral content or satiric purpose. The overall tendency of his work is reductive, and actually destructive. His book is written to amuse, but under the cover of amusement to undermine the positive, humanistic assumptions of Cervantes. Consequently, it is in important respects retrograde. Cervantes' conservatism had allowed him to reach a position which the younger writer's rational, literal-minded moralism obliged him to disapprove of.[4]

Avellaneda alters Cervantes' plan in several important respects. He objects to the richness of Sancho's character, debasing it with the introduction of gluttony and stupidity. He reduces the imaginative element in Don Quixote and tries to tie the whole action much more closely into contemporary social reality. He is very careful about the way in which he motivates Don Quixote's madness, combining chance events such as the arrival of a group of gentlemen travelling to a tournament, with the stupid gullibility of Sancho, who is the first to reintroduce the idea of knight errantry, in order to effect a lapse from sanity in his hero. His alterations result in an overall weakening and loss of interest. As Roger Laufer has pointed out, Cervantes' attribution of *gourmandise* and *gros bon sens* to Sancho is changed to a combination of *gourmandise* and stupidity. The thinness and idealism which Cervantes brings together in Sancho's master Avellaneda changes for thinness and foolishness. So the creative tension within the characters is lost.[5]

Avellaneda is greatly more concerned than Cervantes with relating

---

[4] Avellaneda's identity remains an unsolved literary mystery, so strictly speaking it is unreasonable to refer to him as younger than Cervantes. His relation to Cervantes, however, makes the temptation a strong one!

[5] R. Laufer, *Le Sage ou le métier de romancier* (1971), pp. 89–90.

social and aesthetic values, and one of the most important changes he introduces is to make Sancho the initiator of most of the comic and burlesque action. Don Quixote himself is left much more passive than Cervantes' hero and is manipulated by others, losing a great deal of interest as a result. He is even the social inferior of those who manipulate him. His Dulcinea becomes the hideously disfigured tripe-seller, Barbara, and he loses the creative capacity to make his own reality. It is no surprise at the end of the novel when he is sent to be cured in the madhouse at Madrid.

Cervantes' immediate answer to all this was typically audacious. Following Alémaṇ's hint, he introduces Avellaneda's Quixote into his own continuation. Here the false Quixote and Panza are made to serve a function similar to that for which he created Cide Hamete Benengeli in the first part. In Chapter 60 Don Quixote comes across Avellaneda's book for the first time. He is told by two gentlemen how bad it is and how his character has been traduced. When Altisidora is recounting her experiences in hell, it occurs again, reported as handed about from devil to devil. Finally, in Chapter 72 it features again. Don Quixote, travelling home, meets Don Álvaro Tarfe, one of Avellaneda's principal characters, and confronts him with the fact that the Don Quixote he had met in Avellaneda's narrative was not the real one. Previously Don Quixote had decided to go to Barcelona when he learnt from the two gentlemen that Avellaneda had reported him in Saragossa, so as to give his creator's rival the lie. By Chapter 72 the situation is hopelessly complex. Avellaneda has been telling lies it is clear, but his lies are not simply lies, because otherwise Don Quixote in the *true* history of Cervantes would have been unable to meet and converse with Don Álvaro. Don Quixote makes Don Álvaro sign a deposition to the effect that Avellaneda's hero was not the real man, which he does quite willingly:

Eso haré yo de muy buena gana—respondió don Álvaro—, puesto que causa admiración ver dos don Quijotes y dos Sanchos a un mismo tiempo, tan conformes en los nombres como diferentes en las acciones; y vuelvo a decir y me afirmo qu no he visto lo que he visto ni ha pasado por mí lo que ha pasado.

That I will with all my heart, answered Don Álvaro, for it is very surprising to see two Don Quixotes and two Sanchos at the same time, as alike in their names as they are different in actions; and I repeat and affirm that I have not seen what I have seen and that what happened to me didn't happen.

Don Quixote II, lxxii, p. 1055

Sancho's answer is not calculated to set either Don Álvaro's or the reader's mind at rest: 'Without doubt', said Sancho, 'your worship must be enchanted, like my lady Dulcinea del Toboso. . . .'[6] But this is the perfect answer to Avellaneda's rationalism. It consists in adopting the very techniques of playfulness which his rival had condemned, to show the ineffectiveness and shallowness of the rationalism he proposed as an alternative. If Part I had annoyed him, it is dreadful to imagine what state of mind the unrepentant Part II may have reduced him to.

Yet Cervantes himself is not unaffected by the exchange. His continuation shows that he has moved a long way towards a more literal-minded and rational approach to the structure of fiction. The composite nature of Part I from a structural viewpoint is replaced in the continuation of 1615 by a more consistent but rather pedestrian method. Cide Hamete Benengeli is made to lament the change, 'not daring to launch out into other episodes and digressions graver and more entertaining'.[7] Nor is this the only aspect of change. Don Quixote II shows a far more developed awareness of society as a whole than the first volume, and the focus is more closely arranged, lacking the abstraction as well as the liveliness of the earlier book. Even so, allowing for these changes, and for the fact that Cervantes has effectively answered Avellaneda's main attack, the fundamental principles remain unchanged. Don Quixote II is a development rather than a new departure.

Don Quixote's third sally begins with the famous episode concerning the enchantment of Dulcinea, in which Sancho is shown to have learned and developed the lessons of Book I. At first in charge of the situation, he invents freely, only to be defeated by his own invention. Don Quixote himself, however, at first Sancho's gull, is able to take charge of the situation by extending the idea of enchantment and so to give himself a new lease of life. This is an essential element throughout the book. It shows us a hero older and wiser, though not too wise, who has learnt to temporise with reality. Confronted with the actors who show fight, this wiser Don Quixote withdraws, depending on enchantment

[6] 'Sin duda—dijo Sancho—que vuestra merced debe de estar encantado, como mi señora Dulcinea del Tobosa.' II, lxxii, p. 1055.
[7] '. . . sin osar estenderse a otras digresiones y episodios más graves y más entretenidos.' II, xliv, p. 848.

to cover his retreat. And then, in the incident which may be said in a certain sense to begin the book, he obtains a new lease of life. The combat with Sansón Carrasco, himself disguised as a knight errant, is the confrontation with reality which we have all expected and feared. Ironically, Don Quixote wins, and is thereby reinforced in his illusion about his own prowess. So he is freed to wander again until he meets Carrasco again as the knight of the White Moon. In the meantime he goes on to his anti-climactic combat with the caged lion who refuses to come out. Here again expectations are betrayed. His foolhardiness should be his downfall, the myth of his military effectiveness giving way to the reality of leonine strength. As it happens, however, we might be tempted to see the outcome as supporting another myth—the lion's essential nobility of nature which makes him unwilling to face an ignoble foe. After the encounter with the lion comes that with the man in the green overcoat which brings to an end the exploratory Book I. This embodiment of a Horatian ideal of moderation, naïvely recognised by Sancho as a saint on horseback, helps to bring the two heroes closer within the range of ordinary social experience, but also has the effect of reminding us that concepts such as that which he embodies are never more concrete than states of being which individuals move into and beyond. The knight of the green overcoat is an apt foil to the knight of the lion.

The first event of Book II is an adventure which calls into question the relationship between passion and social circumstances. At Camacho's feast, so much appreciated by Sancho, the rich host is about to be married to Quiteria, in spite of her love for the younger and poorer Basilio. The resolution of this archetypal rivalry between youth and riches is achieved by means of manipulating circumstances. Basilio's apparent suicide is accepted by those present because they know it is adequately motivated in his disappointment and despair. His request that he be married to Quiteria before he dies is accepted because it is eminently reasonable and no more than anyone would be entitled to in the circumstances. When it turns out that Basilio is very much alive, quite unhurt and, of course, married to Quiteria in spite of Camacho and his riches, there is a strong sense that justice has been done. This is a typically romantic investigation of a question of great importance, similar to several other incidents in the novel. The fundamental question of social justice is not solved in its own terms. Instead the techniques of romance are employed mechanically.

In the remainder of this book illusion and imagination are examined more closely after they have been represented as so effective in solving the problems of Basilio and Quiteria. The last event of the book involves a disaster for Don Quixote and Sancho. The episode of the enchanted bark is one of their periodic humiliations, preparing them for the introduction of a new sphere of action in the Duke's court. Until they step into the bark they get by quite well in this book. The episode of the braying competition, when two villages arrange to meet in violent confrontation as a result of a foolish joke, ends in a discomfiture which Don Quixote manages to assimilate quite well. And Cervantes is not concentrating here on his discomfiture at all although he is shown leaving Sancho in the hands of his enemies, but rather on the madness of the villagers under the influence of a communal insult. In the cave of Montesinos Don Quixote has a rare opportunity to extend his imagination unaffected by material considerations. Here in the darkness of the cave and fast asleep, we may be sure, he dreams freely about Dulcinea and her enchantment.

This episode is perhaps the most important single one in the second volume of Don Quixote's adventures. Here for the first time we have an opportunity of knowing what the state of the hero's mind actually is and through it Cervantes makes one of his subtlest statements regarding the mind and its workings. For Don Quixote, completely free here from assault by servant maids, carriers, enraged villagers or domestic animals, reveals his basic unfitness for knight errantry. His dream is absurd. His imaginary world is not only invaded by the more sordid aspects of material reality—Dulcinea needs money; Durandarte's heart needs pickling to prevent corruption—it is also incoherent and bizarre. The mind of the real knight errant, serving goodness, beauty and innocence as the manifestations of spiritual purity and nobility, is very different from this. Here is a condemnation of the elderly Alonso Quijana which must eventually come to be felt.

It is typical of Cervantes' technique that the central point is made only implicitly, however, and that the incident is followed by one which works in another direction. This is the episode concerning Master Pedro and his talking ape, which concludes with Don Quixote's destruction of the puppet show. There are elements here typical of the second volume rather than the first. Especially important is the new readiness of the hero to make financial reparation for his deeds of frenzy. The episode works in a rather similar way, however, to the burning of the books in the earlier book, and the references to Cide Hamete Benengeli. Don Quixote is mad in reacting as he does to the puppet show, but the difference between his behaviour and that of the rest of Master Pedro's audience is only a question of degree. He is mad precisely because the whole paraphernalia is quite so crude and unconvincing that it could not reasonably be mistaken for reality. But if this is so, could it reasonably attract the attention of an audience at all? And if the audience are fools for taking the puppet show seriously, we are bound to ask, where does it leave us, who have to believe in Don Quixote's madness in the first place in order to dismiss it as such? And of course, what ironical light does it throw on the whole episode when we learn that Master Pedro is not what he seems but the Ginés de Pasamonte of the first part of *Don Quixote*! The notorious galley slave reduced to the manipulator of a talking ape is the kind of surprise we should by now have learned to expect.

The events of Book III raise serious problems for the modern reader, who is likely to misread Cervantes' treatment of the Duke and the Duchess who spend so much time in solemn foolery, as satire. This is a difficult point, but perhaps it would be true to suggest that what Cervantes actually thinks of his powerful aristocrats at play cannot be properly understood until his reader has met Roque Guinart in Book IV and so is equipped to remark on a world which has employment for the bandit but not for the grandee. For the time being it is clear that no reflection is being made on the Duke and the Duchess who take Don Quixote and Sancho into their court and treat them hospitably. What the heroes are offered here is an opportunity to express themselves freely and safely by understanding friends who have read the account of their previous adventures and accurately appreciate their combination of virtues and absurdities. Our attitude to the events at their court ought to be affected by the reaction of the churchman who upbraids them for treating Don Quixote seriously and succeeds only in producing sharp confrontation and demonstrating his narrow-mindedness and lack of charity. In the world governed by the Duke and Duchess confrontation is produced only by menials, various of whom are unable to maintain mental and moral balance themselves.

The events of the book consist in a series of tests for Don Quixote and Sancho, out of which the latter comes rather more seriously affected than the former. The important question of the enchantment of Dulcinea is introduced during the night-time masque, ordered for the entertainment of the court. Then follows the adventure of the damsel, which gives the heroes an opportunity for a real-life adventure, involving a trip on a magic horse. In this situation it is Sancho's veracity that breaks down when he produces a Montesino-type lie regarding a flight through the universe, while Don Quixote accepts events at their face value. After this they part company. In his government of the island

Sancho comes to know something of the relationship between reality and desire. That desire is natural we are reminded through the story of the young girl who enlists her brother's help to enable her to see something of the world outside her home. Sancho is able to deal with many different situations. Peasant wisdom helps him solve many judicial problems which involve attempts to distort the truth, but he is quite unable either to master those immediately around him, or his own physical appetites. In the meantime Don Quixote has further opportunities to develop his own character while he resists the flirtatious attentions of Altisidora and at the same time Doña Rodríguez shows us that it is not madness that makes folly, nor sanity that protects the innocent where social advantage is concerned.

Book IV begins with the end of Sancho's governorship, marked by a symbolic burial, from which his master reclaims him. There follows the tournament brought about as a result of the complaints of Doña Rodríguez, whose daughter has been seduced by the son of a rich farmer. Here we expect Don Quixote to be defeated and his whole career to be brought peacefully to an end under the careful government of the Duke. Where Sansón Carrasco failed, surely the lackey who represents the farmer's son will succeed. But the situation takes an unexpected turn when the lackey tries to manipulate fiction in his own interest, confesses himself unwilling to meet the knight and offers to marry the girl. Later we learn that all he got for his pains was a beating on the orders of the Duke, but for the time being all we know is that he has given Don Quixote another reprieve.

After leaving the Duke's court in a mood of confidence and meeting with a group of young people who are consciously playing their own fiction, being shepherds and shepherdesses in the country, Don Quixote is reduced again when he is trampled by a herd of bulls. This is an appropriate preparation for the events to follow, which give him very little opportunity for a reassertion of his madness but develop the political and social themes which have been raised in earlier action. Serious questions regarding the nature of government and its relations to the state of the nation as a whole stand in the background here though they are never raised explicitly. First we meet the bandit leader, Roque Guinart, who successfully defies the power of the State and the town of Barcelona. Roque represents something very like what Don Quixote himself claims to be—the modern knight errant, righting wrongs and directly implementing moral law rather than mundane legality. Roque's existence is itself a comment on the modern State which is unable to assimilate him. Yet it would be untrue to say that he escapes himself without criticism. Part of his motivation is personal. He seeks revenge against those who have opposed him in the past and the inset story of Doña Claudia, who murders her own lover under the mistaken impression that he has been unfaithful, is an implicit comment on the tendency of such passions.

Roque makes a very apt introduction to the final section of the novel, where Cervantes tackles the most serious social and political issues that he had ever touched on. From Roque's world of disorder we pass into the ordered world of the city where the action and the person of the hero are reduced to a level lower than ever before. Here, while Don Quixote is harmlessly mocked by the boys and amused by the triviality of the talking head, we have a last opportunity to reflect on the nature of amusement itself and to be prepared for the romanesque events which precede his final overthrow.

The story of Sancho's neighbour Ricote, touched on before, while Sancho was making his way back from his island, brings us in contact with the major political question of Cervantes' own day, the expulsion of the Moriscos. The way this issue is introduced is very romantic and, one might say, typical of the novelist's whole approach. The sudden and unexpected capture of a Moorish ship on which two drunken Turks put up a pointless resistance, infuriates the captain of the Spanish galleys against the crew and especially their captain. He, it appears, is a she—Ricote's daughter, who has returned to Spain in disguise in the hope of finding means to rescue her Christian lover who has followed her to Barbary disguised as a woman. The surprising nature of their story, the charm of her manner and the additional surprise of Ricote's appearance in confirmation of what she says, win the hearts of listeners who combine to persuade the captain against his design of hanging her. The incident ends with the notables of Barcelona deciding to petition the court for her exclusion from the expulsion order.

Cervantes says nothing about the edict of expulsion except that it was justified from an administrative point of view. Yet he presents it in such a way that it appears, not only to us, but also to the characters in the novel, as humanly unacceptable. Even here he is anti-rationalistic, against the impulse towards purification of the nation which was destroying the nation as he knew it. For Ricote is presented as a Spaniard, like his daughter; and in their particular case, which is all we have, the administrative solution makes nonsense of social facts.

After this incident the reintroduction of Sansón Carrasco brings about Don Quixote's final downfall as a knight errant. A momentary recovery under the influence of the pastoral ideal is followed by a symbolic trampling by hogs. The disenchantment of Altisidora, bringing with it the disenchantment of Dulcinea, brings the end of the action one inevitable step nearer. But of course what we are approaching is not merely the end of the action, but the end of Don Quixote, and with the end of Don Quixote the death of Alonso Quijana. This inevitable event is Cervantes' last answer to Avellaneda. Don Quixote dies because his nature is not as the rationalist would have it. His personality is integral; his motivation towards knight errantry intimately tied up with his motivation to live. As one dies, so the other ceases. And the trouble which Cervantes takes to ensure that he remains dead is not the result of authorial pique against would-be imitators but the proper care of a writer who has brought to its close a completely integral life and a completely integral statement about human existence in general. The dignity and completeness of Don Quixote as a character is at the centre of Cervantes' vision and the foundation stone of his novel. To destroy the one, as Avellaneda had done, would be to destroy the other.

2 After Cervantes: Romance and Reason in the Seventeenth Century

If the generally predominant diagnosis of the causes of the novel's development were correct we should expect to have seen a gradual development throughout the seventeenth century, perhaps especially in England. In the seventeenth century there is certainly a steady development of many of the factors which are commonly referred to as the conditions of the novel's rise: that is, the final abandonment of the Ptolemaic system, introduction of new philosophic ideas and scientific methods, an increase of interest in the individual as such and the development of economic factors which were eventually to lead to the development of the capitalist system, and finally the social flexibility dependent on them. In spite of all these factors, however, and in spite of the fact that in *Don Quixote* the novel as a literary form has clearly shown its capacity to exist right at the beginning of the century, its development in the decades which followed Cervantes' death was irregular and slow.

The fact was that in spite of the development of factors which might have been considered favourable to the novel, the climate in seventeenth-century Europe was unfavourable. The reasons for this differ from country to country, but the overall pattern is clear. The steady development of rationalistic attitudes meant the abandonment of the humane secularism of Renaissance writers and with it that confidence in the capacity of fiction to adequately reflect on the human condition which had been so large an element in Cervantes' achievement. The abandonment of medieval systems of thinking was not for many years followed by a willingness to develop fiction as an instrument of analysis and investigation. In one form or another authority imposed itself on

26

fiction, preventing its development into the novel. In England, where the abandonment of older attitudes was so strikingly achieved during the Civil Wars and the Commonwealth, the framework of theology became stronger than ever. Milton's development is from the neo-Platonist idealism of *Comus* towards theology and ultimately biblical history as a frame of fiction. Bunyan, for all his contribution to the history of realism as a literary technique, could see no purpose for fiction outside the frame of religious experience. Significantly, England had developed no strong romance tradition of its own, and in spite of attempts during the Restoration to revive it through translation and original composition, English fiction during the century was almost negligible. It is in France, where the romance tradition is stronger, that we see real development of fiction in such a way as to reflect the development of the nation's cultural history during the period. But here fiction succeeds as a result of factors which work against the generally accepted explanation of the mechanisms involved.

Seventeenth-century France was not without political disturbance and even civil wars. The confused disputes of the Ligue were followed by the wars of the Fronde in 1648 and 1651. But these later conflicts were rather the result of resentment against a dominant and successful centralising movement than the indications of a powerful challenge to royal authority. The political, social and cultural life of seventeenth-century France all show clear signs of the effect of this continuing tendency which dominated the life of the period and the following one. The emergence, and the failure, of new forms of prose romance are closely connected with this movement. The literary culture of the whole country was shaped according to the interests of the monarch and the new social classes which were brought into being to serve its interests. The process may be compared with the parallel movement which occurred in Spain, where the rationalising and centralising impulse was confused with conservative intellectual, social and economic tendencies, effecting a general decline in the nation's energies and a complete cessation of the literary activity which had produced the picaresque literature of the century's early decades. In France centralisation was a progressive movement, developing the nation's resources, and it went hand in hand with the development of the nation's intellectual life. The result was a situation where a powerful urge towards fiction existed, firstly in the old romance traditions, which were given new political and social content, and secondly in the new forms of comic romance, which reflected on the immediate social reality of an increasingly self-conscious society. But as for the novel, the form of fiction which comments on contemporary reality only by means of representing it, it was a different matter. The novel remained possible at any moment, sometimes realising itself as a result of chances of different kinds, but always under pressure from the most powerful forces at work in society of the time.

The best introduction to the history of the seventeenth century is a reading of Avellaneda's *Don Quixote*, because Avellaneda is in several ways representative of the contemporary writer. In the first place, as a writer of fiction, he occupies a false position, because he does not approve of fiction itself. Avellaneda is a rationalist. According to his reading of man's nature the all-important faculty is the judgement which makes possible the proper use of will. He takes up Cervantes' fiction partly just because he disapproves of Cervantes' whole sensibility, but also because Cervantes' central characters appeal to him. Don Quixote is mad, and so lacks judgement. Sancho lacks judgement for different reasons. Together they can be used to reflect the all-important norms of social and intellectual life. The trouble is that Avellaneda's conception of madness is so mechanistic that it leaves no room for the sort of fictional possibilities that are open to Cervantes.

The same is true for many other writers of the period. Seventeenth-century writers either project a heightened version of standard man in the romance hero or depict a reduced version in the peasant and the madman. Whichever path they take, their basic attitudes to man's nature are the same. There is an interesting passage in one of the most important romances of the period, John Barclay's *Argenis* (1621). John Barclay was an important and interesting character. A Scot, of French descent on his mother's side, he was an accomplished Latinist and represented an old tradition of European scholarship. In his youth he worked at the court of James I, in whose interests he published his satirical fiction *Euphormion* (1603–7). Madness is employed in this work as a means of introducing satirical observations, but certainly not as a method of heightening our sense of social or intellectual normality. *Argenis*, however, is a very different work, written in the interests of the French court rather than the English, and finished while Barclay was at the Papal court at Rome. Here he makes a quite gratuitous digression in order to introduce a character who believes that he is the hero, Polyarchus. Polyarchus himself is not what he seems, but the King of France, in love with Argenis whom he has earlier met while himself disguised as a girl. He is being sought by the troops of King Meleander and a rumour spreads to the effect that he has been caught. It turns out, however, to be Heraleon, the man who thinks he is

Polyarchus, who has been captured by peasants while fleeing from royal troops. What Cervantes would have made of this mixture of disguises dazzles the imagination, but Barclay seems entirely unaware of the possibilities in the situation he has created. He is fixated on the didactic function, which is introduced by means of a dialogue in which the King questions an unidentified sage concerning the nature of madness. The answer given in the rather confusing contemporary English translation is as follows:

> The divisions of the braine, quoth he, are loose in such men, and too apt, by their own thinnesse, to receive the images of things which wee call phantasies; these being once imprinted in that thinne substance, and obnoxious to them by its owne lightnesse, whithersoever it be moved, it is therefore hard to blot out againe: because, for the most part they delight with a kind of sweetnesse, and doe moreover give as it were a tincture to the mind, not otherwise changed into other colours, but by violent succeeding shapes of several things. It is impossible therefore, that such braines should be ever idle, being alwayes immoderately either sad or merry, by the violence of intruding thoughts. But if these men encline especially to any one affection, they still have it in their minde, and still feele it with delight, being present before the eyes of their understanding; whether it be pride, or covetousenesse, or impatience of revenge, or whatsoever our troubled desires lay before us. And being this way of themselves enclined, if any thing touch them on that part, they are presently disturbed; that what they have a long time desired to be, they beleeve is so indeed: neither now doe their imaginations (since their minds by custome are overcome) present that thing as wisht for, but as true and present.
>
> *Burclay his Argenis*, I, trans. Kingesmill Long (1625), p. 46

Sometimes, Barclay's sage opines, the overall effect is good because 'the fault of their minds being spent upon one desire, gives them leave more quietly and almost without prejudice, to contemplate and understand other things: and lastly, to live like other men. . . .' So he allows medically for the case of an Alonso Quijana, but this is not his main purpose. That is rather to reflect on the state of the human mind in general in the context of the social and political preoccupations of King Meleander. The latter, sore because of his inability to deal with powerful, rebellious subjects, comments that all men suffer the same disease:

One thinks there are no gods; another that all things are gods: Hee thinkes nothing so good, as pleasure; and hee, that the gods punish not vice: to conclude, few men but are madder than Heraleon; but onely that more covertly, or agreeably to the world's *Genius* is their frenzie: and so much the more to be lamented, because they will not shake off their madnesse, and Heraleon cannot.

Barclay his Argenis, p. 47

The particular form of disease, we notice, is a sort of constitutional lightness or instability, amounting to an inability to control different aspects of one's own nature. And it is interesting that this quasi-physiological analysis is brought forward not merely to explain delusion, but also moral viciousness. At the root of everything, according to Barclay, is the need for an educated steadiness of mind which is the condition of moral, social and political health.

Perhaps it may be surprising to some readers that this analysis of man's nature and state is fundamentally similar to that put forward by the greatest philosopher of the period. We associate Descartes, through the *Discours de la méthode* (1637), with modernism, thinking of him as one of the great moderns whose work represents an important advance in the process by which philosophy learnt to concern itself with the human mind and physical sciences with rigorous examination of phenomena. But in the treatise on human passion, *Les Passions de l'Ame* (1649), Descartes presents a different aspect of his thinking, showing essentially the same combination of rationalism and social orthodoxy that motivated the romances of the period.

Briefly summarised, Descartes' view was that the blood underwent a kind of combustion in the heart, leading to the production of certain refined particles called '*les esprits animaux*'. These find their way to the brain and either go from there through the proper channels direct to the muscles, along the nerves, or direct themselves to the soul, in its seat in the pineal gland, in the brain's very centre. Descartes' exposition of the nature of passion is rather confused by his use of different terms for the same things and by his failure to be precise about the *manner* of the soul's action. However, he distinguishes two functions of the soul, which are those of willing and awareness — '*volontez*' and '*perceptions*' or '*connoissances*' — which are to be thought of as respectively actions or passions of the soul. Passion, one might perhaps say, is the soul in a particular state of awareness, which may be excited in it by impressions in the senses conveyed along the nerves, or be derived from itself. The usefulness of these passions consists in the fact that

they allow the soul to contemplate an object or idea steadily. Their
danger is that they preoccupy the soul for too long and usurp its active
function. Only the judgement can protect the soul from its passions and
form the basis of virtue. One might almost go so far as to say that for
Descartes judgement *is* virtue.

Passions may be fought with other passions, but not with security or
long-term effect. The only proper method is by using the '*Propres
armes*' of the soul—'firm and determined judgements concerning the
knowledge of good and evil, according to which she has resolved to
conduct the actions of life'. Most men, Descartes thought, do well
enough by means of false judgements which allow them to resist
passions other than those on which they are founded. But on the other
hand:

> ... il y a pourtant grande difference entre les resolutions qui proce-
> dent de quelque fausse opinion, et celles qui ne sont appuiées que sur
> la connoissance de la verité: d'autant que, si on suit ces dernieres, on
> est asseuré de d'en avoir jamais de regret, ni de repentir; au lieu qu'on
> en a tousjours d'avoir suivi les premieres, lors qu'on en decouvre
> l'erreur.

> ... there is nevertheless a great difference between the resolutions
> which proceed from some false opinion, and those which are based
> only on the knowledge of truth; so much so that if one follows the
> latter one is assured of having nothing to regret or to repent; whereas
> one always does have after following the former once one has
> discovered the falsity.
>
> *Les Passions de l'Ame* CXLIX (1649), *Oeuvres de Descartes*,
> C. Adam et P. Tannery (1969), XI, pp. 367–8

Much later in the treatise Descartes returns to this point again to
underline the fact that the only source of real happiness in life comes
through the integrity of the soul, which is the only basis of a controlled
enjoyment of the passions:

> Et affin que nostre ame ait aussi de quoy estre contente, elle n'a
> besoin que de suivre exactement la vertu. Car quiconque a vescu en
> telle sorte, que sa conscience ne luy peut reprocher qu'il ait jamais
> manqué a faire toutes les choses qu'il a jugées estre les meilleures
> (qu'est ce que je nomme icy suivre la vertu), il en reçoit une
> satisfaction, qui est si puissante pour le rendre heureux, que les plus

violens efforts des Passions n'ont jamais assez de pouvoir pour troubler la tranquillité de son ame.

And in order that our soul may also have reason to be content she need only follow virtue exactly. Because whoever has lived in such a way that his conscience cannot reproach him with ever having failed to do all the things which he has judged to be the best (which is what I here call following virtue) he receives a satisfaction from it, which is so effective in making him happy that the most violent efforts of the Passions never have enough power to trouble the tranquillity of his soul.

Les Passions de l'Ame CXLVIII (1649), *Oeuvres*, pp. 442–3

Fortunately this happy state, Descartes assures us, is available to all because the soul can be trained, like a dog, so that even the most feeble-minded may learn to acquire an absolute empire over themselves with the employment of *assez d'industrie*.

We have the evidence of Molière and Racine to assure us that the predominance of mechanistic views of human character in seventeenth-century France was nothing but favourable to the development of certain kinds of drama. Descartes' ideal was clearly the *honnête homme* of contemporary salons, whose highest exercise of reason was manifested in his complete adjustment to social and intellectual manners of the court circle. In at least two comedies, *Dom Juan* (1665) and *Le Misanthrope* (1666), Molière deeply questioned the idea of *honnêteté*, but it is nevertheless true to say that it is fundamental to his achievement as a dramatist whose whole stance depends on certain assumptions held in common with his audience. Racine's drama, on the other hand, largely concerns characters who either find themselves in situations where Descartes' solution to the problem of passion is impracticable, or centres on the factor which Descartes left out of account—that is, the problem of temperament. *Britannicus* (1669) might almost be read as an explosion of Cartesianism effected from within. Nero can be swayed towards virtue. His judgement can be affected, his emotions manipulated, but the basic factor in his character is a temperamental inclination towards evil. The play ends with the foreboding speech of the character who had depended most on Cartesian methods of character training, the soldier Burrhus, doomed himself by Nero's ravening appetite for destruction.

Racine's view of character may be said to challenge Descartes', though the difference between them is more a matter of mood than of

opinion. In the case of Madame de Lafayette, there is no such difference. Her one great achievement in fiction, the *nouvelle, La Princesse de
Clèves* (1678), shows what could be done within a fictional mode on the
basis of a mechanistic view of human psychology. Her achievement
depends on the adjustment of character types drawn from romance to a
dramatic plot. It also depends on the fact that Madame de Lafayette
adopted a highly formal court setting which gave psychological justification for a level of dignity in her characters and a degree of reserve in
her role as narrator which are essential conditions of the level of
intensity which she maintains. Her methods might have been further
developed within the *nouvelle*, whose special characteristics were
favourable to it, but were certainly not available for development in the
novel at large. Her success, in fact, is sufficiently exceptional to alert us
to the fundamental difficulties experienced by the writer of fiction in her
period. We may notice also that her work, and that of Molière and
Racine, belongs to the second half of the century. In the period
immediately after Cervantes—the period of Avellaneda, it would not
be unfair to call it—the characteristics of French fiction in general are
liveliness, persistence and ineffectiveness in equal proportion, each
quality the inevitable counterpart of the others.

THE NEW ROMANCE

Through Honoré d'Urfé's *Astrée* (1607–27) the Renaissance traditions
of pastoral extended well into the seventeenth century: and of course,
d'Urfé's enormously successful work was greatly popular for decades
after his death, though read then perhaps primarily as a *roman à clef*. In
fact, however, the refined Platonism of d'Urfé's work is quite untypical
of the period, which is dominated by a new type of romance which
reflects a rationalism and cultural centralism completely foreign to the
aristocratic d'Urfé. In the years between 1620 and 1670 there grew up
and flourished a new genre of romance, sometimes referred to as
'heroic', which drew its methods from earlier writers like Heliodorus
and Ariosto but aimed directly at affecting the sensibility of contemporary man. This genre, initiated by Barclay, either attempted to imitate
the methods of history, or actually claimed itself to be historical. Its
function was ultimately, however, political. So it used history, but
could not rely on historical fact. Truth was acceptable only if carefully
dressed. And for the same reason that it was political, it was also
closely restricted to contemporary manners and modes of thought.

That is, it was designed to serve the cultural purposes of a centralising establishment associated with the monarchy and its chief servants.

This is made very explicit in Barclay's *Argenis*. Here Meleander, King of Sicily, is troubled with rebellious subjects, one of whom seeks the hand of his daughter, Argenis. She is also wooed by Polyarchus and Archombrotus, the former King of France and the latter eventually revealed as the Prince of Mauritania and her own half-brother. Argenis represents the state of France, the events of the novel reflect the events of the reigns of Henry III and Henry IV of France. One character represents Barclay himself—the poet, Nichopompus—and he expresses severe disapproval of the rebellious subjects of Meleander, including the Huguenots and the rebellious noblemen of the Ligue. His companion Antenorus, however, warns him against incorporating this disapproval in a threatened historical account of the troubles of Meleander's reign because he says that to write a true account would provide the king's enemies with dangerous material and would leave the reader's judgement open to influence from the opposite point of view. Nichopompus replies by saying that he envisages a kind of history which will work on the reader's passions and so involve his interest in the acceptance of the right opinion and which will reveal only so much of the truth as is discreet. In other words, he plans a romance, and is executing his plan in *Argenis*:

> I will compile some stately Fable, in manner of a Historie; in it will I fold up strange events; and mingle together Armes, Marriages, Bloodshed, Mirth, with many and various successes. The Readers will be delighted with the vanities there shewne incident to mortall men; and I shall have them more willing to reade me, when they shall not find me severe, or giving precepts. I will feed their minds with divers contemplations, and as it were, with a Map of Places. Then will I with the shew of danger stire up pittie, feare, and horrour and by and by cheere up all doubts, and graciously allay the tempests. Whom I please I will deliver and whom I please, give up to the Fates. I know the disposition of our Countriemen: because I seeme to tell them Tales, I shall have them all: they will love my Boke above any Stage Play or Spectacle on the Theatre. So first, bringing them in love with the potion, I will after put in wholesome hearbes: I will figure vices and vertues; and each of them shall have his reward. While they reade, while they are affected with anger or favour as it were against strangers, they shall meet with themselves; and finde in the glasse held before them, the shew and merit of their own fame, It

will perchance make them ashamed longer to play the parts upon the stage of this life, for which they must confesse themselves justly taxed in a fable. And that they may not say, they are traduced; no man's Character shall be simply set downe; I shall find many things to conceale them, which would not well agree with them, if they were made known. For, I that bind not myself religiously to the writing of a true History, may take this liberty. So shall the vices of the man be struck: neither can any man take exceptions, but such as shall with a most shameful confession discover his own naughtinesse. Besides, I will have here and there imaginary names, to signifie several vices and vertues; so that he may be as much deceived, that would draw all in my writing, as he that would nothing, to the truth of any late or present passage of State.

Barclay his Argenis II (1636), pp. 192–3

Antenorus greets this passage with delight, rubbing his hands together with glee and assuring Nichopompus that his work would delight posterity. We can imagine something of the same reaction from Cardinal Richelieu himself, as he worked to subdue the literary activity of the whole country to the interests of the State.

Subsequent romances were less clear in their political motivation than *Argenis*. Increasingly, as the century wore on, they became historical rather than political in their inspiration, but their basic aesthetic remained the same, and they also worked in the same direction, towards confirming social, cultural orthodoxy. According to those who wrote these increasingly interminable works, the ordinary human being was fundamentally unreliable. He could be persuaded to reason only by being deceived, and only the romance could deceive and inveigle him for a sufficiently long time. So it became lengthy itself, embodying contemporary ideas of what was pleasing to the imagination but inspired by no adequate shaping spirit. In the first place, its inspiration came from without: it was fictional not as end in itself, but as means to something else. Secondly, it was fundamentally dishonest because it claimed to be historical but was unable to accept historical truth. Thirdly, it was absurd, because contemporary ideas of *bienséance*, which amounted to a fixation with contemporary manners, prevented the development of consistent fictions.

According to the ideas predominant during the Renaissance and affecting writers like d'Urfé, Sidney and Cervantes, fiction appealed to a strong, positive element in the human spirit, reflecting man's immaterial, spiritual qualities. This view lingered on in the seventeenth century, but only feebly. So Fr Langlois, in his interesting pamphlet, *Le Tombeau des Romans* (1626), quotes Scaliger's *Excitations contre Dardan* in support of fable:

> Il faut que tu scaches, adioustet'il, que notre entendement est de sa nature infiny. C'est pour quoy il appete les choses plus esloignées & estranges & se delecte és choses fauses & en la peinture des monstres, d'autaunt que tout cela surmonte & franchit les vulgaires limites de la verité. L'intelligence humaine méprise la prescription de certaines fins, tant sa capacité est ample. Aussi le sage mesme loüe la perfection de la peinture, quoy qu'il scache qu'elle est fausse, aymant mieux une belle image peinte, qu'une reelle & vivante parfois. Car les choses semblent estre mieux contrefaites par l'art que faictes par la nature. C'est ainsi que les fictions nous plaisent & se font admirer de nous. L'admiration ne doit pas estre plustost appellee fille d'ignorance que mere de science.

> You must know, he added, that our understanding is of its nature infinite. This is the reason why it desires the most exotic and strange things and delights in false things and in the painting of monsters, in as much as all that surmounts and passes beyond the vulgar limits of truth. The human intelligence despises the prescription of certain limits, so ample is its capacity. Also the wise man himself praises the perfection of the painting, although he knows it is false, sometimes liking a beautiful painted image better than one real and living. Because things seem to be better counterfeited by art than made by nature. It is thus that fictions please us and make us admire them. Admiration should no sooner be called daughter of ignorance than mother of science.

> *Tombeau des Romans* (1626), pp. 92–3

This is not an argument that Langlois puts forward on his own behalf. The context is a two-sided debate which he claims to put together having just come from a company where he learnt that the Garde des Sceaux was refusing to license the publication of romances. The attitude current in the early and middle years of the seventeenth century was much nearer to that formulated by Desmarets de Saint-Sorlin in the preface to his *Rosane, histoire tirée de celles des Romains et des Perses* (1639):

> La Fiction ne doit pas estre considerée comme un mensonge, mais

comme une belle imagination, et comme le plus grand effort de
l'esprit; et bien que la Verité semble luy estre opposée, toutefois elles
s'accordent merveilleusement bien ensemble. Ce sont deux lumieres
qui au lieu de s'effacer l'une l'autre et de se nuire, brillent par l'esclat
l'une de l'autre.

La Verité de l'Histoire toute seule est seiche et sans grace, et se void
toujours traversée par les espines que la fortune insolente jette en sa
chemin; d'autre costé la Fiction toute seule, telle qu'elle est dans les
Romans, est vaine et chimerique et n'a aucun soustien: Il faut que
l'une corrige l'autre, et que les adoucissemens qu'elles s'entre-
donnent, elles paroissent ensemble pleines d'utilité et de charmes.
Nostre esprit ayme la Verité: mais il n'est pas fasché qu'on la pare et
qu'on enrichisse. . . .

Fiction must not be considered as a lie, but as a beautiful imagination, and as the greatest effort of the spirit; and though Truth seems
to be opposed to it, they always agree marvellously well together.
They are two luminaries which instead of effacing each other and
harming each other, shine brilliantly together.

Historical Truth alone is dry and graceless and always seems itself
thwarted by the thorns which insolent Fortune throws in its path; on
the other hand, Fiction alone, such as it is in the Romances, is vain
and chimerical and has nothing to sustain it; One must correct the
other so that through alleviating each other they appear together full
of utility and charm. Our soul loves Truth: but it is not disturbed that
it should be embellished and enriched.
Rosane (1639); H. Coulet, Le Roman jusqu'à la Révolution II (1968),
pp. 40–41

The verb parer, to adorn, embellish, appears frequently in contemporary discussions of this sort, giving an indication of the extent to which
the whole usefulness of fiction consisted in its ability to make truth
more presentable. It is also important to notice, however, that the
combination of truth and fiction, history and romance, actually had the
effect of destroying both. The idea of vraisemblance worked together
with that of bienséance to ensure quite grotesque results. Aristotelean
theory regarding the balance of possibility and probability in art were
twisted into an argument that seeming true was more important than
being true; and bearing the prejudices of the audience in mind, what
was to seem true had to correspond to contemporary ideas. The final
result was a hopeless blending of historical or pseudo-historical data

and contemporary fashion in manners and morals.

The highest development of this 'heroic' mode was in the romances of Madeleine de Scudéry. She worked with her brother Georges who was important as a dramatist and whose *L'Amour tyrannique* (1638) had received official support from Richelieu against Corneille's *Le Cid*. Between them brother and sister developed theory and practice of romance writing to new heights of rationalistic absurdity. The preface to *Ibrahim* (1641) gives us the highest development of the theory of *vraisemblance*; and Chapter 10 of *Clélie* (1654–60) a conversation on fable which outlines the whole range of faculties required by romance-writing:

> Il faut, pour ainsi dire, estre le créateur de son ouvrage: il faut sçavoir l'art de parer la vertu, et de ne la montrer pas comme une chose difficile à practiquer. Il faut non seulement connoître le monde de la maniere que le doit connoître celuy qui fait une Histoire, mais il faut encore sçavoir le bel usage du monde, de la politesse, de la conversation; l'art de railler ingenieusement. . . . Mais sur toutes choses il faut sçavoir ôter à la Morale ce qu'elle a de rude et de sec, et luy donner je ne sçais quoy de si naturel et de si agréable qu'elle divertisse ceux à qui elle donne des leçons.

> He must, so to speak, be the creator of his work: he must know the art of embellishing virtue and of showing it as not a difficult thing to practise. He must not only know the world in the manner in which it must be known by one who is writing a History but must also know the ways of fine society, courtesy and conversation; the art of mocking ingeniously. . . . But above all things, he must know how to remove from Morality what it has of crudity and unattractiveness and to give it something so natural and so agreeable that it amuses those to whom it gives lessons.

> *Clélie* (1654–60); H. Coulet, *Le Roman jusqu'à la Révolution* II (1968), p. 56

We could say that the attitude represented here amounts to the decadence of the tradition initiated by Barclay half a century before. The political impulse has disappeared as political and social stability has become more and more firmly established. What remains is the determination to write to one class of people, and to identify their interests and their manners with those of the human race in general. Madeleine de Scudéry had absolutely no historical sense, no objectivity, no idea of society as a whole. Not only could she not have written a novel, she could not even have written a good romance: she had no respect for fiction as such, and a completely mechanistic idea of composition.

Madeleine de Scudéry's romances went on being read for decades, in France and in England. They were pattern books to the clumsy and ignorant provincial well into the following century. But they suddenly ceased being written somewhere around the decade from 1670 to 1680 and were replaced by another fictional form, the *nouvelle* or *petit roman*, which flourished up to and just beyond the end of the century. They were important enough while they lasted to demand a larger place in a history of romance or of fiction in general than we have been able to give them. Their importance for us derives not so much from their quality as fiction but from their value as evidence for the state of literary sensibility during the period from 1615 to 1670, revealing the interplay between different factors in contemporary intellectal life which kept writers away from the novel and made it impossible for the achievement of Cervantes to be imitated or understood.

COMIC ROMANCE

Heroic romance was not, of course, the only fictional product of the seventeenth century; and it is to its counterpart that historians of the novel generally turn when they attempt to trace the development of the genre. There are two sources of confusion in this field. Firstly, there is a long-established tendency to look back to the seventeenth century not for signs of the presence of the novel as such but for signs of the development of the techniques and attitudes which were to be developed in the novel in later periods. Secondly, students of the novel in general tend to assume that it is through the comic romance or anti-romance of the seventeenth century that the later novel developed, whereas in fact these forms flourished only within the shade of heroic romance and suffered the same basic limitations.

A work which figures largely in many accounts of the development of the novel in this period is Furetière's *Le Roman bourgeois* (1666). This is an important work, which no historian can afford to ignore. It is original in bringing the narrative focus to bear on the middle sections of the social scale and its methods involve lively characterisation, the imitation of ordinary speech patterns and representation of the material conditions of life in contemporary Paris. Furetière writes with wit and a sharp eye for the reductive aspects of human behaviour. But his work remains within the frame of satire. It develops no sustained narrative interest. Scenes of satire and social comedy stand out sharply, especially in the first part, which treats the comic wooing of the bourgeoise Javotte, but this action is brought to no proper conclusion and the second part of the fiction develops the wholly satirical relationship between Charroselles and Mlle Collantine. *Le Roman bourgeois* is neither romance nor novel and except with respect to its technique of characterisation, tells us little about the way the novel developed that could not be equally well learnt from the comedies of Molière.

It is more tempting to turn to fictions which come more fully into the category of anti-romance, protesting against the extravagances of the heroic romance itself, especially because their presence seems to lend strength to the argument that the novel developed as a protest against a romance misrepresentation of reality. What they actually show, however, even at their best, is how short a distance a writer may travel when his motive in writing is merely dissatisfaction with a particular literary mode. The anti-romance was based on fundamentally the same ethos as the romance. The difference between them is that the writer of anti-romance has an even more literal-minded tendency than his romance counterpart. And this eventually leads him into a position which is every bit as absurd.

Charles Sorel's *Le Berger extravagant* (1627), which is a very coherent and well-planned work, shows this most clearly. Sorel starts from a similar position to that of Cervantes, though he claimed not to have been influenced by him. He develops, however, a rationalist critique of *Don Quixote* which had enormous influence and remained widely current well into the next century. *Don Quixote*, he argues, lacks *vraisemblance*. He criticises the Duke's attentions to Don Quixote in the second part, the matter of Sancho's government, the idea of the priest and the barber's leaving home to wander after the hero, and the behaviour of Sansón Carrasco. Above all, he criticises the romanesque element in the novel:

> Mais en fin pour dire tout en un mot ce que je pense de l'histoire de Don Quichotte, elle n'a garde de faire beaucoup contre les Romans, veu que mesme elle est entre meslée d'une infinité de contes fort romanesques et qui ont fort peu d'apparence de verité, si bien que comme telle, elle peut estre mise au rang de tant d'autres qui ont trouvé icy leur attaque. . . .

But finally, to say in one word what I think of the history of Don

Quixote, it has not taken care to do much against Romances, seeing
that it is even intermingled with an infinity of very romanesque tales
which have very little appearance of truth, so that as such it can be
put in the same rank as so many others which have been here
attacked. . . .

   Remarques sur les XIIII livres au Berger extravagant (1639), p. 547

In fact Sorel's position is basically the same as Avellaneda's, though he
employs a different method. He claims to be rationally consistent and
accuses Cervantes of inconsistency and on this basis sets out to depict
the adventures of a young bourgeois who is under the delusion that he is
a shepherd and inhabits a pastoral landscape.

   His scheme is certainly worked out with great consistency. Everything that happens to Lysis is possible if not probable, and his response
to these events is perfectly consistent. So for someone obsessive in his
preoccupation with the terminology of pastoral, it is relatively credible
that the conflagration of his hat in his mistress's presence should seem
to be caused by the fiery beams of her eyes. As Avellaneda does, Sorel
takes great care to keep his hero's antics firmly within a framework of
normal behaviour and motivation provided by other characters. Like
Avellaneda, he depends on a normal character, who acts as a foil to his
hero, and he composes his action of much the same sort of pantomime
as Don Álvaro Tarfe provided in the earlier work. The result, of course,
is a fundamental dullness which ruins the book as a fiction. Sorel
conceives of Lysis' delusion as a simple disorder of the mind, which he
restores at the end by rational argument. The only interest which his
story provides is the relatively shallow comic interest which arises in
the discrepancy between event and interpretation. The events themselves can develop no interest, and no other characters in the book can
draw our attention consistently.

   Before he has got very far into *Le Berger extravagant*, in fact, it is
more than likely that the reader will be asking himself why Sorel ever
wrote it at all. Sorel himself was uneasy about this and was sensitive to
the accusation that he had merely written another of the romances
which he claimed to be attacking:

   Au reste je me moqueray de ceux qui diront qu'en blasmant les
   Romans je fay un autre Roman. Je respondray qu'il n'y a rien de
   fabuleux, et qu'outre que mon Berger represente en beaucoup d'en-
   droits de certains personnages qui ont fait des extravagances sembla-
   bles aux siennes, il ne luy arrive point d'avantures qui ne soyent

veritablement dans les autres Autheurs: tellement que par un miracle
estrange, de plusieurs fables ramasses, j'ay fait une Histoire veritable. Quant à l'ordre de ce recueil extra ordinaire, il est à la mode des
plus celebres Romans, afin que ceux qui se plaisent à les lire ne
dedaignent point de le lire aussi, et s'y trouvent ingenieusement
surpris.

For the rest, I care nothing for those who will say that in criticising
Romances I am making another Romance. I will answer that there is
nothing of the fabulous about it, and apart from the fact that my
Shepherd represents in many places certain personages who have
committed extravagances similar to his, no adventures happen to
him which are not truly found in other Authors: in such a way that by
a strange miracle I have made a true History from many fables
gathered together. As for the order of this extraordinary collection, it
is in the manner of the most celebrated Romances, in order that those
who are pleased by reading them will not disclaim to read it also, and
will there find themselves ingeniously surprised.

Preface, *Le Berger extravagant* (1640)

Taken as a whole, so far as I can see, this amounts to saying that
although he may be accused of writing a romance, he has written a
romance in order to please those who like romances! Sorel is obviously
unhappy here, and with good cause! The essence of his argument is
that pastorals and other romances lack *vraisemblance*, or logical
consistency, and are therefore ridiculous. He allows nothing for the
interest or validity of fiction in its own right. It must seem true in order
to achieve some non-fictional end. To make this point Sorel creates a
fiction in which an individual is mocked for taking fiction literally. But
in fact there is very little to choose, in the final analysis, between Sorel
and his own hero. Experience of reading the book itself tells us every
moment that we have to read it as *fiction*, not as if *literally* true—in
fact, in exactly the same way as we read *Don Quixote*, or any other
romance. That is, requiring consistency, but not *vraisemblance* in the
way the Sorel applies it in his criticism.

When Sorel tried his hand at other fiction he was more successful,
and the one time when he wrote fiction freely as such he produced one of
the undisputed novels of the period. Significantly, however, this was
his first literary work, produced at the age of twenty-one, before he had
developed his own rationalistic critique. It is interesting too that this
Histoire comique . . . was produced at a time when he was in close

contact with the only section of the community which put up an effective intellectual resistance to the centralising tendency in contemporary life. This came from the small group of *libertins* whose importance is indicated by the fact that they drew the attention of the monarch himself. Molière was just acceptable, perhaps, but Théophile de Viau was certainly not, and was accordingly banished in 1619 for free-thinking and in 1625 for blasphemy and obscenity. It was Théophile who produced, in his *Fragments d'un histoire comique* (c. 1620), the first attempt to produce a comic history independent of burlesque or anti-romance. Not surprisingly, he left it unfinished, because it would have been completely unpublishable at the time. A later, obscurer, and more unfortunate figure, clearly like-minded, was Claude Le Petit, who was executed for pornographic writing in 1662. Here again there is a connection with an independent approach to fiction which leads clearly in the direction of the novel. Le Petit's *L'Heure du berger* (1662) is no more than the report of a brief amorous encounter basically similar in structure to one of the romanesque *nouvelles* which Scarron used in *Le Romant comique*, but it represents a significant step towards a straightforward treatment of contemporary experience outside the frame of comedy, and is quite unlike anything produced by more cautious contemporaries who died in their beds.

Sorel tried later to conceal his relationship with this group. He never publicly owned his authorship of his *Histoire comique . . .* and he revised it twice to make it less objectionable to the orthodox. He continued in the attempt to write straight fiction, but once he became orthodox himself he had lost the impetus which brought him success. His *Polyandre Histoire comique* (1643) remains well worth reading from an academic point of view. This book was deliberately contemporary and completely in accordance with the author's critical views. The central character, Polyandre, is a typical *honnête homme*, representing the social, cultural norm of the period. Around him are grouped several more or less eccentric and non-conforming characters: Orilan, in love with all women; Gastrimargue, parasite and pedant; Musigene, penniless poet and grotesque. There are two sources of interest. The first is the antics of Néophile, the son of a fabulously rich financier, whom Polyandre is to teach *honnêteté*. The problem here is that once Néophile has come to heel nothing more of interest can happen to him and his adventures fade into the past. The second source of interest is the wooing of Aurélie by Polyandre, temporarily frustrated by the suits of Néophile and his father, Aesculan. As a focus of interest, however, this also fails to develop. Had it done so, in fact, it would have drawn Sorel away from his basically satirical standpoint into a treatment of a love relationship and the tensions involved in it. The potential for this is certainly there, but just as certainly incapable of development. The narrative energy of *Polyandre* in fact is derived entirely from studies of individuals who depart from the norm represented by the central character, who is quite incapable of generating action himself. There is nothing, after all, for the honest man to do but *be* honest. Sorel left the work unfinished, and it is easy to see why. To continue it would have been merely to re-do what he had already done. He was unable to develop any significant fiction within the framework of his own critical thinking.

Apart from *L'Histoire comique . . .* there is only one other fiction in the period up to 1670 which is entitled to the name of novel, and this is Scarron's *Le Romant comique* (1651 and 1657). Scarron is quite unique in the period because he alone may be said to have understood Cervantes and to have grown beyond the frame of rationalist burlesque to understand the relationship between romance concepts and the reality of human motivation. Scarron focuses on the novelist's perennial problem concerning the nature of experience and, like many others throughout the novel's history, he exploits the techniques of fiction in order to explore the nature of experience. But he failed to finish his *Le Romant comique* because he could not do so without confirming the romance patterns he was manipulating and so going against the very essence of the work. No other solution was available to him within the framework of intellectual experience open to even the most sensitive novelist in his period. Together with Sorel he proved beyond dispute that the novel was still possible in the seventeenth century, that is, not crude or naïve or proto-realistic, but mature and sophisticated in its own right. But then, Scarron and Sorel are the exceptions who survive in spite of the rule of reason and the supremacy of the centralising cultural pressures which dictate the whole shape of the fictional universe in their day.

L'HISTOIRE COMIQUE DE FRANCION (1623)

L'Histoire comique de Francion, published only eight years after the second part of Don Quixote, when the author was in his twenty-first year, has a claim to be considered one of the most original works in the history of the novel. It could certainly claim to be, among other things, a more successful comic epic in prose than *Tom Jones*, more than a hundred years before Fielding invented the term. With every sign of truthfulness Sorel denied that he had been influenced at all by *Don Quixote* but confessed to the importance of his reading of the picaresque tales of Spain. His achievement, in fact, consisted in combining an inspiration derived from the picaresque with a Rabelaisian vision of life as a whole and adapting to it a structure borrowed from classical epic. Sorel's view of life is humorous. He sees man as essentially a comic animal, but at the same time he is aware of a very strong pressure, partly social and partly philosophical, to find a way of transforming the animal into a creature of dignity and spirit. Sorel has little interest in anything that could be called morality, no sense of the importance of inner experience. His concern is with the bearing of his characters. Consequently his novel is mechanistically structured, varying in focus but always bearing on contemporary reality, always concerned with contemporary conditions of life. *Francion* shows none of the romance's tendency towards the abstract, but constantly tests the conceptual element against experience itself.

In an age of rationalism Sorel's criticism—the most important of his generation as far as fiction is concerned —is rationalistic. What sets him apart is a constitutional interest in the representation of things as they are. This survived his becoming respectable and is prominent even in his later, scholarly work. In one striking passage he shows that he sees right through the weakness of the contemporary argument that fiction is superior to history because it can improve on life: 'Have they well considered', he asks of critics who support this view, 'of what they dare advance? They must then believe that everything is given up to some blind chance. Do they not know that it is God who ordains everything which happens here below?'[8] Fiction merited his respect only in so far as it was straightforward representation of life as it actually was. 'Good comic and satirical romances', he thought, 'rather seem to be images of history than all the others':[9]

Les actions communes de la Vie estans leur objet, il est plus facile d'y recontrer de la Verité. Pource qu'on voit plus d'hommes dans l'erreur et dans la sottise. . . . Or comme il y a tousjours beaucoup de

[8]'Ont-ils bien pensé à ce qu'ils osent avancer? Il faut donc qu'ils croyent que tout est abandonnée à quelque aveugle hazard. Ne scavent-ils pas que c'est Dieu qui ordonne de tout ce qui se fait ici bas. . . ?' *De La Connoisance des Bons Livres, ou Examen de Plusiers Autheurs* (1671).

[9]'Les bons Romans Comiques et Satyriques semblent plûtost estre des images de l'Histoire que tous les autres.' *La Bibliotheque Francoise*, 2nd ed. (1667), p. 188.

Sujets pour de telles Pieces, on rencontre là plûtost le genre vray-
semblable, que dans les Pieces Héroïques qui ne sont que fiction,
puisqu'il y a peu d'hommes qui méritent d'être estimez des Heros,
c'est à dire quelque chose entre les Dieux et les hommes; Mais avant
que de chercher la pure verité on s'arreste à ses ombres et à ses
figures.

. . . the common actions of Life being their object, it is easier to find
Truth there. Because one sees more men in error and foolishness. . . .
But as there are always plenty of subjects for such Pieces, one more
often finds there the *vraisemblable* genre than in the Heroic pieces
which are only fiction, since there were few men who merited to be
called Heroes—that is to say, something between men and Gods;
But sooner than seek pure truth people stop with its shadows and its
images.

La Bibliothèque francoise (1667), 2nd ed., pp. 88–9

As we have already seen, Sorel did not succeed in his maturity as he did
with *Francion*, in spite of the refreshing clarity and literal-mindedness
of his criticism. What was missing in his later years was the element of
irresponsibility, the comic abandon of *Francion*, but this was no more
than one half of the reason for this success; the other lay in that interest
in *naïveté*, one could almost say, in realism, which was present
throughout his life.

It seems fairly clear that the primary impulse behind *Francion*
derived from Sorel's reading of the picaresque, and perhaps especially
the work of Quevedo and Alemán, whom he mentions in his text and to
whom his debt is obvious. What they seem to have suggested to him is
that 'low actions' could be susceptible of a literary treatment that was
something more than simply comic, arousing interest in themselves.
One of his characters, listening to Francion's narration of his own life
story, urges him to continue with his school-time adventures, referring
him to the example of the picaresque:

Ignorez vous que ces actions basses sont infiniment agreables, et que
nous prenons meme du contentement a oüyr celles des gueux et des
faquins comme de Guzman d'Alfarache et de Lazaril de Tormes,
comment n'en recevray je point à oüyr celles d'un Gentilhomme
escolier, qui fait paroistre la subtilité de son esprit et la grandeur de
son courage des sa jeunesse.

Do you not know that these low actions are infinitely agreeable and that we even get enjoyment from hearing those of beggars and rogues like Guzman d'Alfarache and of Lazaril de Tormes, how should I not accept those of a Gentleman at school, who makes apparent the subtlety of his spirit and the grandeur of his courage since his youth.

Histoire comique de Francion (1623); *Romanciers du xvii Siècle,* ed. A. Adam (1968), p. 180[10]

What is interesting here is the combination of 'low actions' with heroic qualities, a combination which it is assumed can be found in actual experience in the life-story of a gentleman. This is the motivation behind Sorel's determination to provide what he calls 'an image of human life', which could be provided within the framework of the comic and satiric mode. His defence of this method involves a rejection of the commonplace arguments of most of his contemporaries:

N'est il pas vray que c'est une tres agreable et tres utile chose que le stile comique et satyrique. L'on y void toutes les choses dans leur naifveté. Toutes les actions y paroissent sans dissimulation, au lieu que dans les livres serieux il y a de certains respects qui empeschent de parler de cette sorte, et cela fait que les Histoires sont imparfaites et plus remplies de mensonge que de verité.

Is it not true that the comic and satiric style is a very agreeable and useful thing? One sees there everything in its naïveté. All actions there appear without dissimulation, whereas in serious books there are certain considerations which prevent discussion of this kind, and this means that Histories are imperfect and more filled with false-hood than with truth.

Histoire comique de Francion, p. 1321[11]

Naïveté and comedy together are the key elements in Sorel's whole view of fiction, acting together to bring him to a position from which he could see the adventures of his hero not simply as picaresque or comical but as something which could be organised into a coherent criticism of contemporary life—in other words, a novel.

Another element was important, however, and this was Sorel's sense that fiction as he imagined it could be employed with a direct social

[10]The two examples, *Guzman* and *Lazaril,* are an addition to the 1626 text of *Francion.*
[11]This passage is an addition to the 1633 text.

purpose, employed in order to shape a view of contemporary life which life itself was almost demanding. *Francion* has in fact a more immediate social relevance than any other novel of its period. Sorel was aware of change taking place in society around him, which involved the destruction of a whole way of life previously associated with the gentleman and he used his fiction so as to project a new ideal, a new code of behaviour in a world where the gentleman's place was not only very different but was much more insecure than it had previously been. The young gentleman, Francion, Marquis de la Porte, is chosen as the novel's hero for two reasons. Firstly, for his name, which suggests frankness and French-ness, and for his typically noble qualities. He is an apt representative of what is best in the nobility of France. Secondly, because his liveliness and playfulness make him a suitable hinge on which to turn a good deal of comic action. Francion's father represents a way of life which he is aware is passing away. Brought up to be a soldier, he returns from the wars to his Breton estate to find his social position undermined in a world which is increasingly organised according to financial considerations and which is dominated by the servants of the State rather than by people of noble blood. Consequently he sends his son to Paris to study and to adjust himself to this new world. Sorel's interest in him derives from his ability to survive and to adjust, adapting old cultural and social values, based on the idea of birth and breeding, to the new world.

Sorel's idea of the gentleman very much belongs to his age. He writes in the interests of aristocracy and his idea of virtue has a strong social element relating to manners rather than to morality. He pays lip-service to a more elevated conception, telling us in his 1626 Preface: 'He who is a peasant and who lives well as a peasant seems to me more praiseworthy than he who is born a Gentleman and does not perform the appropriate actions.'[12] However, he actually sees an absolute difference between the one and the other based on the gentleman's superior refinement. Only the gentleman can raise himself to a level of fully human dignity, away from comparisons with the animal world. So, he tells a friend, the gentleman must take care in the matter of love-making, employing an elevated vocabulary, even though his aim may eventually be that of the peasant:

. . . nous le faisons bien en autre maniere, nous usons bien de plus de

[12] 'Celuy qui est paysan et qui vit fort bien en paysan, me semble plus loüable que celuy qui est nay Gentilhomme et n'en faict pas les actions.' 'Aux Grands', p. 1260.

caresses qu'eux, qui n'ont point d'autre envie, que de saouler leur appetit stupide, qui ne differe en rien de celuy des brutes, ils ne le font que du corps, et nous le faisons du corps et de l'ame tout ensemble, puisque faire y a . . . puisque les mesmes parties de nostre corps que celles du leur se joignent ensemble, nous devons remuer la langue, ouvrir la bouche et deserrer les dents comme eux quand nous en voudrons discourir, mais tout comme en leur copulation qu'ils font de mesme façon que nous, ils n'apportent pas neantmoins les mesmes mignardises et les mesmes transports d'esprit, ainsi en discourant de ce jeu là, bien que nostre corps face la mesme action qu'eux pour en parler, nostre esprit doit faire paroitre sa gentilesse, et nous faut avoir des termes autres que les leurs: de cela l'on peut apprendre aussi que nous avons quelque chose de divin et de celeste, mais que quant a eux ils sont tout terrestres et brutaux.

. . . we do it in a very different manner, we use many more caresses than them, who have no other desire than to surfeit their stupid appetite, which differs in nothing from that of the brutes, they do it only with the body, and we do it with the body and the soul together since it has to be done . . . since the same parts of our bodies as those of theirs join together, we must move our tongues, open our mouths and unclench our teeth like them when we wish to discuss it, but just as they behave in the same way as us in their copulation, but do not bring to it the same delicateness and the same spiritual transports, so in discussing that affair, although our bodies may perform the same action as theirs, in order to speak of it our spirit must make its gentility apparent, and we have to have terms other than theirs: from that one could also learn that we have something of the divine and the celestial, but that as for them they are all earthy and brutish.

Histoire comique de Francion, pp. 321–2

Other qualities are important to Sorel than those which come under the heading of social and cultural refinement. He takes care to establish Francion's courage, stoicism, sense of proportion, self-control, but as the above passage indicates, none of these is interesting as such or traced in its connection to human nature as such. Sorel's hero is primarily a gentleman, that is, he adjusts his character and his demeanour according to an entirely externalised code, which marks his membership of the class of the elect, above those with money, with power or even with talent.

This conception of the gentleman is the most important single idea in

Francion, but the action is nevertheless wide enough to extend to all social classes and to give an impression of society as a whole from the point of view of the values embodied in the hero's character. The adventures of the hero from birth to marriage to the Italian heiress, Nays, are held within a loosely epic structure which allow precisely the kind of shifting focus which Sorel's plan requires.

Book I begins *in medias res*, with a situation which sets the tone for the whole novel. We are introduced abruptly to a climactic tableaux scene which is at the centre of the Book and which brings before us a whole range of human passions and conditions—greed, criminality, lasciviousness, ignorance and complacency. The separate parts of the tableau are drawn from *fabliaux* material—the impotent old cuckold, contributing to his own downfall, the over-smart lover, the passive wife-mistress, satisfied in spite of everyone else's discomfiture. Valentin, the husband, is tied to a tree in the woods, where he has gone to seek a hopelessly lost potency. Catherine, the male/female, servant/robber, is hanging above the château moat, exposed to the wonder of an audience of peasants from a nearby village. One of the other robbers is hanging with Catherine, a third has escaped with Francion's money, the fourth has had his unwillingness rewarded in Laurette's bed, while Francion himself is lying in the moat, seriously hurt by a blow on the head received when his rope-ladder had been unfastened by Catherine. The reaction of the peasants to this revelation is not the least important part of the comedy, especially as they decide that Francion has been engaged in sorcery and force him to flee from the village in a wagon.

This opening situation presents us with a glimpse of humanity from a completely reductivist viewpoint and provides a frame within which the character of Francion is to expand. The Book ends with Francion's meeting with Count Raymond at a village inn and with his explanation of the events which had brought him to the château of Valentin. The relationship between these two is the most important factor at this stage of the novel because it is used as the means by which we understand the nature of Francion's character and at the same time it provides justification for the narration of events which precede the beginning of the action.

Book II begins, however, with the comic introduction of the old bawd, Agathe, who takes what advantage she can of the hero's amorous sleep-walking. She interrupts the development of Francion's narrative with an account of her own adventures which is justified by the fact that it gives us a chance to know more about Laurette and so ties earlier events with those still to come in the immediate future. In itself it is interesting, too, because of what it tells us about human motivation and behaviour, especially in the matter of love. Agathe herself is a moral lesson which might have come from the verse of Villon, the walking grave of her own beauty, but still driven by sexual impulses which she cannot satisfy.

At this point, when Agathe has brought us up to date on the background of Laurette, and so provided commentary on Francion's own narration, Francion goes with Count Raymond, whose identity he does not know, to his château, where he entertains him with the story of his life. This includes an account of the background of his family and his childhood, showing the development of the primary impulses of adventurousness, generosity and bravery in his character. This is continued with his experiences at school in Paris, which are reminiscent of the unfortunate adventures of Pablo Buscon in the school of Quevedo's El Cabra. Here Sorel breaks off Francion's narrative and introduces a reference to the heroine, Nays, by means of a portrait which has been lent to Raymond by an Italian nobleman who is staying with him. Nothing is made of this at the time, but it shows the way in which Sorel is determined to keep the various threads of his action present in the reader's mind, even while he is dealing with events so long in the past. It is what he later learns of Nays that persuades Francion to go to meet her and so takes him away from Raymond's château into the next phase of action.

The description of Francion's adventures in Paris gives Sorel a chance to show the formation of his hero's character in process, and at the same time to introduce a good deal of satire of contemporary manners and institutions which is directly relevant to his hero's situation. In the first instance he develops the character of the pedant Hortensius as a foil to Francion, the truly educated man. Hortensius is at once ridiculous in his pedantry and absurd in his social aspirations, and is provided with a foil himself in the madman Collinet. Collinet's intermittent madness makes him less ridiculous than Hortensius's permanent foolishness. Francion, on the other hand, gradually develops in dignity, sophistication and nobility of spirit. The first step to this is shaking off the pedantry of school. He tells his ex-tutor near the end of the book: 'The best book that you could see is experience of the world.'[13] Studying this, and trying to develop his natural faculties, without vulgar prejudice, has given him a combination of learning and charm which stamps his character as a man. In Paris, after he has

[13] 'Le plus beau livre que vous puissiez voir . . . c'est l'experience du monde.' P. 455.

finished at the University, his money is stolen from him and he has to cope with adversity and public contempt. In this atmosphere he acquires the measure of stoicism which he assures Raymond is an essential ingredient of nobility: 'It is to have a soul which resists all the assaults which fortune can mount against it, and which mingles no baseness among its actions.'[14]

Gradually Francion's noble bearing enables him to establish himself in Paris. He practises as a poet and comes to understand the best of contemporary poetry and criticism. He also sets up a society for the establishment of gentlemanly conduct and as its leading spirit also establishes himself financially as a gentleman-follower of the nobleman Clerante. This relationship opens up a new sphere of action and enables Sorel, through Francion, to comment on contemporary manners among the highest classes in the capital city in his day. The development of the relationship between Clerante and his mistress, Luce, in which Francion himself plays an ambiguous role, gives us an insight into the nature of love in this environment. Further insight comes through the story which Francion tells of an anonymous nobleman's attempt to win the love of a doctor's daughter and the attempted assassination which follows, revealing a degree of brutality and ignobleness which Francion has set himself to reduce. Between these two episodes we have a parody of the Horatian interlude in a retreat to the country which is crude and farcical. Here, in a world lacking refinement, Francion feels at liberty to indulge his playfulness by heightening our awareness of peasant brutishness. The central episode is provided by an event in which they disguise themselves as peasants, attend a wedding and put a laxative in the soup. The fun begins when the guests are dancing in the courtyard of the château. There is little attempt here at satire—no correction of vices, but rather the further development of Sorel's fundamentally comic view of unaccommodated man.

At this point Sorel resumes control of the narrative in describing an incident which clearly marks Francion off from the peasants and allows him to show the essential nobility he has acquired. In order to find out what his present attitude is, Raymond begins a discussion about the theft of Francion's money years before, which had reduced him to great hardship. Francion shows that he is quite above bearing malice for such a small occasion for such a long time although he has no wish to meet the thief, whoever he might be. Raymond takes Francion's reply as offensive, reveals that he himself was the thief, and leaves the room,

[14] '. . . c'est avoir une ame qui resiste a tous les assauts que luy peut livrer la fortune, et qui ne mesle rien de bas parmy ses actions.' P. 252.

threatening vengeance. Francion is confined to his room, without his clothes, waiting to see what Raymond intends to do but warned by a servant that he intends to kill him. When another servant comes in the morning to dress him, Francion has an admirable opportunity to show that he is above base fear of death and can control his response to personal danger:

> Je ne sçaurois quitter mon humeur ordinaire, quelque maleur qui m'avienne, dit Francion, et puis je vous asseure que je ne redoute point un passage auquel je me suis dès long temps resolu, puisque tost ou tard il le faut franchir. Je ne me fasche que de ce que l'on me veut faire mourir en coquin.

> I would not change my ordinary mood whatever misfortune might happen to me, said Francion, and besides, I assure you I have no fear of a passage concerning which I have been for a long time resolved, since sooner or later it must be undertaken. I am only annoyed that they want to put me to death like a rogue.
>
> *Histoire comique de Francion*, p. 306

It turns out, however, that what Francion is actually being prepared for is a rather well-mannered orgy involving the gentlemen of the neighbourhood, their wives or mistresses and Laurette, who has been specially brought by Agathe under the pretence that she is going to visit a local shrine. After several days of this, Francion parts for the spa at which Nays is waiting for the young nobleman she has come to France to marry, not yet knowing that he has recently died.

The plan is, of course, that Francion will try to ingratiate himself with Nays and marry her instead of the unfortunate deceased, but on his way he has further comic adventures. The first is an encounter with an innkeeper and his errant wife who claims that he is incapable of satisfying her sexually. Francion's cure for their problem is to witness the fact that the innkeeper can perform satisfactorily and to leave them with threats and financial rewards to ensure their living together amicably in the future. Next is an incident in which Francion meets a gentleman who is afflicted with avarice and pretensions to social elevation and uses one vice to counteract the other. He visits him and claims relationship, so involving him in expense. During the night the host's daughter, prevented from marrying by her father's meanness, takes her lover into the house. The father confronts them, sword in hand, under the impression that he will find Francion's men stealing his money, which is locked in that room. Here again we have a farcical situation, though this time also a potentially tragic one. Francion, however, makes use of the event to show Du Buisson the results of his meanness and ends by convincing him that generosity pays.

Nothing more happens before Francion meets Nays, who sensibly decides to make the best of the fact that Floriandre is dead and is very impressed with Francion's politeness and charm. They travel slowly towards Italy and the inevitable marriage but Sorel finds a way of postponing it by having Francion imprisoned by his rivals. His train splits up, seeking him. Nays is disillusioned and goes on to Rome without him, and Francion is turned loose in the Italian countryside, penniless. Here he lives as a peasant for some time and gives Sorel a chance to provide a parody of the Arcadian romance. Francion encounters a number of typical characters in a number of amorous adventures—the innocent shepherdess, the lustful married woman, the jealous shepherds—all of whom could have come straight from Boccaccio's *Decameron*.

This phase of the novel is brought rather clumsily to an end when Francion is mid-way through an affair with the daughter of a rich bourgeois. Leaving her at night, he is caught up in the confused events which follow the rumoured betrayal of the town. This incident ends with the execution of the man responsible for spreading the rumour. It shows a good deal of skilfulness on Sorel's part in assimilating exemplary material and adapting it as plot machinery, but is worked into the novel only mechanically. At this stage, in fact, Francion's character has faded into the background, the narrative impulse has flagged, and Sorel is developing satirical and humorous interests that reduce the cohesiveness of his fiction. We lose sight of Francion's motives when he lingers in Italy and in France, without making any attempt to get back to Nays. Instead he takes pleasure in manipulating the various individuals and groups he comes into contact with, eventually setting up as a wise man and giving Sorel a chance to work in more *fabliaux* material. So Francion tells his landlord, who is curious about his wife's chastity, to tell her that the magician has said that all cuckolds will turn into dogs in the morning. Unable to keep the secret, she tells her friends, and the morning sees the town's whole female population examining their husbands. In the landlord's case, he discovers her guilt, but goes on also to discover her innocence. Of the two occasions on which she was unfaithful, one was caused by her ignorance and the second by her care for his interests. Like a wise man, the host settles down content. Another marriage situation is settled by an ancient device. A girl's midnight visitor is to be discovered by her putting a cross on his forehead. She asks his name, finds that he is the man she fancies anyway and tells him of the trick. He puts a cross on the foreheads of his sleeping companions as well and the slow-witted father has to seek Francion's help again. The discovery made, a potentially dangerous situation is again averted by common sense, and it ends in marriage instead of violence.

It is only a chance meeting between Francion and one of his gentle-man followers who has been seeking him through Italy and France, that withdraws Francion from this situation and gets him to Rome. From that point on there is little to stand in the way of his marriage to Nays and final acquisition of social stability and a place in the world befitting his talents and abilities. Sorel's sense of the integrity of his subject is restored to him at this point. He brings Hortensius back into the action as a foil to Francion, partly to relieve our sense of Francion as an adventurer, partly to strengthen our awareness of the fitting connection between rank and talent. The ridicule of Hortensius is based on the fact that he combines ignorance of the world with social pretentiousness and a perfectly apt situation is found for him when supposed envoys arrive for him from Poland with the news that he has been elected to the vacant throne. As king-elect Hortensius is embarrassed because he has no money, no clothes, and no manners. His case is inversely analagous to Francion's, who is acquiring rank and money but who is equipped to benefit from the situation. Once this digression has come to an end, there is little, at least in the novel's first version, to prevent the marriage itself and the end of the action.

As the later parts of his novel indicate, Sorel's commitment to the business of representing the texture of contemporary life was not consistently strong. Lacking a means of introducing his comic and satiric material naturally as he develops the action, he is willing to abandon it almost completely for the sake of bringing in stories and situations drawn directly from other forms of comic literature. That this weakens the interest of *Francion* is beyond dispute. Yet at the same time it weakens it without destroying it. The structure of *Francion* allows a shifting narrative focus and the way in which action is built up around the central character permits a constant movement from the centre outwards in the construction of a comic vision of life as a whole. Sorel might have maintained firmer control, but the basic framework of his novel is intact. Later revisions did not help him to improve it, though at times he attempted to increase the element of psychological motivation behind changes in narrative direction. At the centre of *Francion* is the idea of man as a gentleman, an idea of man as moulding himself according to a pattern which is not justified by experience but imposed on experience by a number of social and cultural pressures working together. Sorel's purpose is to show how character may be moulded according to this pattern and at the same time to depict the absurdity of human nature in other forms. His basic idea of gentility is not greatly different from that of his contemporaries, which found its expression in the heroic romances. What saved him from the romance was the irreverence he shared with the *libertins*, the interest in sexuality, and his perception of the insecurity of the concepts which were supposedly dominant in contemporary social life. These factors motivated his turning to comedy in the first place, but they also ensured that the comedy should be the comedy of contemporary life and they governed the choice of a central character who could be seen putting together his own character amidst the flux of social living. In other words, they made Sorel a novelist.

LE ROMANT COMIQUE

Coming to *Le Romant comique* from *Francion*, the reader will notice that Sorel and Scarron have a good deal in common. Their basic values are similar; they are both strongly committed to the idea of the gentleman as combining the best of the old heroic qualities associated with the nobility and the new refinement of the period. They are similar too in that they project these values against a comic background in which human passions unmoderated by refinement and unelevated by nobility of sentiment appear crude and violent, amusing and frightening, by turns. The difference between them in literary terms derives from the way in which Scarron reacted to the writing of Cervantes. Like Sorel he seems to have been strongly influenced by the picaresque. Before he produced *Le Romant comique*, he is supposed to have contemplated writing a romance in which the hero ended on the gallows. But in the novel he actually wrote the influence of Cervantes is clearly predominant over that of the picaresque. In *Le Romant comique* there is also a much stronger romanesque element than there is in *Francion*. Its particular quality derives, in fact, from the way in which the element of reductive comedy is related to this romanesque element in a manner suggested by Cervantes and yet radically different from his own method in *Don Quixote*.

Scarron makes several disclaimers of any intention of writing in the same mode as the romances, claiming quite aggressively at times to be free from aesthetic considerations by virtue of his own foolishness. The reader questions Scarron's narrator at his own peril, as we see at the beginning of his 'Histoire de L'Amante Invisible':

> On dira icy de quoi je me mesle. . . . Sçaçhe le sot qui s'en scandalise que tout homme est sot en ce bas monde, aussi bien que menteur, les uns plus et les autres moins; et moy que vous parle, peut-estre plus sot que les autres, quoy que j'aye plus de franchise à l'avoüer, et que mon livre n'estant qu'un ramas de sottises, j'espere que chaque sot y trouvera un petit caractere de ce qu'il est, s'il n'est pas trop aveuglé de l'amour-propre.

> I will be asked here why I concern myself with this. . . . Let the fool who is offended at it know that every man is a fool in this base world, as well as a liar, some more and others less; and I who am speaking to you, perhaps a bigger fool than the others, though I may have more frankness in admitting it, and that my book being nothing but a heap of follies, I hope that every fool will find there a little representation of what he is, if he is not too blinded by self-love.
> Le Romant comique (1651 and 1657); Romanciers de xviie Siècle, ed. A. Adam (1968), pp. 552–3

Another warning, at the beginning of Chapter xii, informs the sensitive reader that he would find nothing in the novel but foolishness, even if it were to grow as long as Mlle de Scudéry's Le Grand Cyrus, and puts forward a novel version of the claim to mix amusement and instruction: 'Without filling my Book with examples to imitate, by painting actions and things at one time ridiculous and another time blameworthy, I will instruct and divert in the same way as a drunken man. . . .'[15] But Scarron's commitment to comedy is by no means as strong as these aggressive interjections would suggest. He still has a rooted investment in standards of behaviour more or less elevated, just like Sorel, but he has gone one step beyond Sorel in the direction of Cervantes and has come to see his own standards as forms of conceptualisation of questionable relation to experience itself. Consequently he seeks to present what we could call romanesque elements concerning characters definitely above the comic level in conjunction with elements of comedy and

[15] '. . . sans emplir mon Livre d'exemples à imiter, par des peintures d'actions et de choses tantost ridicules, tantost blasmables, j'instruiray en divertissant de la mesme façon qu'un yvrogne. . . .' P. 575.

violence. They are never allowed to assimilate one to another but are kept in a sort of dialectic relationship, existing independently but overlapping at many points.

Scarron's basic method is the establishment of a romance action which is then deliberately fragmented and over which is imposed a sub-plot reflecting the manner of the picaresque tales and the burlesque representation of a group of characters not necessarily involved in either plot. *Le Romant comique* is not a picaresque story, even in structural terms, though it is episodic. It is held together by virtue of the fact that it narrates primarily the adventures of a group of actors, all of whom are of equal importance as members of the group and so as subjects of the author's attention. The romanesque plot and the picaresque interest develop against the larger action and within its limits, which are stretched only by means of the different stories which certain characters tell. Scarron also interweaves a number of more or less romanesque *nouvelles* into the body of the work, by this means extending and elaborating his own commentary on the human condition. Then he also adds his often caustic and aggressive commentary which constantly reminds the reader that he is dealing with a fiction whose capacity to interest and intrigue him in spite of its absurdity is itself a reflection on the nature of human experience.

The central story of *Le Romant comique* could well have been told as an extended *nouvelle* with strong elements of the romance. Its central characters are a young man, whom any discerning reader will immediately understand to be the rightful but displaced heir of a Scottish lord, and the legitimate but unrecognised daughter of a French nobleman. To give the young hero his stage name, by which he is known throughout the book, Destiny is rejected by his supposed father and mother and brought up, thanks to the good offices of his godfather, as a gentleman, with the two sons of a local nobleman. With one of these youths he cements a firm friendship, but with the other, the brutal Sainct-Far, he is only on terms of indifference. Together they go to Italy, where Destiny is left behind at Rome because of illness and meets Estoile/Leonora and her mother Mlle de Boissiere when he saves them from the unwelcome attentions of a Frenchman who later turns out to be the villainous and brutal Saldagne. After falling in love with Estoile and falling out of favour with her mother, although he has narrowly escaped murder at Saldagne's hands on their account, Destiny makes a campaign with the Papal forces and returns to France with Verville and Sainct-Far.

At this point Destiny's fate gets entangled with that of the two brothers. Verville becomes involved with one of Saldagne's sisters, the intrigue is discovered and in the confusion which follows one of them narrowly escapes rape at the hands of Sainct-Far. A duel follows in which Verville and Destiny confront Saldagne and Sainct-Far. The duel is interrupted but ends with Destiny's losing favour with Verville's father and a marriage being arranged between the two brothers and the two sisters.

This support withdrawn, Destiny decides to travel in search of his fortune, but on his way out of France he meets Estoile and her mother again. They are coming back to France to meet her father but have been robbed on the way and are glad to accept Destiny's help a second time. They go together to Paris via Orleans, helped by Rancune, whom they meet on the way. In Paris they hear that the French nobleman is now out of favour and has left the court and gone to Holland where they follow him, but not before they have encountered Saldagne again and Destiny has been robbed of a box containing a portrait of Estoile's father. Arriving at the Hague they find that her father has gone to England. Mlle de Boissiere falls ill, Destiny loses his money and they decide to join a troupe of players.

After this, having arrived at Le Mans with the actors, they continue to be plagued by Saldagne and are also involved with the villainous La Rappiniere, under-sheriff of Le Mans, who has actually been responsible for the theft which happened in Paris. Estoile's friend Angelica is abducted by Saldagne in mistake for her but released when Saldagne accidentally comes across Estoile herself. With Verville's help Destiny rescues Estoile and through the agency of another friend, he recovers the stolen box from La Rappiniere. This is the point Scarron had reached at the end of the second volume. All that actually remained to be concluded in the third volume, which he was writing when he died, was the punishment of La Rappiniere, who is heading for the gallows, and of Saldagne, whose dreadful violence is gradually bringing him closer to destruction, and the discovery of Destiny's birth, together with Estoile's recognition and their marriage.

Le Romant comique contains two similar stories which are related by central characters—the history of La Caverne, Angelica's mother, which is never finished, and that of Leander, a young man who joins the troupe to follow Angelica. There are also four independent *nouvelles* which are rather loosely tied in to the narrative. The action of the novel, however, does not run through these stories although it does give rise to them and make them psychologically necessary. It actually begins with the arrival of the troupe at Le Mans and concerns the events of their stay there, mixing up separate narrative passages with the adventures which arise from the foolishness of Ragotin and the poet, the malice of Rancune, and the various relationships between different members of the players' troupe and the inhabitants of the town and surrounding area. The episodic nature of the plot and the way in which the various stories are split up ensures that none of these elements obtains supremacy over the others. As a result of this *Le Romant comique* has to be read as a sequence of different modes. Its contents cannot be added up to make a sum. It offers a view of reality which is attainable only in constant movement from one mood to another.

The novel begins with a self-contained unit of four chapters which introduce the players as they come into Le Mans and present a fast-moving series of actions and confrontations, in which the character of La Rappiniere as a rogue and Destiny as a hero are firmly developed. Any suggestion that what we have to expect is a developing action, however, is quickly allayed by the burlesque report of La Rappiniere's nocturnal encounter with a goat. And Chapter V 'Which doesn't contain much', beginning with a warning that the book will focus on no single hero: 'since there is nothing more perfect than a Hero of a book, a half dozen Heroes, or so-called heroes will do more honour to mine than a single one, who perhaps would be the one least spoken of. . . .'[16] The chapters which follow accordingly complicate the narrative thread by introducing the other players and particularly Estoile. At the same time Scarron introduces the comic event of the litters, which all gather together in the same place, indicating that mere force of coincidence can produce situations stranger than romance. This incident is also important because it is the chance of so many litters being in the same area at the time that saves Estoile from Saldagne.

At this point the action pauses while Scarron introduces the first of his *nouvelles*, which is supposedly narrated by the comic Ragotin, who has just been introduced to the readers for the first time. Ragotin, with Rancune, is one of the most important characters of the novel, though he is not engaged in the central action at all. The little man suffers from pride and anger as much as the old player from malice and La Rappiniere from the tendency towards insolence and rapine. All three exemplify the power of these emotions in the human character. Ragotin particularly is a kind of anti-hero, reflecting on the motives and manners of those involved in the central action the strange light cast by

[16] '. . . puisqu'il n'y a rien de plus parfaict qu'un Heros de livre, demy-douzaine ou soy-disant tels feront plus d'honneur au mien, qu'un seul, qui seroit peut-estre celuy dont on parleroit le moins. . . .' P. 540.

his burlesque adventures. Especially, but by no means exclusively, by Ragotin, a number of animals are brought into the action and take their place at odd moments as the equals of the human participants, very much heightening the reductive effect.

The *nouvelle* attributed to Ragotin is the 'Histoire de L'Amante Invisible', which shows us how Scarron has reacted to Cervantes and how he has developed Cervantes' themes in his own way. The hero of the *nouvelle* is a young Spanish gentleman of noble lineage who has acquired all the physical and moral attributes of the ideal of his class. The story provides an unexpected test for him which questions the extent to which he is capable of behaving correctly in a situation from which the social and intellectual factors which usually prop up judgement are absent. In the first instance he is approached by a lady who refuses to show her face but offers him love and riches. His judgement confused, he nevertheless falls in love with her. Shortly after he is approached by another lady who tries to awaken doubt in his mind concerning his invisible mistress and announces that she also loves him. Then he is spirited away by four masked men and taken to a magnificent castle, where he is presented with the same temptation by another beautiful woman. This is a straightforward test of constancy, but also something more. Scarron interweaves into his text many references to the romances and to *Don Quixote*. He makes it quite explicit that we are to think of what is happening to Dom Carlos as a species of enchantment, and makes enchantment serve the same purpose as Cervantes. That is, it creates an atmosphere in which we can become aware not merely of the relationship between the concept of constancy and the character of Dom Carlos, but also of the importance of the concept as a constituent part of the reality of character itself. Dom Carlos succeeds in proving his constancy and remains faithful to the unseen mistress. He is, then, constant. But it turns out that the seen and the unseen mistress are actually one and the same person, so that if he had been unfaithful to the one it would merely have been confirmation of his love for her. The test he had survived is one in which the judgement and social interests have been deliberately weakened and confused in order to give him an opportunity of showing how far he could remain constant to an idea; and circumstances suggest to us, as the story concludes happily, that this is the only ultimate proof of the possession of constancy at all.

Immediately after this *nouvelle* there is an abrupt change of mood, as we move into a burlesque episode in which Ragotin's anger is repaid by physical humiliation and the loss of his hat, and this in turn leads into an aesthetic discussion regarding the possibility of turning Ragotin's *nouvelle* into a play. Here Destiny shows his judgement in aesthetic matters while Ragotin reminds us that the judgement required to criticise literature is essentially the same as that which governs conduct. The proximity of this discussion to the story of Dom Carlos is not without importance. Destiny, after all, is a Dom Carlos in a minor key; and the connection is made closer by Ragotin's decision to love one of the actresses, without being able to make up his mind which one!

Only at this point, at the beginning of Chapter XII, does the story of Destiny and Estoile begin to come out into the open, but it is interrupted by the outbreak of a disturbance in a neighbouring room in which several naked people are engaged in a battle in total darkness. Their situation is ludicrous enough—they are fighting without, for the most part, knowing the reason, which is inadequate in itself, and they are continuing to fight only because of the darkness. It becomes more ludicrous, and more significant to us, when it draws in other characters, including Destiny, ending only with the entrance of La Rappiniere in his capacity of law enforcement officer and creditor of the host.

So Destiny is drawn into these very unheroic events just before he becomes the narrator of his own story. He takes this as far as the time when he falls out of favour with Mlle de Boissiere in Rome, as a result of the behaviour of Sainct-Far. Then, immediately after he has broken off, we hear the continuation of the adventure of the litters and learn how Saldagne, confused by the number of litters and made furious by his disappointment in missing Estoile, kills the servant who had brought the information about her mode of travelling. The savage violence of this scene is itself modified, however, by the comic reaction of the curé of Domfront whose litter Saldagne has stopped. Confused by fear and self-interest, the curé is convinced that Saldagne is one of his neighbours with whom he has a legal process and who now wishes to assassinate him, and he deposes to this effect to La Rappiniere after the event. The whole episode ends with the capture of one of Saldagne's servants, but before Destiny continues his story we are introduced to two new characters who are to be important members of the group—that is, the charlatan and his Spanish wife. Then Destiny's story continues, but before he can go beyond the marriage of Verville and Sainct-Far he is interrupted again by a burlesque serenade which Ragotin has laid on for Estoile. This event, which ends badly for the little man, as usual, intermingles two sexual themes—the conceited love-making of Ragotin and the sexual antics of the dogs which disturb the serenade.

The narrative now returns to the present while the group perform their play, go to the gaol to interview the captured servant and Ragotin continues to make a fool of himself with Angelica and La Caverne, insisting on gallantry which is painful to them and ends in his humiliation. In Chapter XVIII we return a third time to Destiny's story, which he brings up to the time when he and Estoile join the players. Here we notice something which is a feature of Scarron's narrative everywhere but in the *nouvelles*. That is, the abandonment of what we might think of as the normal proportions of narrative and the development of insignificant events at the expense of action. Destiny's report of their journey to Holland, for example, is hurried into a few lines: 'Finally, we left Paris for Peronne, went to Brussels and from Brussels to the Hague. . . .'[17] Yet in the same narrative we are given a long account of their comic entry into Orleans, which has no significance in itself. The effect, of course, is to reduce our involvement with the emotions of the central characters in their exigencies and increase our sense of the connection between their adventures and the world inhabited by Ragotin and La Rappiniere.

At the end of Destiny's account we return to the present again with the loves of Roquebrune and Rancour for the charlatan's wife and Ragotin and Roquebrune's ridiculous adventures on horseback on the way to a marriage where they are to help in the celebrations. Through this marriage a new character is introduced, who is to be important in the central action; this is the lawyer, M. de la Garouffiere, whose conversation with the players gives Scarron an opportunity to assert standards of naturalness in fiction above the extravagant sublimity of the romances. This in turn introduces another *nouvelle*—'A Trompeur, Trompeur et Demy', which reflects directly on the values involved in the central story. Its young hero, in spite of poor appearances, impresses a rich young widow with his '*riche mine*', his '*bonne mine*', '*esprit*' and general merit. Accordingly, she gives him her love and offers him marriage, and when he is unfaithful takes the initiative to win him back by manipulating circumstances in her own favour. The story might contain a lesson for Destiny and Estoile regarding the way they should deal with their own circumstances. It plays an important part in Scarron's statement regarding the way in which tragic extremes can be avoided where common sense and courage prevail.

Immediately after the ending of this story the romantic circumstances of the central story reassert themselves with the abduction of

[17] 'Enfin nous partismes de Paris pour Peronne; de Peronne, nous allasmes à Bruxelles et de Bruxelles à la Haye.' P. 637.

Angelica by Saldagne. The first volume of the novel ends here, and the second begins with the pursuit of Angelica's ravishers by Destiny. At once the heroic tone is reduced in a most significant way by the incident in which a naked madman leaps from a tree and rides behind the hero! Then, when Destiny loses his way and stops, the forward-moving impulse of the narrative breaks up into accounts of the burlesque adventures of Rancune and Ragotin. The central story is further modified too at this point, through the story of Angelica's mother, La Caverne, which shows how crude and dangerous situations are quite compatible with perfectly ordinary circumstances and how the basic situation of the abducted heroine can be present even where there is no element of physical force. Typically, here Scarron uses the comic interruption of a greyhound into the women's room to break off the story and separate the past from the present in terms of tone rather than time.

Now Destiny meets the servant Leander, hears more about Angelica, and also learns Leander's own story, which again reflects on his own. Leander and Angelica are also lovers, also separated by circumstances, which he is thinking of trying to overcome by heroic action. Significantly Destiny dissuades him and advises a moderate manipulation rather than outright confrontation, stressing the difficulties which could lie in their path on purely practical grounds. Following this good advice, the comic dimension of the novel reasserts itself with a series of fights and violent confrontations. Firstly, there is a violent altercation between the local schoolmaster and the brother of the dying innkeeper which is begun on a point of honour and carried on while the man is actually passing away. Then we hear stories from the curé about the avarice of the innkeeper which provide amusing evidence of how ideas motivated by basic personality traits can conquer even the demands of flesh and blood. The innkeeper's avarice and stupidity rise to the heights of heroism itself when he asserts that he will not rise again if it means being buried in a good sheet! His body becomes the occasion of further adventures when Rancune uses it to frighten Ragotin. No sooner is the fight which follows this patched up but Ragotin is in more trouble and showing us again what power anger has in the absence of discretion. But of course, Ragotin here is no more than the foil to Saldagne, whose greater power and consistency make him more dangerous. The line between them is one in which we pass from laughter to fear in successive degrees, not according to the nature of the passion but the circumstances which accompany it.

With Chapter XI, 'Amongst the least Amusing of the Present

Volume', we are at the centre of the novel's second part and we learn
that Angelica has been released and Estoile captured in her place.
Before we can be certain of what has been happening, however, the
narrative sequence is characteristically broken. Angelica's story is held
back by trivial circumstances, and we have to wait until Destiny meets
Vervielle in a neighbouring town before we can be sure of what has
happened to the heroine. Two chapters later we learn from Estoile's
own words how she was led away. Meanwhile, through Chapters
VIII-X we have been learning more about Destiny after the reintroduction of Garouffiere and the wedding party. Destiny can prove himself
again a man of wit and sense with Garouffiere and at the same time free
himself from the grotesque attentions of Mme Bouvillon by his combination of politeness and common sense. The adventure ends in physical
humiliation for her, but not for the hero.

After Chapter XIII another *nouvelle* is inserted into the narrative,
this time by Garouffiere—'La juge de sa propre cause'. This is the most
romanesque of all the *nouvelles*, which Scarron has adapted from his
source so as to throw emphasis on abduction and threatened rape, but
which again brings us round to realise how external violence can be
contained and controlled by sense and virtue. Though the hero's love
for the heroine and his determined constancy start off a chain of
circumstances which involve great risk and danger for them both, they
also are the means by which he is made happy at the end. The exercise
of noble qualities by those who possess them—primarily by characters
whom Scarron introduces into the *nouvelle*—brings the action to a
happy conclusion.

After the ending of 'La juge de sa propre cause' there occurs a
confrontation with La Rappiniere who is shown as possessing the same
qualities of mind as the wicked Moor in the *nouvelle*, so the two
dimensions of narrative are again brought together. Then follows
Ragotin's encounter with the gipsies and the peasant relatives of the
madman who had assaulted Destiny. This episode develops into an
examination of identity and its relationship with passion. Ragotin is in
a situation far more disturbing than that of Shakespeare's Christopher
Sly or the enchanted characters in *The Tempest*, or Don Quixote on his
way back to the Duke's court. But Ragotin, instead of questioning his
circumstances or his relationship to them, acts instinctively, under the
influence of his characteristic passion. Fleeing from the peasants and
meeting a group of clergymen and nuns, he instinctively assaults them.
Instead of asking himself the question which they ask him—what is he
doing?—Ragotin rushes on and encounters another humiliation, a

ritual beating and stinging by bees. Had Ragotin questioned his own
identity, or the nature of his circumstances, this would not have
happened. But he is brought into danger by precisely that factor which
preserves him from doubt, and consequently, though he is not clinically
mad, he suffers just as if he were.

In the remainder of the novel as Scarron left it, two further adventures of Ragotin frame a last *nouvelle*, 'Les Deux Frères Rivaux'. The
first of these, beginning with a quarrel in the theatre with the phlegma-
tic giant, Le Grand Baguenodiere, proceeds to involve the whole theatre
in an absurdly chaotic situation and ends with Ragotin biting the leg of
someone who has had the misfortune to fall on top of him. The *nouvelle*
which follows is read during a dinner which Ragotin gives the troupe in
pursuance of his amorous designs. Once again, it reflects on situations
of violence and danger and suggests that persistence, courage and
determination can make head against adversity. The two brothers of
the title find themselves in the house of the one of two sisters whom they
both love in circumstances so confused that they are almost bound to
lead to a tragic conclusion. But even though danger presses, the
situation is resolved happily, through quite natural means. That is,
characters who have been straightforward and honest with each other
throughout the action, retain their ability to avoid misunderstanding in
spite of circumstances. At the moment when all five of the central
characters confront each other and misunderstandings are thickest,
Dorotée breaks through every entanglement and the action unravels
itself in a series of clauses which follow in simple grammatical and
logical succession:

> Dorotée se jetta aux pieds de son Pere et le conjura de l'entendre. Elle
> luy conta tout ce qui s'estoit passé entre elle et Dom Sanche de Sylva
> devant qu'il eust tué Dom Diegue pour l'amour d'elle. Elle luy apprit
> que Dom Juan de Peralte estoit en-suitte devenu amoureux d'elle, le
> dessein qu'elle avoit eu de le desabuser et de luy proposer de
> demander sa soeur en mariage, et elle conclut que, si elle ne pouvoit
> persuader son innocence à Dom Sanche, elle vouloit, dez le jour
> suivant, entrer dans un Convent pour n'en sortir jamais. Par sa
> relation les deux freres se reconneurent. Dom Sanche se raccommoda
> avec Dorotée, qu'il demanda en mariage a Dom Manuel; Dom Juan
> luy demanda aussi Feliciane, et Dom Manuel les receut pour ses
> gendres avec une satisfaction qui ne se peut exprimer.

> Dorotée threw herself at her father's feet and begged him to hear her.

She told him everything thathad taken place between herself and Dom Sanche de Sylva before he killed Dom Diegue for love of her. She informed him that Dom Juan de Peralte had fallen in love with her afterwards and told him the design she had to make him realise how things stood and to propose that he ask for her sister in marriage, and she ended by saying that if she could not persuade Dom Sanche of her innocence, she wished to enter a convent the following day, never to come out again. Through her account the two brothers recognised each other. Dom Sanche was reconciled with Dorotée, whom he asked in marriage from Dom Manuel; Dom Juan also asked him for Feliciane, and Dom Manuel received them as his sons-in-law with a satisfaction greater than could be expressed.

Le Romant comique, p. 794

After this nothing remains but the ending of the second volume on a comic note, which is achieved through a final humiliation of Ragotin. Sleeping during the reading, with his head beneath his knees, and sometimes raising it to show he is awake, Ragotin attracts the attention of a horned ram who is used to being teased by louts who hang around the inn. The ram charges, Ragotin wakes up, before he can realise what is happening, the animal charges again, and Ragotin leaves the inn '*en furie*' at the laughter of the company.

This final glimpse of Ragotin reminds us of the fact that the difference between a ram and a man is not quite so great in physical terms, or even in emotional terms, as might have been thought. Ragotin and the ram, both following their nature, are on surprisingly equal terms in their encounter. And this is an idea which Scarron never wishes us to keep for long out of the forefront of our minds as we read about the adventures of Destiny and Estoile. *Le Romant comique* embodies an ethos which is fundamentally optimistic, suggesting that man may raise himself to a level of nobility of feeling and action and may also, by the exercise of reason, sense and consistency, free himself from servility to circumstance. On the other hand, Scarron is more than an optimist. He has learnt from Cervantes that the relationship between concepts and character is problematic, and he throws round his positive statement about human life a veil of comedy through which we are constantly aware of human beings as unheroic creatures, living in a world which is dangerous or comic in so far as it is made so by force of their own passions. It is not surprising that it is unfinished, because the act of finishing it, of bringing Destiny and Estoile into the haven of nobility, La Rappiniere to the gallows and Ragotin and Saldagne to the disaster from which they can hardly be protected, would have settled the mood once and for all. The resolution of the plot would also have been a resolution of the tension between different aspects of human life and different values. The primary quality of *Le Romant comique* is that these are kept apart. Scarron's actual statement is accessible only through the process of reading, the process of moving through one to another, not by means of coming to a fixed point which can exist only at the end of a work of fiction.

3 The Fall of Romance: The Development of French Fiction after 1670

The factor that marks the later decades of the seventeenth century off as a separate period in the history of the novel is the decline of heroic romance and the emergence of the shorter *nouvelle*, and around that a coherent body of critical doctrine. The theory which accompanied the rise of the *nouvelle* has a distinctively modern appearance. It is to a certain extent anti-romantic and seems to bear witness to a distinctive shift in sensibility in favour of the realistic modes of writing which were to develop during the following century. This impression is strengthened, moreover, by the fact that it was out of the word *nouvelle* that the English word novel developed, which suggests a continuous development from the one form to the other.

However, the theory of the *nouvelle* needs to be read with great caution, and even the development of the term 'novel' is not so straightforward as it might seem. *Nouvelle* became 'novel' during the early decades of the eighteenth century while the French *nouvelles* of preceding decades were being translated and imitated. At the same time other modes of writing, in origin non-fictional, were being drawn into the sphere of fictional composition and the result of the whole process was the development of a new mode for which the term 'novel' was a useful description. But the terms 'novel' and 'romance' ran side by side throughout the eighteenth century in England and they were only separated out towards the century's end as a result of the development of Gothic romance, which had to be distinguished from the more realistic work of other writers. Even so the novel went on being called romance well into the nineteenth century and the tendency to oppose the two terms as representing conflicting approaches to fiction and to life is a distinctively modern development.

In France the opposite happened, and this needs to be borne in mind by the English reader. Though the *nouvelle* replaced the romance in seventeenth-century France it came to be thought of as a type of romance itself, though distinguished from romance in general by its smaller scope and simpler structure. Eventually it was felt to have specialised itself to such an extent that it was unsuitable as a term for describing the new forms of fiction which were appearing in the early eighteenth century. So the French fell back on the older word, remembering its flexibility in an historical context and noticing its ability to connote the *fictionality* of the work concerned rather than pointing to a particular quality in its *mode* of representation.

The sudden decline of the heroic romance is well documented. Heroic romance had never lacked enemies. We remember the charges laid by Sorel in *Le Berger extravagant* and recognise them again in the more famous formulation of Boileau's *Dialogue des Heros de romans*, traditionally thought to have been written as early as 1665, though not published till 1713, out of respect for Mlle de Scudéry. But charges which had not impinged seriously before 1665 seemed to carry great weight in the later years and were thought by contemporaries to account for the romance's decline and the accompanying rise of the short *nouvelle*. The contemporary view in its orthodox form is summarised by Bruzen de la Martinière in his *Introduction generale a l'étude des sciences et des belles letters* . . . (1731):

> On se lassa enfin de ces longs Romans; divers Auteurs, comme *Desmarets* dans son *Ariane*, Gombaut dans son *Endimion*, etc, avoient déja composé des Romans plus courts qui faissoient moins languir l'impatience des Lecteurs; on vit enfin parôitre la *Princesse de Clèves, Zaïde* et autres petits ouvrages qui acheverent de dégôuter le public de ces intrigues éternelles qui n'avoient de dénouement qu'au dixième volume. Scarron donna son *Roman Comique*, l'une des meilleures choses qu'il ait produites. Il publia aussi quelques *Nouvelles Espanoles* assez courtes pour qu'un volume en contienne plusiers. Madame *de Villedieu* amusa à son tour le public par de jolies Historiettes qui ont été recueillies en corps d'ouvrage, et fit tomber la vogue qu'avoient eue *Clélie, Cyrus, Cassandre*, et tous les autres grands ouvrages.

Eventually people tired of these long Romances; various authors, like Desmarets in his *Ariane*, Gombaud in his *Endimion*, etc. had already composed shorter Romances which did not make the Readers' impatience languish so much; at last the *Princesse de Clèves, Zaide* and other short works appeared which succeeded in disgusting the public with these eternal intrigues which were not unravelled until the tenth volume. Scarron published his *Roman comique,* one of the best things he produced. And also some *Nouvelles Espanoles* short enough for a volume to contain several. Madame de Villedieu in her turn amused the public with her pretty *Historiettes* which have been collected together in one body of work, and made the vogue which *Clélie, Cyrus, Cassandre* and the other great works had had, decline.

Introduction general . . . 'Des Romans' (1731), p. 266

The *nouvelle* which gradually made its appearance during the seventeenth century was a short fiction centred around a love intrigue. It developed partly from the Italian *novella,* partly from native French sources — particularly influential was the *Heptameron* (1558), by Marguerite de Navarre. Most important of all was the Spanish influence because it was in Spain in the first instance, in the hands of Cervantes (whose *Novelas Ejemplares* appeared in 1613), and of several other writers whose work was increasingly translated into French in the later part of the century — Perez de Montalvan, Castillo Solorzano, Cespedes y Memeses and Maria de Zayas — that the form was fully developed. Translation and original composition were closely intertwined in France, but gradually, from Sorel's publication of his *Les Nouvelles francoises* (1623) and *Nouvelles choisies* (1645), the form developed strongly, especially through the work of Scarron (*Nouvelles oeuvres tragi-comiques,* 1655) and Segrais (*Les Nouvelles francoises,* 1656). Initially slow, in the hey-day of heroic romance, from the mid-century on it gained ground steadily so that as one modern critic describes it: 'From 1656 on scarcely a year was to pass which did not see some collection of *nouvelles* or some separate *nouvelle* appear, and for a long time it was to be the *nouvelle* which dominated in the domain of fiction.'[18] Or, as it is resoundingly put by another writer, whose word may rest authoritative: 'By contrast with the years 1600–1650 the genre takes its revenge on the romance. This revenge is striking, total, since

---

[18] 'A partir de 1656, il ne se passera presque pas d'année qu'on ne voie paraitre, soit quelque recueil de nouvelles, soit quelque nouvelle isolée, et ce sera pendant longtemps la nouvelle qui l'emportera dans le domaine des fictions.' G. Hainsworth, *Les 'Nouvelles Exemplaires' de Cervantes en France au xviie Siècle* (1933), p. 100.

the long affected romance disappeared once and for all from the literary scene.'[19]

The *nouvelle* defined itself against a quite explicit series of demands. Together with the complaints about the vices of the romance—lack of *vraisemblance*, over-use of coincidence, too great a distance from the reader—went positive demands for more naïveté or straightforwardness in narration, the use of contemporary subjects and contemporary names. A typical debate is to be found in Segrais's *Nouvelles francoises ou les Divertissemens de la Princesse Aurélie*. The Princesse, though she declares herself pleased with d'Urfé: 'What is there better done, more touching and more natural that the fine imaginings of *L'Astrée?*'[20]—has fault to find with the works of her contemporaries:

> Mais à dire le vrai, les grands revers que d'autres ont quelquefois donnez aux veritez historiques, ces entrevûës faciles et ces longs entretiens qu'ils font faire dans des Ruelles entre des hommes et des femmes, dans les Pays où la facilité de se parler n'est pas grande qu'en France, et des moeurs tout-à-fait francoises qu'ils donnent à des Grecs, des Persans ou des Indiens, sont des choses qui sont un peu éloignées de la raison. Le but de cet art étant de divertir par des imaginations vraisemblables et naturelles, je m'étonne que tant de gens d'esprit qui nous ont imaginé de si honnêtes Scythes et des Parthes si genereux, n'ont pris le même plaisir d'imaginer des Chevaliers ou des Princes François aussi accomplis, dont les avantures n'eussent pas été moins plaisantes. . . .

> But to tell the truth the great reverses which others have given to historical truth, those easy interviews and long conversations which they bring about between men and women in bedrooms, in countries where the facility of conversing is not great as it is in France, and completely French manners which they give to Greeks, Persians or Indians, are things which are a little remote from reason. The aim of this art being to amuse by *vraisemblable* and natural imaginings, I am astonished that so many men of wit who have imagined such honest Scythians and such generous Parthians, have not taken the

---

[19] 'Par rapport aux années 1600–1650, le genre prend sa revanche sur le roman. Cette revanche est éclatante, totale, puisque le long roman précieux disparait finalement de la scène littéraire.' R. Godenne, *Histoire de la Nouvelle françoise aux xvii*[e] *et xviii*[e] *Siècles* (1970), p. 103.

[20] 'Qu'y a-t-il de mieux fait, de plus touchant et de plus naturel que les belles imaginations de l'Astrée.' P. 17.

same pleasure in imagining French Chevaliers or Princes equally accomplished whose adventures would not have been less pleasant. . . .

Les Nouvelles francoises ou les Divertissemens de la Princesse Aurelie (1656), 1722 ed., p. 19

In the discussion that follows, the possibility of contemporaneity and naturalness are canvassed. Gelonide cites the example of Spanish *nouvelles*, which are no more disagreeable—'for having heroes called Richard or Laurens'. She sees no reason why one should not have adventures 'extremely natural, tender, and surprising' about the Wars of Paris just as well as about the War of Troy. Uralie objects to this idea the fact that people would not be able to acccept characters in fiction whom they could not meet in the world around them, but Aplanice rejoins with a distinction between public and private action: 'But have all the accidents which have happened in the battles which have taken place been published?'[21] Her argument is central to the definition of theory which accompanied the appearance and development of the *nouvelle* as a form:

A-t'on divulgué toutes les galanteries qui se sont faites dans la vieille Cour, et sçaura-t'on toutes celles qui se font aujourd'hui? Au reste, commes ces choses sont écrites, ou pour divertir ou pour instruire, qu'est-il besoin que les exemples qu'on propose, soient tous des Rois ou d'Empereurs, comme ils le sont dans tous les Romans? Un particulier que les lira, conformera-t'il ses entreprises sur des gens qui ont des Armées, des qu'il leur plaît, ou sa liberalité sur des personnes qui prodiguent les pierreries; car les diamans et les grosses perles ne manquent jamais aux Heros mêmes qui ont perdu leur Royaume. . . .

Have they disclosed all the intrigues which took place in the old Court, and are all those which take place today known? Besides, as these things are written either to teach or to amuse, is there any need for the examples they put forward all to be those of Kings or of Emperors, as they are in all the Romances? Will a private person who reads them model his enterprises on those of people who have armies whenever they please, or his generosity on that of people who are prodigal of jewels: because diamonds and large pearls are never

[21] 'Mais a-t-on publie tous les accidens qui sont arrivez dans celles qu'on a données?' P. 23.

lacking even to Heroes who have lost their kingdoms. . . .
Les Nouvelles francoises . . . , pp. 23–4

On the model implied in this debate the Princess Aurélie and her companions attempt each to relate a narrative—that is, as Aurélie later puts it: 'to recount things as they are and not as they should be'.[22] Aurélie would leave the idealism of the 'grand Roman' for something which has some of the sound of realism:

> Qu'au reste il me semble que c'est la difference qu'il y a entre le Roman et la Nouvelle, que le Roman écrit ces choses comme la bienséance le veut et à la maniere du Poëte, mais que la Nouvelle doit un peu davantage tenir de l'Histoire et s'attacher plutôt à donner les images des choses comme d'ordinaire nous les voyons arriver, que comme notre imagination se les figure.

> That besides it seems to me that the difference between the Romance and the Nouvelle is that the Romance describes things according to *bienséance* and in the manner of the Poet, but that the Nouvelle must hold a little more to History and rather concern itself with giving the images of things as we ordinarily see them happen, than as our imagination figures them.
>
> *Les Nouvelles francoises . . .* , p. 165

It was not only, however, against the Romance that the *nouvelle* came to be distinguished. Contemporary discussion reveals the fact that it was associated with modernity and with the cause of the Modern as opposed to the Ancient. Both partners in the famous debate about the merits of Mme de La Fayette's *La Princesse de Clèves* (1678) agree in this respect. J-B-H. Du Trousset de Valincour in his *Lettres . . . sur le sujet de la Princesse de Clèves* (1678), makes one of his characters categorise the *nouvelle* together with the epic poem and heroic romance—'those which are mingled with truth' as distinct from ancient and modern comedy where everything is invented—and subordinates it to the rules of criticism, especially those of *vraisemblance* and *bienséance*, but is embarrassed when asked whether Virgil and Homer can stand the same kind of examination. He is not prepared to abandon the rules, but is completely modern in his interpretation of them. On the other hand his opponent, J. A. de Charnes, in his *Conversations sur la*

[22] '. . . de raconter les choses comme elles sont, et non pas comme elles doivent etre.' P. 165.

critique de la Princesse de Clèves (1679), is far more aggressively modern, freely criticises the ancients on rational grounds, insists that the *nouvelle* is a modern genre and demands its own rules:

> Mais je dois vous dire présentement, que les Histoires Galantes, qu'on fait aujourd'hui, ne sont ni dans l'une ni dans l'autre de ces deux especes. Ce ne sont pas de ces pures fictions, ou l'imagination se donne une libre étenduë, sans égard à la verité. Ce ne sont pas aussi de celles ou l'Auteur prend un sujet de l'histoire, pour l'embellir et le rendre agréable par ses inventions. C'en est une troisiéme espece, dans laquelle, ou l'on invente un sujet, ou l'on en prend un qui ne soit pas universellement connu; et on l'orne de plusiers traits d'histoire, qui en appuient la vrai-semblance, et réveillent la curiosité et l'attention du Lecteur.

> But I must tell you at present that the Histoires Galantes that are made today, are included in neither one of the species. These are not pure fictions, where the imagination stretches itself freely, without regard to truth. Nor are they those where the Author takes a subject from History to embellish it and make it agreeable by his inventions. It is a third species of fiction, in which one either invents a subject or takes one which is not universally known; and one ornaments it with various features from history, which lend it *vraisemblance*, and awaken the curiosity and the attention of the Reader.
> *Conversations sur la critique de la Princesse de Clèves* (1679), p. 129

Charnes goes on to make a strong claim for the new form of fiction against older romance and to insist that it be judged according to its own rules:

> Les faiseurs de Romans, aprés Heliodore, ont pris des moyens plus naturels et plus vrai semblables, et ils ont été supportez plus long-tems: mais ces avantures regulieres et melées avec trop d'art les unes dans les autres, nous ont enfin lassez dans leur livres; et nous ne trouvons agréables sur nos theatres ces fictions ingenieuses, que parce que l'action des personages qui se font voir sur la scene, supplée en quelque maniere à l'incredulité que nous avons pour les choses qu'ils représent. Enfin nos derniers Auteurs ont pris une voye qui leur a semblé plus propre à s'attacher le Lecteur, et à le divertir; et ils ont inventé les Histoires galantes, dont je vous ay fait d'abord le description. Ce ne sont plus des Poëmes ou des Romans assujettis à

l'unité de tems, de lieu, et d'action, et composez d'incidens merveilleux et meslez les uns dans les autres: Ce sont des copies simples et fidelles de la veritable histoire, souvent si ressemblantes, qu'on les prend pour l'histoire meme. Ce sont des actions particulieres de personnes privées ou considerées dans un estat privé, qu'on développe et qu'on expose a la veüe du public dans une suite naturelle, en les revestant de circonstances agreables; et qui s'attirent la créance avec d'autant plus de facilité, qu'on peut souvent considerer les actions qu'elles contiennent, comme les ressorts secrets des évenemens memorables, que nous avons apris dans l'Histoire.

The makers of Romances, after Heliodorus, have taken more natural and more *vraisemblable* means, and they have been supported longer: but these regular adventures, too artificially mingled with each other, have finally tired us of their books; and we only find these ingenious fictions agreeable in our theatres because the action of the characters which present themselves on the stage in some way helps out the incredulity we have for the things they represent. In fact, our recent Authors have taken a path which has seemed to them more appropriate to interest the Reader and to amuse him; and they have invented the *Histoires Galantes*, which I have already described to you. These are neither Poems nor Romances subject to unity of time, of place and of action, and composed of marvellous incidents intermingled together: They are simple and faithful copies of true history, often so lifelike that they are taken for history itself. They are particular actions of private persons or persons considered as in a private estate, which are developed and are exposed to public view in a natural sequence, clothing them with agreeable circumstances; and which evoke credibility with so much the more facility because the actions which they contain can often be considered as the secret springs of memorable events, which we have learnt from History.

Conversations sur la critique . . . , p. 134

De Charnes adds one more phrase of great importance which completes his formulation of a completely modern and consistent critique of the *nouvelle.* Speaking of the type of action proper to the form he again distinguishes it from the action typical of the older romance: 'It concerns a coherent story, which represents things in the way they come about in the ordinary course of the world.'[23]

[23] 'Il s'agit d'une Histoire suivie, et qui represente les choses de la maniere qu'elles se passent dans le cours ordinaire du monde.' P. 136.

Here we have the fullest and most consistent adumbration of the theory which accompanied the rise of the *nouvelle,* and a clear indication that the change in taste which caused and accompanied it related to the type of action rather than to the type of material. The essential thing about the *nouvelle* is its relative simplicity of action, the central intrigue with which it begins and ends rather than the interlaced effect of romance action. In this respect the *nouvelle* largely lives up to its theory, but only in this. It has been fairly remarked that all the criticisms addressed by Sorel in his *Le Berger extravagant* against the heroic romance could equally be addressed to the *nouvelles* of the years from 1671–99. R. Godenne puts it squarely: 'Everything happened as if the *nouvelle* were allowed only one function: that of being a reduced version of a romance.'[24] Even Sorel, most given to *naïveté* and naturalness in his criticism, wrote of the *nouvelle* and the romance in 1667 as distinguished fundamentally not by manner but by extent.[25] With a theory relating to content and manner which prefigures the theory of the later novel, the *nouvelle* was actually a form of romance, very far from permitting the development of novel-type structures or novel-type realism. Why this was so is to be explained by the function it served and the view of life and society which underlay it.

HISTORY AS FICTION: THE THEORY AND PRACTICE OF THE ABBÉ DE SAINT-RÉAL

The discrepancy between the theory and practice of the *nouvelle* can be explained by reference to the closely linked development of the concept of history. History and fiction are never far from each other at any time during the seventeenth century. In a rationalistic age the use of historical material was felt to justify the fictional treatment; and at the same time preoccupation with *vraisemblance* rather than truth encouraged a fictional treatment of historical subjects. The heroic romance itself had been 'historical', partly in imitation of the epic and Renaissance poetic romance and partly because of its moral and political

[24] 'Tout se passe comme si l'on n'accordait à la nouvelle qu'une fonction: celle d'être une reduction d'un roman.' *Histoire de la Nouvelle françoise aux xviiᵉ et xviiiᵉ Siècles* (1970), p. 120.
[25] 'Mais puis qu'elles ne represent que de certaines accidens de la vie, ainsi que sont quelques Relations veritables, pour chercher un entier divertissement, nous devons avoir des Relations plus amples, lesquelles on appelle des Romans Parfaits, ou des Roman Heroiques. . . .' *La Bibliothèque Francoise,* 2nd ed. (1667), p. 181.

function. But in the hands of those concerned with heroic romance the idea of history had only the very slightest connection with actuality. Just like romance itself, contemporary history was directed entirely towards achieving a certain effect on the reader. It was conceived of basically as a rhetoric rather than a science. Even at its most scientific, moreover, it leant towards fiction. According to Gomberville, primarily remembered, of course, as the author of *Polexandre* (1632–7):

> L'historien est obligé de dire particulièrement toutes les affaires publiques qui nassent dedans les Estats, comme les guerres civiles, les rebellions, les entreprises sur les Estrangers, ou des Estrangers, les divisions de Religion, les souslevemens des Princes, et des peuples, et les conquests, sans oublier le plus secret des interests et des raisons qui ont obligé les uns et les autres a prendre les armes.

> The historian is obliged to give particular relations of all the public events which arise within States, like civil wars, rebellions, ventures against foreign countries or on the part of foreign countries, Religious divisions, revolts of Princes and peoples, and conquests, without forgetting the more secret of the interests and the reasons which have obliged the one or the other to take up arms.
> *Discours des vertus et des vices de l'Histoire, Et de la maniere de la bien escrire* (1620), p. 112

Given the contemporary state of knowledge, a programme like this was an invitation to invention. The result, as might have been expected, was that there was little difference between contemporary romance and contemporary history except the predominance of love as a motive and a subject for debate.

The appearance of the *nouvelle* is connected with a development in the idea of history. '*Nouvelle*' and '*Histoire*' were largely interchangeable in the titles of contemporary fictions and it is interesting that what happened in England with the development of the two versions of the latter word to refer to fiction and history proper did not take place in France. Rather the idea of fiction and factual accounts became hopelessly confused—as did the accounts themselves. In the first instance this development reflected growing interest in causal processes, in human motivation and in the nature of human events. So, as the Abbé de Saint-Réal described it, History was to concern itself less with externals and more with essential matters:

Cependant, le veritable usage de l'histoire ne consiste pas à scavoir beaucoup d'évenemens et d'actions, sans y faire aucune réflection . . . car scavoir, c'est connôitre les choses par leurs causes. Ainsi scavoir l'histoire, c'est connôitre les hommes qui en fournissent la matiere; c'est juger ces hommes sainement: étudier l'histoire c'est étudier les motifs, les opinions et les passions des hommes, pour en connôitre tous les ressorts, les tours et les détours, enfin toutes les illusions qu'elles scavent faire aux esprits, et les surprises qu'elles font aux coeurs.

Meanwhile, the real use of history does not consist in knowing many events and actions, without making any reflections on them . . . because to know is to understand things through their causes. So to know history is to know the men who provide the material; it is to judge men soundly; to study history is to study the motives, the opinions and the passions of men, in order to recognise all their impulses, their turns and twists, in fact all the illusions with which these can bewilder the mind, and to capture the heart.

'De l'Usage de l'Histoire' (1671), Oeuvres (1730), I, p. 2

Saint-Réal was acutely conscious of the difficulties which beset the searcher after truth. The corruption and instability of human nature was such that constant attention and self-examination was necessary for the historian. So he explains after one of the anecdotes which lie at the centre of each of the seven discourses that make up his essay 'De l'Usage de l'Histoire' (1671):

Cet example fait voir ce qui a été dit tant de fois, et qu'on ne peut trop redire pour apprendre à s'en garder, qu'on ne scauroit croire combien peu de chose nous pousse, et peu de chose nous arrête; que quelque profession que nous fassions de penetrer le fond des affaires, cela nous arrive assez rarement; que dès que les paroles ont quelque chose qui rebute, on n'examine plus rien; que quelque force de raisonne-ment dont nous nous vantions, la premiere impression des sens nous entrâine presque toujours. Soit paresse, soit foiblesse, soit hazard, il n'est point de motif si étrange, qui ne puisse être trouvé raisonnable; point de circonstance si vaine, qui ne soit capable de nous déter-miner; point de consideration si absurde, qui ne puisse nous émouvoir.

This example demonstrates what has been said so many times and which we cannot too often repeat so as to learn to protect ourselves from not believing what small things motivate us and inhibit us; that whatever profession we might make of penetrating to the depth of affairs, we rarely succeed in doing so; that as soon as the words have something which disheartens us, we enquire no farther; that whatever force of reasoning we boast of, the first sense impressions almost always inveigle us. Whether it be laziness, weakness, or chance, there is no motive so strange that it may not be considered reasonable; no circumstance so trivial that it may not be capable of making up our minds; no consideration so absurd, that it may not move us.

'De l'Usage de l'Histoire,' pp. 7–8

So far, the modern reader might exclaim, so good! But he need go no farther into Saint-Réal's short thesis than the first discourse to discover that the author's apparently healthy intellectual scepticism is in fact part of a shallow and restricted rationalism, and that his interest in history is purely in so far as it can serve certain moral and ultimately social ends, and, furthermore, that the way it is designed by Saint-Réal to serve those ends brings it into inseparably close relationship with fiction itself.

According to Saint-Réal man is motivated by four basic passions which subsume all others—Folly, Malice, Ignorance and Vanity, and is also governed by the force of Opinion, which is more powerful than other factors. The study of history is essential because it is only through the infinite number of exempla it provides that we may come to know the extent of human sinfulness and folly. Saint-Réal opposes the Platonistic arguments sometimes brought forward in defence of romance by saying that there are very few people in whom the love of beauty is strong enough to act as a motive. On the other hand, nature has implanted in us a *complaisance* to study the vices of ourselves and others and this *complaisance* may be made use of by the historian to educate our judgement. Judgement, of course, for Saint-Réal, is the central mental faculty and the means of correcting our moral nature:

Car enfin, c'est principalement à cette faculté, qu'il appartient de découvrir nos défauts, et d'y faire réflexion, pour connôitre exactement la nature de notre âme, et sa maniere de proceder.

Because in fact it is principally to this faculty that it belongs to discover our faults and to make reflexions on them, in order to know exactly the nature of our soul, and its manner of proceeding.

'De l'Usage de l'Histoire,' p. 37

In practice, however, Saint-Réal's judgement is astonishingly shallow and prejudiced. The historical content of his thesis is confined to anecdote, arbitrarily interpreted according to his own requirement. So, for example, the first point is supported by stating that the Sultan of Turkey's motive in offering financial support to Henry IV against the Ligue was simple dislike for the word Ligue. Saint-Réal does not mention whether it was the French word or the Turkish word which the Sultan disliked, whether his hatred was for the word or what he took to be its significance. Nor does he cite authority for his assertions; nor allow any other element of motivation to enter into his case.

In fact Saint-Réal's work is a perfect example of the kind of thinking which lay behind the fiction of the period, with its over-dependence on romanesque elements, its strained motivation, crude manipulation of exotic effects and circumstances and its constant tendency to idealisation and generalisation. At the very centre of his work there is a passage which explains the whole attitude, not only to history but to life in general. A rationalist, he is a rationalist in the service of contemporary manners and the social order of which he is a part. Just as he spent his whole life vacillating between one patron and another, clearly conceiving both literary and clerical professions as secondary in importance to the requirements of the social order in general and his social position in particular. Saint-Réal is a man of his period. Even though rumoured to be a *libertin*, his literary work is rigidly orthodox and his whole mental outlook reflected in his attitude to the opinion which in all societies other than his own distorted men's perceptions. The logical result of his rationalism was a scepticism which would have undermined the far more important moral function of literature. So, even though he attacks the force of opinion, he sticks firmly by the idea of *bienséance*, which governs the representation of men and human affairs:

Car il est constant qu'il y a dans les hommes une idée naturelle de bienseance; mais cette idée quelque naturelle qu'elle soit, ne laisse pas de pouvoir être effacée par les préjugez de l'enfance, l'éducation et la coutume.

Because it has been established that there is a natural idea of *bienséance* in men; but no matter how natural this idea may be, it can nevertheless be effaced by prejudices of childhood, education and custom.

'De l'Usage de l'Histoire,' p. 56

Saint-Réal takes his stand on the ground provided by *bienséance* against all who would use reason to attack orthodoxy:

Si donc nous l'accusons dans ces recontres, si les libertins prennent, de cette bizarrerie de moeurs, occasion d'établir leur incertitude generale de toutes choses, et leur blasphêmes contre la lumiere naturelle; ce n'est pas qu'ils ayent trouvé, après un examen solide, que c'est la faute de la nature: mais c'est qu'il faut necessairement qu'ils avouent, que c'est la sienne, ou la nôtre; et l'amour propre, et la vanité ne les laisse guere balancer entre ces deux partis.

If then we are apprehensive in these encounters lest the libertines take occasion of this extravagance of customs, to establish their general uncertainty of all things, and their blasphemies against the light of natural reason, it is not that they have found, after a solid examination, that it is the fault of nature: but it is that they have to admit either that it is hers or ours, and *amour-propre* and vanity hardly permit them to hesitate between the two sides.

'De l'Usage de l'Histoire,' p. 58

In these passages we see the explanation of the contradictions implicit in Saint-Réal's work. As a historian, he was in fact a romance-writer; and as the author of *nouvelles*, he was trapped within a supposedly historical frame of action. In his *Dom Carlos* and *Conjuration de Venise* he made such a confusion of fact and fiction, external event and added motivation and commentary, that it was impossible for his contemporaries to unravel it. His work could not be read as history, nor as fiction, but as something which shared the nature of both and which concerned itself with a dimension of experience which could be reached through neither on its own. The consideration which governed Saint-Réal, and in this he is typical of many contemporaries, was his desire to work directly on the sensibility of the reader. His work existed to stimulate the reader's judgement but at the same time to weave round it the framework of *bienséance*. It is not too much to say that for Saint-Réal, and for many writers who used fiction more freely, both fiction and history existed in order to create *bienséance* in the reader. Consequently they might or might not approach the direct representation of human behaviour, as the case might be. What they had to do was to stimulate the reader's sense that reality coincided with official accounts of it. Ultimately this is the function of the seventeenth-century *nouvelle*: and of course, in an atmosphere where such a form could flourish, the novel as such could hardly breathe.

BEYOND THE *NOUVELLE*: ACTUALITY AND FICTION

If we look outside the framework of the *nouvelle* for works which come closer to the method and aims of the novel in this period we are not wholly disappointed. There are a good number of semi-fictional works which are often described as heralding the development of the novel in the following century. There are works which combine directness of manner with structural crudity, which may be used as evidence for the development of realist techniques, but which also tell us a good deal about the cultural factors which governed the writing of fiction at the time. Significantly, they are attempts at memoirs or autobiography which turn to fiction as a means of organising experience. One of the earliest is *Le Page disgracie* of Tristan l'Hermite (1642–3), which contains sharply realistic though often primarily humorous writing, especially in the early sections describing his adventures as a page. Later passages describing his love for an English girl whose family he serves, read strangely. They lack some of the usual technical elements which novelists use to achieve *vraisemblance*, yet at the same time they do give the impression that the situation is a factual one receiving fictional treatment rather than the reverse. In later sections we return to the humorous adventures, leaning towards burlesque and *fabliaux*-type situations.

Tristan always writes clearly and effectively, without any romanesque element and with the apparent intention of rendering an event in its actuality. But he was unable either to provide a coherent shape for his autobiographical material from within, or to impose a fictional pattern from without. Only two actions emerge as shaping factors: firstly, the encounter with an alchemist whose return we constantly expect; secondly, the love-affair with the English girl, which later fades into the background. Tristan's life, it is clear, had no shape for him in itself, and was incapable of being organised within any of the narrative frames offered by contemporary fiction.

Much the same may be said of a work which is more often mentioned in histories of the novel than Tristan's work, though with less justification—the *Memoires de M. d'Artagnan* (1700) by Courtilz de

Sandras (1644–1712), which later made the basis of Dumas Père's *Les Trois Mousquetaires* (1844). Courtilz's work, again partly biographical, draws on a wider narrative range than Tristan's, and lacks a good deal of the latter's clarity. The *Memoires* reflect contemporary conditions of life and imperfectly but sharply embody the sensibility of a racy, brutal, sometimes sentimental age, combining biography, scandal, memoir and novel of adventure. But again, they lack coherence, even as an account of contemporary life, and as a criticism of it they are completely naïve.

Approaching Count Anthony Hamilton's *Memoires du Comte de Grammont* (1713), we are coming to material still more familiar to historians of the novel. Hamilton's account of his brother-in-law's life, supposedly partly from dictation, has often been considered as a more or less accurate account of manners at the court of the later Stuarts. Much of it is factual without doubt, and all of it is presented in sharp detail with a strong sense for the individual scene and even at times for the concatenation of incidents which makes up an adventure. Hamilton/Grammont is also capable at times of treating the feeling of characters at odds with their environment, as well as the behaviour of those whose lack of sensitivity enables them to thrive within it. Once again, however, the *Memoires* lack shape. Grammont's love for Hamilton's sister, who is eventually to become his wife, is worked up to some extent, but in no way is it capable of enclosing the action as a whole. The book's essence is anecdote, reflecting a world but incapable of shaping it.

These semi-fictional autobiographies show very clearly that individual experience was not felt to be capable of organising or explaining itself, even though it was strongly enough developed to demand expression. Consequently they tell us why the narrative frames later to be typical of the novel as a form could not be developed at this time. What they do not tell us is why the novel could not draw on other narrative frames so as to satisfactorily explain contemporary experience within the social and moral values predominant at the time. Looking for an explanation of this failure, we find ourselves face to face again with Don Quixote and Sancho Panza.

THE RETURN OF DON QUIXOTE

A concern for the use of fiction as a means of criticising contemporary experience did exist in these later years of the seventeenth century,

quite independent of the *nouvelle* and the biography. Springing out of
the same rationalist habits of thought which vitiated the work of most
writers of romance and *nouvelle*, it seems to have arisen among the
social class and even among the individuals most affected by the
contemporary religious movement, Jansenism, which combined moral
severity with insistence on grace. It expressed itself not directly but
through attempts to imitate and modify the achievement of Cervantes.
So in the later years of the seventeenth century Don Quixote rode again,
not once, but many times, each time until the last increasingly difficult
to recognise.

There is a sharp contrast here between England and France, which
reflects on the conditions as they affected the writing of fiction at this
time in both countries. A renewed interest in Cervantes' work was
common to both countries in the last three decades and around the turn
of the century. But in England Cervantes' work was burlesqued rather
than imitated. In the hands of Milton's nephew, John Phillips
(1631–1706), significantly of the anti-Puritan party and a translator of
Calprenède and Scudéry, *Don Quixote* was drastically adapted to an
English scene and a lower social and literary level. The beginning of his
translation is typical of the whole and almost unrecognisable:

> In some part of *Mancha*, of which the Name is at present slipt out of
> my Memory, not many years ago, there liv'd a certain Country
> Squire, of the Race of King *Arthur's* Tilters, that formerly wondered
> from Town to Town, cas'd up in Rusty old Iron, with Lance in Rest,
> and a Knight-Templers Target; bestriding a forlorn *Pegasus*, as Lean
> as a *Dover* Post-Horse, and a confounded Founder'd Jade to boot.
> Beef-steaks stew'd in a Nasty Pipkin, with a Red-Herring to taste his
> Liquor a Nights; Fasting and Prayer a Fridays, parch'd Pease a
> Saturdays with a Lark now and then a Sundays to mend his
> Commons, consumed three parts of his Estate. . . .
>   *The Life and Atchievements Of . . . Don Quixote* (1686), p. 1

Ned Ward's metrical version, published in 1711, takes the same
tendency much farther, and has to be read to be believed. His representation of Alonso Quijana's niece and housekeeper is as good an example
as any:

> Besides the *Don*, the number Three,
> Made up his Christian Family:
> But these had in their sev'ral Stations,

So many rare Qualifications,
That they could turn their Hands to any
Performance, as if thrice as many.
        The first, a young depending Niece,
Of Female Flesh a pretty piece,
A freckly kind familiar Lass,
Just Rotten Ripe for Man's Embrace,
Could dance a *Minuet* or a *Bory*,
Sing an old Song or tell a Story,
Upon his Spinet chime the Tune,
Of *Happy Groves*, or *Bobbing Joan*. . . .
        Next her, a pale-fac'd wither'd Slattern,
Of Piety the very Pattern,
Her Age full Forty Five or more,
Her Station that of House-keeper;
A Dame that understood by Halves,
To make fine Sweetmeats, Pickles, Salves:
Could also Dress and heal with Art,
Kibe'Cut or Bruise in any Part. . . .
But above all her boasted Gifts,
With which she made such sundry Shifts,
She had a Fiddle, as some say,
On which Her Master us'd to play,
Which Did his Am'rous Freaks supply,
And charm'd him from the Nuptial Tye. . . .

The Life and Notable Adventures of . . . Don Quixote . . . Merrily
Translated into Hudibrastick Verse (1711), pp. 8–10

Such quite excruciatingly bad verse is no evidence of a very refined sensibility, but we ought not to dismiss Ned Ward's attempt without noticing the extent to which it illustrates a predominant tendency in English culture at the time. England had no romance tradition of its own, but it had developed a tradition of burlesque stronger than the French equivalent in proportion as the political impulse behind it during the Restoration period was stronger. Behind the work of Phillips and Ward lies Samuel Butler's *Hudibras* (1663–78), a burlesque satire of the Presbyterians. The models for Butler were Sorel's *Le Berger extravagant* and Scarron's *Virgile travesti* (1648–52). It is significant that Butler was unable to imitate their other fictions, and that the interest in *Don Quixote* which he and others showed should have been overcome by their fondness for burlesque and coarse parody.

In France at this time it seems to have been much easier to think of the possibility of developing forms of fiction which were primarily representative of the conditions of contemporary living. Consequently there are several attempts during the last decades of the seventeenth century to amend and extend *Don Quixote* so as to make it accord with contemporary values and reflect contemporary reality. These attempts emerged against a background of rationalist criticism of Cervantes and were impeded by the same factors which prevented the development of the *nouvelle* into the novel. But at the same time they seem to have been the means by which fiction as Avellaneda conceived it was mediated into the novel as we know it.

So far as I know it is impossible to be precise about the nature of the connection between this movement in contemporary fiction and the Jansenist movement in general, though it is quite certain that there was such a connection. Perhaps it is true to say that the development of forms of fiction which directly and straightforwardly represented the reality of contemporary life was the result of the impact of rationalist critical principles upon a sensibility deeply affected by Jansenist habits of thought. It is difficult not to imagine that Jansenist concern for the education of youth had something to do with it. Certainly it is true to say that Jansenist writers, though followers of Descartes in general, have a preoccupation with the realities of passion and with the internal life of man that must have helped to draw them towards forms of literature which could be used to achieve a convincing analysis of human character in contemporary circumstances.

However this may be it is interesting to notice that the appearance of Filleau de Saint Martin's four volume translation of *Don Quixote* between 1677 and 1679 was widely associated with Port Royal, centre of the Jansenist movement, and even attributed to the central figure in the Jansenist controversy, 'le Grand Arnauld', in spite of the Jansenists' well-known tendency to disapprove of imaginative literature.[26] Immediately after this there appeared a very trenchant criticism of *Don Quixote* from another writer associated with the Jansenists. This was Pierre Perrault's *Critique du livre de Don Quichotte de la Manche* (1679). Perrault came from an influential family, all the members of which were high-ranking administrators and authors in their own right. They were associated with Jansenism either as individuals or through their brother Nicholas, who was one of the seventy doctors

[26] For the most notorious expression of this disapproval, see P. Nicole, *Les Visionaires* (1667), which produced Racine's famous attack in his *Lettre à l'auteur des Hérésies imaginaires* (1666).

excluded from the Sorbonne with Arnauld during the persecution of the Jansenists. The family also showed a strong interest in the natural sciences. Pierre himself, 'receveur des finances' in Paris, also composed numerous pieces concerning physics and mechanics. His brother Claude, 'architecte de l'Académie des sciences', was responsible for *Memoires pour servir a l'histoire naturelle des animaux*. Pierre's criticism is basically an extension of the arguments of Sorel and others before him, though he is more thorough-going and literal-minded. He claimed to have made a general critique of all the book contained:

Par laquelle je fais voir des absurditez, contrarietez, Impossibilitez, Indecences, malhonnestetez, langeurs et longeurs de stile et de narration, Inutilitez, bassesses, neglicences, manque de Jugement et d'invention, fanfaronnerie et vanite de l'autheur avec son peu de capacité et suffisance.

By which I demonstrate the absurdities, contradictions, Impossibilities, indecencies, crudities, heavy and boring features of style and of narration, Irrelevances, lownesses, carelessness, lack of Judgement and invention, swaggering and vanity of the author, with his deficiency of capacity and ability.
Critique du livre de Don Quichotte... (1679); ed. M. Bardon (1930), p. 72

Avellaneda would have been delighted! Perrault has a lot of small points to make. He criticises Cervantes' vanity in the preface to Part II; condemns Cervantes for saying there were so many windmills in Part I; finds inconsistencies of dating. Most seriously of all, however, he develops Avellaneda's attack on the serious, romanesque parts of the book. And in the course of doing this he moves away from the traditional position and adumbrates, not the consistent comedy of Avellaneda and Sorel, but a new, realistic form of art. His criticism derives from the common assertion regarding *vraisemblance* and *bienséance*:

. . . il peche contre les deux principales et plus necessaires conditions d'une histoire inventée, comme est celle de ce livre, qui sont la vraysemblance dans les Incidens et la bienseance dans les discours des personnages suivant leurs caracteres.

. . . he sins against the two principal and most necessary conditions

of an invented history, such as this book is, which are *vraisemblance*
in the Incidents and *bienséance* in the discourses of the personages
according to their characters.

Critique . . . de Don Quichotte . . . , p. 101

Then he elaborates his argument, distinguishing two categories of
fiction—the 'Poetique', which includes heroic romance and pastoral,
and the 'Comique':

> . . . cette maniere dis je Comique est tout oppossée à celle la, car elle
> ne represente rien qui ne soit au naturel et conforme a la facon
> ordinaire de vivre sans exageration, sans figures, sans hyperbolles,
> sans fictions, Et autant que toutes ces choses là servent d'ornement
> au Poetique, autant sont elles un reproche au Comique quand elles
> s'y rencontrent.

> . . . this manner I call Comic is completely opposed to the other,
> because it represents nothing which is not natural and conforms to
> the ordinary way of life, without exaggeration, without figures,
> without hyperboles, without fictions. And as much as all those
> things serve as ornament to the Poetic, so they are a reproach to the
> Comic when they are encountered there.

Critique . . . de Don Quichotte . . . , p. 117

This definition is the basis of his worst charge against Cervantés—that
having chosen to write a comic romance rather than a poetic, he should
not have mixed the two genres. The reason why he should not, though
this is implicit rather than clearly stated, is the usual rationalistic idea
that fiction should either set out a recognised ideal, or be read as if
literally true. But this idea is no longer acting in Perrault's mind so as to
form his taste. The idea of comic romance which he actually describes
shows that he is not only preoccupied with reality as a thing of
importance in itself, but with representation of reality:

> N'est il pas vray que nostre autheur a du choisir pour la sienne celle
> que J'appelle Comique et non la Poëtique. Et s'il a choisy la Comique
> comme il est facile de le juger, ne l'a t'il pas du rendre conforme à la
> verité? ne l'a t il pas du rendre possible en toutes ses parties? n'a t il
> pas du en bannir tout le merveilleux? ne faire que des incidens
> ordinaires, ne se servir que de raisonnemens simples, et telz qu'on les
> fait dans le cours de la vie? Tous les personnages qu'il y a introduitz

n'ont il pas du suivre ces regles là? n'ont ils pas du raisonner comme l'on fait ordinairement? penser comme les autres hommes, parler de mesme, avoir les mesmes desirs, les mesmes considerations et precautions?

Is it not true that our author should have chosen for his that which I call Comic and not the Poetic. And if he has chosen the Comic as it is easy to judge it, ought he not to have made it conform to truth? ought he not to have made it possible in all its parts? ought he not to have banished from it all the marvellous? only have made ordinary incidents, only have employed simple arguments and such as are made in the course of life? Ought not all the characters he has introduced follow those rules? ought not they reason as is ordinarily done? think like other men, speak the same, have the same desires, the same considerations and precautions?

Critique . . . de Don Quichotte . . . , p. 118

Bearing in mind the evidence provided by the work of Tristan and Hamilton, it is fairly easy to see that the fulfilment of this programme was virtually impossible in the late seventeenth century. It is ironic that those who were influenced by it were forced into the task of re-writing *Don Quixote* itself rather than composing original fictions. Within their works they show a good deal of imaginativeness and invention, but in spite of this they are unable to break out of the strait-jacket of imitation into the novel itself—unable at least, that is, until they had served their apprenticeship and paid their own perverted form of homage to the creator of Don Quixote.

FILLEAU DE SAINT MARTIN

The first of these writers was Filleau de Saint Martin, whose translation of Cervantes' work had drawn forth the comments of Perrault. Like his successors he takes a good deal of trouble to achieve *vraisemblance*. So he begins by explaining the provenance of these further adventures of Don Quixote. Having altered the end of his translation to dispose of Cervantes' account of Don Quixote's death, he attributes the new account to an Arab by the name of Zulema, converted and christened Henriques de la Torre, who leaves his manuscript behind him when he goes to the Indies. He begins the actual narration by carefully documenting Don Quixote's restoration to sanity, after which he depicts him taking care to maintain his mental stability by an ordered life on approved patterns. One of his first actions is to dispose of his books, and then:

> Sa maison ainsi purgée, aussi-bien que son imagination, il s'appliqua à faire un jardin, et de tems à la pêche ou à la chasse; et tout cela avec moderation, de crainte qu'un grand mouvement ne lui troublât le tête, qu'il se trouvoit lui-même un peu afoiblie.

> So, his house purged, as well as his imagination, he applied himself to make a garden, and occasionally in fishing or in hunting; and all this with moderation, for fear that a great agitation might disturb his head, which he himself found a little weakened.
> *Continuation de L'Histoire de L'admirable Don Quichotte* (1697),
> *Histoire de L'admirable Don Quichotte* V (1713), p. 4

Unfortunately, Filleau continues, the precautions are in vain. A fever contracted while hunting is further excited by the discharge of muskets by a file of soldiers intending a salute to Don Quixote. He is encouraged in his insanity by Sancho, and aided by him, sets off again on his adventures.

Before they leave home, however, there are two significant developments. Firstly, we have the arrival of Dorotée, who is now the Duchess of Albuquerque, since the death of Fernando's brother and who is on the way to take possession of a château they have recently inherited. Secondly, we have Sancho's decision to become a knight himself, having fallen in love with Dorotée, followed by a burlesque episode in which he kills a pig, which he identifies as an enchanter called Dom Grognard. Filleau comments at this point:

> On n'a jamais bien pû savoir de Sancho, s'il croïoit absolument ce qu'il venoit de dire, ou s'il se l'étoit imaginé; mais il y a aparence que, gâté par les visions de Don Quichotte, dont il avoit pris les maximes et les manieres, et qu'un peu d'invention se joignant à son imagination déja troublée, il voiöit les choses autrement qu'elles n'étoient. Quoi-qu'il en soit, nous le verrons toujours de même dans la suite, où il nous prépare une belle foule d'extravagances.

> It could never be found out from Sancho whether he completely believed what he had just said, or if he had imagined it; but it seems

that, spoilt by the visions of Don Quixote, whose ideas and manners he had imitated, and a little invention joining his already troubled imagination, he saw things other than they were. However it may have been, we shall always see the same in what follows, where he is preparing a fine crowd of absurdities for us.

Continuation de . . . Dom Quichotte . . . V, p. 81

This is derived directly from what Cervantes says about Don Quixote's vision in the cave of Montesinos, but Cervantes introduces it in order to make a point about the nature of the imagination and its relation to reality. Filleau, like Avellaneda, considers reality in itself to be unproblematical and consequently he misses the point of Don Quixote's madness altogether. In fact he goes so far as to transfer the madness almost entirely to Sancho. Filleau cannot conceive of a character being both wise and foolish at the same time, or reconcile Don Quixote's social position with his being the hero of burlesque adventures. In his eyes the mere fact that Sancho is a peasant prepares him for the role of fool, and in his version it is Sancho who gets beaten, not Don Quixote at all. The latter's role as a spokesman, on the other hand, is very much strengthened and he becomes surprisingly stable and effective in the world of action.

Leaving aside the elements of pantomime, the action of the novel is rather restricted. After a short stay at Basilius' house, Don Quixote and Sancho go on to a château belonging to a husband and wife whom they meet in their travels and assist. The bulk of the narrative is taken up with interpolated stories which are carefully interwoven with the actual present of the narrative and in which Don Quixote is made to comment on the nature of man and his condition in a way obviously approved by the author. Finally, however, the narrative becomes hopelessly confused, as the author loses control of the place and time-setting of the events he is dealing with and the narrative breaks off.

The first inset story of importance concerned the marriage of Gamacho's niece with Osorio, who is given up to an insane jealousy which makes him maltreat his wife and act in a totally ludicrous and dangerous manner. His cure is achieved as a result of the shock of meeting with Don Quixote, being roughly treated by him (Don Quixote is under the impression that Osorio has presented himself to challenge him), and lectured regarding jealousy. It is clear that Filleau chooses jealousy partly because it is a pressing social problem, but also because it is a passion which comes closest of all to the condition of madness. In jealousy, after all, the mind persuades itself that what is not, is, and consequently provides an example of the passions taking over not only the judgement but also the soul. Don Quixote understands the case perfectly. His own mental derangement does not prevent him from making a coherent diagnosis of Osorio's case which combines medical and moral considerations. Of man he says:

Il doit pecher par sa nature, parce qu'elle est corrompuë; mais il doit se relever par la raison, qui sert de contre poids à ses passions. Malheureux en cela que toutes les choses visibles sont pour lui des objects de concupiscence, capables de l'ébranler, de le mettre en mouvement, et de lui faire de dangereuses chutes: mais heureux en ce que son esprit, tout indivisible et tout imperceptible qu'il est, s'elévant jusqu'à son origine, en se dégageant de la matiere, peut connoître le neant des choses humaines; renverser toutes les fausses idées qui lui viennent des sens, et détruire et anéantir les flateuses impressions que les objects exterieurs lui ont laissées. Qu'on ne dise donc plus que les passions sont trop fortes, qu'elles nous emportent d'un mouvement rapide, et que la raison est trop faible pour tenir l'homme dans l'équilibre. C'est qu'il se precipite lui-même dans la recherche de voluptez sensibles et qu'il neglige sa raison; de crainte que le convainquant de sa propre honte, elle ne le tire malgré lui d'une erreur qui lui plaist, et ne l'attache à des objects pour que il n'a point de goût, tout sublimes qu'ils puissent être.

He must sin by his nature, because it is corrupt, but he ought to raise himself by his reason, which serves as a counterpoise to his passions. Unfortunate in that all visible things are for him objects of concupiscence, capable of shaking him, of exciting him and of making him undergo dangerous falls: but happy in that his spirit, all indivisible and imperceptible as it is, rises towards its origin, in disengaging itself from matter, can recognise the nothingness of human things; overturn all the false ideas which may come to him from the senses, and destroy and annihilate the flattering impressions which external objects have left him. So let it not be said that the passions are too strong, that they carry us away with a rapid movement, and that the reason is too weak to keep man in equilibrium. It is that he precipitates himself in the search for voluptuous sensations and neglects his reason; fearing that, convincing him of his own shame, she will draw him in spite of himself from an error which pleases him, and attach him to objects for which he has no taste, no matter how sublime they may be.

Continuation de . . . Don Quichotte . . . , p. 192

Now that Osorio is saved from this position, Don Quixote goes on to explain his falling into error in the first place as resulting from his having married from concupiscence and avarice, which passions dragged with them, fear, suspicion, jealousy, injustice and violence.

This treatise of the nature of man, combining medical and moral and social elements, is followed by a similar disquisition on the nature of Providence. Leaving Basilius' house, Don Quixote attacks a smithy which turns out to be the refuge of a gang of bandits, and puts them to flight. Not long after he and Sancho attack and overcome another man who has been trying to rape a woman they find tied to a tree. Her story follows at some length and involves the events of the later part of the volume. She is called Eugenie and is married to Valerio, whose château is nearby. She has attracted the love of both Valerio's brothers, who have successfully attempted her abduction. Just at the point when, Valerio lying unconscious at her feet, the more brutal of them is about to rape her, a large bear rushes out of the forest and carries him off. Nothing more is heard of him except his horrible screams. The other brother and his companions being drawn off after hearing noises, one of them returns, intending to offer Eugenie violence on his own account. He too is drawn away and is returning to complete the action when he is intercepted by Don Quixote.

All the characters involved in this affair retire to a neighbouring inn, where Valerio recovers and is transported to his own home. Not, however, before Don Quixote has delivered some authoritative remarks on the whole story.

Don Quichotte, charmé du recit d'Eugenie, de la beauté de son esprit et de la justesse de ses termes, lui donna des louanges excessives, mais il loüa encore plus sa vertu, en disant que c'étoit ce qui lui avoit atiré la protection du Ciel, et des marques si visibles de la vengeance divine sur les plus coupables de ses ennemis.

Don Quixote, charmed with Eugenie's narration, with the beauty of her *esprit*, and with the justness of her terms, gave her excessive praises, but he praised her virtue even more, saying that it was this which had attracted the protection of Heaven, and such visible marks of divine vengeance on the most culpable of her enemies.

Continuation de . . . Don Quichotte . . . , pp. 316–17

Sancho's response, we may note, is to offer to hang Pedrario, the captured offender, if the authorities are short of a hangman, showing blood-thirsty tendencies which are further developed by Robert Challes. Don Quixote, however, has much more to say. He takes the whole story, as we are evidently intended to read it, as a reflection on the nature of the human condition and makes it the text for a comment on divine justice:

> ... c'est un des plus grands secrets de la Providence de Dieu; qu'ayant toujours les yeaux ouverts sur la conduite des hommes, il retient si long-tems le glaive suspendu sur la tête des impies, et laisse l'innocence dans l'oppression. que les méchans vivent dans la prospérité et dans l'abondance, et les bons gémissent acablez de miseres, et comme le rebut de la nature; mais que le triste état de ceux-ci, à parler selon le monde, leurs persecutions, leurs soufrances, sont le veritable caractere de ceux qu'il aime et que le bonheur imaginaire des autres, et l'abus qu'ils en font, est une marque infaillible de sa haine.

> ... it is one of the greatest secrets of the Providence of God, that having the conduct of men openly in sight, it retains the sword so long suspended over the heads of the impious and leaves the innocent under oppression. That the wicked live in prosperity and in abundance, and the good groan, weighed down with misery, and like the refuse of Nature; but that the sad state of the latter, speaking as the world speaks, their persecutions, their sufferings, are the true character of those he loves, and that the imaginary happiness of the others, and the abuse that they make of it, is an infallible sign of his hatred.

Continuation de . . . Don Quichotte . . . , p. 318

On this occasion, moreover, Don Quixote goes far beyond his brief and he matches the disquisitions which Cervantes gave him on the Golden Age, on arms and letters, with an attack on the whole contemporary world of late seventeenth-century France, on the corruption of judges, the wickedness of those in authority and the sinfulness of all men:

> ... il conclut qu'après avoir long-tems atendu le pecheur le Ciel irité de ses crimes, et encore plus de son impenitence, devenoit un ennemi implacable, et ne manquoit pas d'exercer sur lui la vengeance qu'il avoit amassée dans le trésor de sa colere; que l'oppression qu'il

souffre dans ses Elus n'etant qu'une épreuve qu'il fait de leur patience
après les avoir long-tems vû gemir dans l'aveu de leur propre
impuissance et de leur coruption, il ne manquoit pas aussi de
recompenser leur vertu dès ce monde, et que ces recompenses ne sont
qu'un prélude, et comme un avant-goût de celles qu'il leur prépare de
tout tems dans la gloire éternelle.

. . . he concluded that after having a long time awaited the sinner, a
Heaven irritated by his enemies, and yet more by his impatience,
would become an implacable enemy, and would not fail to exercise on
him the vengeance which it had amassed on the treasury of its anger,
that the oppression that it suffered in its Elect being no more than a
test which it made of their patience after having seen them a long time
groan in acknowledgement of their own weakness and their corruption, it would not fail to recompense their virtue in this world, and
that these recompenses were only a prelude, and like a fore-taste of
that which it prepared for them for all time in eternal glory.

Continuation de . . . Don Quichotte . . . , p. 322

Readers who fail to recognise Don Quixote in the preacher Filleau
presents to us, can hardly be blamed. We are very far here from the
original character, but the distance we have travelled is deeply significant of Filleau's concern with religious and social orthodoxy. The story
of Sainville which follows and concludes his book stresses this further.

Sainville is a typical example of the *honnête homme*. The story which
is told about him concerns the uneven course of his love for Sylvie,
whose unexplained marriage to another man has occurred some time
before. When the narration begins she has been fleeing into Spain to
escape from her husband and both he and Sainville have been wounded
by the bandits led by Valerio's brothers. The story about Sainville
seems to be rather similar to that of Valerio and Eugenie except that it
throws emphasis on the male instead of the female and gives a good deal
of weight to his honest conduct in a variety of situations. What is most
striking about it, however, is Filleau's total inability to manage it
coherently. It is narrated by one of the women who are accompanying
Sainville and she begins it *in medias res* at the point when, some time
after Sylvie's marriage, Sainville unexpectedly meets the woman he
had previously loved in Paris, when she deceives him as to her identity
and then asks for his help to free her husband, who has been imprisoned
in Naples. When he is half-way through telling the story of recent
events to *this* woman they are interrupted by the noise in the street of a

carriage in which two women are being driven away against their will.
Sainville rushes out and engages one of the men and is imprisoned for
the night. One of the women turns out to be Sylvie. They have a
demi-éclaircissement and just as Sylvie is about to go on with her story,
so explaining her behaviour, the French girl who is relating the story is
interrupted by the arrival of a carriage outside. At this point, merciful-
ly, Filleau must have given up, for he ends the volume with Sainville's
adventure in mid-air.

CONTINUATION AT TWO REMOVES

The continuation of Filleau's continuation, published after his death, in
1711, was stated on the title-page to be by him but external and internal
evidence seem to attribute it rather to Robert Challes, later a novelist in
his own right. Challes introduced a new note into the fiction, but also
continues the main lines of Filleau's work. He shows perhaps more
imagination and succeeds in interpolating his *nouvelle* material rather
better, but is if anything farther than Filleau from the stance of
Cervantes.

In the first place Challes reduces the dignity of Sancho even further.
He is made more bloodthirsty and quite uncharacteristically explains,
when several robbers have been rendered helpless: 'Good, good . . .
more bodies and fewer eaters; kill, kill, sirs, or I am going to hang them
immediately. In saying this, he dismounted, went towards them, and
going up to one whose sword was broken, thrust his own through his
body.'[27]

Later on, when he is injured after firing an over-charged musket,
Sancho is subjected to a treatment which goes far beyond even Avellaneda's pantomime situations. Told that urine is the only cure for
gunpowder wounds, and having it confirmed by Dorotée, he is persuaded to allow himself to be urinated on by the servants.

> . . . et comme il ne pouvoit voir leur operation, le plus hardi, ou plutôt
> le plus efronté d'eux tous, ala se mettre a genoux auprés de lui, et lui
> lâcha sur le visage le superflux de son humidité; tous les autres en
> firent autant après lui, et inonderent l'infortuné Sancho le plus

[27] 'Eh bon, bon, dit Sancho, plus de morts et moins de mangeurs; tuez, tuez,
Messieurs, ou je m'en vais les pendre tout à l'heure. En disant cela, il mit pié à
terre, ala à eux, et s'aprochant d'un dont l'epée étoit cassée, lui passa la sienne
dans le corps.' P. 119.

copieusement qu'ils purent à la décharge de leurs reins. Ruy Gomez dit que malicieusement ils lui en lâcherent quelque portion dans la bouche, que le Chevalier avala malgré lui.

. . . and as he could not see the operation, the boldest, or rather, the most shameless of them all went to kneel near him, and released on his face the superfluity of his humidity; all the others did as much after him, and inundated the wretched Sancho as copiously as they could with the discharge of their kidneys. Ruy Gomez says that they maliciously let some portion of it go in his mouth, which the Chevalier swallowed in spite of himself.[28]

> *Continuation de l'admirable Don Quichotte . . . , Histoire de*
> *l'admirable Don Quichotte* VI, (1711), p. 136

Further adventures Sancho is made to undergo are drawn more or less directly from either Cervantes' first or his second parts but there they are attributed to Don Quixote. As with Filleau, it is clear that for Challes Sancho's social position and lack of refinement make him the recipient of adventures beneath the dignity of Don Quixote. This goes so far that Challes deprives Sancho of his sexual innocence, preserved so far by all those writers who had treated his character.

Don Quixote remains the author's spokesman, and continues to be surprisingly effective in dealing with robbers and other violent men. Challes introduces a lighter tone into his book, however, and instead of the elevated moral tone of the first continuation, we have here disquisitions on love. Considerable space is taken up by a discussion on the relative methods of loving in France and Spain and two inset *nouvelles* relate to the nature of sexual love. In *Le Jaloux trompé* traditional material regarding a lover disguised as a serving woman, and a chastity belt which he persuades the husband to make his wife wear, lead to a happy ending. *Le Mari prudent* shows a wise man's method of dealing with a young and erring wife. After the latter story Don Quixote, in his capacity of protector of the weaker sex, gives a long discourse on the nature of jealousy and a strong attack on the double standard in sexual matters.

Surprisingly enough Challes succeeds in unravelling the narrative

[28]The Ruy Gomez mentioned here is the supposed narrator who has acted as redactor of the accounts of Zulema; his papers find their way to the Spanish court, are bought by a Frenchman and so brought to France. This is typical of the involved and pointless fooleries which elaborate Cervantes' humour without understanding it.

mess Filleau had left him with. He makes the carriage whose arrival had ended Filleau's book turn out to be that of Dorotée and her husband and he quickly introduces the Duke of Médoc, their friend and the governor of the Province, identified with the Duke who had entertained Don Quixote in Cervantes' second part. Together the gentlemen clean up the nest of bandits and see justice done to them and jointly agree to bring Don Quixote back home safely. So they invent an elaborate pantomime which involves great humiliation for Sancho and punishment for a long list of offences, some of them committed in the versions of earlier writers and which depends on the arrival of the barber, the priest, Sansón Carrasco and Dulcinea. Typically Challes takes care to relate her to contemporary reality: 'the truth is that she was very pretty and well behaved and of a lively disposition.'[29] Don Quixote is persuaded that she is to become a nun and ordered to return home. Then he is enriched by secret contributions from the gentlemen and after Sancho receives a few more humiliations, they both set off home. Challes, it seems, intended to end the story by making him repent in the same way that Cervantes himself did. However, in the published version the ending was altered to make a point that might have come from the pen of Le Sage. Mistaking a cold stream for Merlin's fountain in the Ardennes, they both drink copiously to free themselves from love—for Dulcinea and Teresa. Fever and pleurisy ensue, and although Sancho survives, Don Quixote dies, providing a chance for a dig at contemporary medical practices: 'After eight blood-lettings and a great number of bottles of herb tea, he died in the arms of his priest with all the sentiments of a good Christian.'[30]

POSITIVELY THE LAST APPEARANCE?

Challes' continuation of Filleau, perhaps because it was too closely tied to its model, is rather old-fashioned considering its date of publication, though it could well have been written any time in the interval between 1711 and the appearance of Filleau's book in 1697. A few years before Alain Le Sage had published what it is not too much to call his own continuation, even though it was basically a translation and adaptation of the work of Avellaneda (1704). Significantly, Le Sage levels the kind

[29]'La verité est qu'elle étoit fort jolie, fort sage et avoient beaucoup d'esprit.' P. 354.
[30]'. . . après huit saignées et grand nombre de bouteilles de tisane, mourut entre les bras de son Curé avec tous les sentimens d'un bon Chrétien.' P. 500.

of criticisms against Cervantes which had been made by Sorel in his *Le Berger extravagant* two generations before and more recently elaborated by Perrault. Cervantes' version lacks *vraisemblance*, according to Le Sage—though the attack is mounted against Benengeli and by another character. 'El Curioso Impertinente' comes under heavy attack, particularly for the handling of the episode when Anselmo hides to watch his wife and does not come out when she seems to offer violence to herself and when he comes to Leonora's door and, finding it locked, does not break it open. The death of Anselmo, who had enough strength to start the letter and yet dies before he finishes it, is even worse, according to this character:

> Disons donc, reprit la dame, que l'auteur a manqué de génie; et que ne sachant comment dénouer son histoire, il a pris le parti de choquer la nature et la vraisemblance; ne pouvant imaginer un événement ingénieux mais naturel, pour faire connôitre à Anselme l'intelligence secrète de sa femme et de son ami.

> Let us say then, resumed the lady, that the author lacked genius; and that, not knowing how to bring his story to a conclusion, he decided to shock nature and *vraisemblance*; not being able to imagine an ingenious but natural incident, to make Anselmo discover the secret understanding of his wife and his friend.
> *Nouvelles avantures de Don Quichotte* (1704); *Oeuvres de Le Sage* (1821) x, p. 362

Other charges relate to the management of the episode of the galley slaves and of that in which Dorotée bewails her misfortunes in the wilderness for the benefit of the listening priest and barber.

It is not surprising that an author who felt like this about Cervantes should have subjected Avellaneda to considerable revision. And although Le Sage stays faithful more or less in the early sections, he gradually moves away from his model in the direction of a *nouvelle*-type action, involving a love plot, turning on displaced social identity. He reduces the religious element in Avellaneda from the first, considerably redrafting the story of the Prioress who is miraculously protected by the Virgin. He also omits another novel altogether and inserts one of his own in its place, replacing the dismal but exemplary *Wealthy Unfortunate* with the *Histoire de don Raphael de Bracamonte*, though it does not do him a great deal of credit. Most important, however, he introduces a great deal of new material which concerns the adventures of 'la belle Engracie', her long-lost brother and their respective loves, which serves to hold the later part of the *Nouvelles Avantures* together.

Most interestingly, however, all Le Sage's modernism does not prevent him from entering farther into the spirit of Cervantes than either Filleau or Challes were able to do. As Roger Laufer, one of his most brilliant modern critics, put it, it was in imitating Avellaneda that Le Sage acquired the critical sense that Cervantes possessed much more naturally. Although Filleau and Challes had juggled about with various narrators and thrown doubt on the whole process of narration, they did so in the interests of rationalistic simplicity. Le Sage, on the other hand, shows himself aware of the kind of issue which Cervantes develops. He invents, for example, an episode in which Sancho, who has cheated over the performance of a spell which will free the Infanta Burlerine from a troublesome beard by eating and drinking in bed under cover of darkness, is persuaded that he must actually have dreamt that he cheated, on the basis of the fact that the beard did disappear. Then while he takes great care to end his account of Don Quixote's adventures naturally, having him shot in a casual and highly predictable encounter with the Holy Brotherhood, in the report of his death he brings back into the character of Sancho a great deal of what had been lost: Sancho's lament could not have been written by Avellaneda, Filleau or Challes:

> Oh mon bon seigneur et mon mâitre, s'ecria-t-il en pleurant à chaudes larmes! C'est donc cette fois-ci que nous sommes séparés! Nous ne nous reverrons plus que dans la grande vallée! Ah pauvre orphelins, votre père est mort! Les princesses auront beau crier, personne n'ira les secourir; et la chevalerie va tomber pour le coup, puisqu'elle a perdue le chevalier qui l'étayoit. Helas! que ferais-je sans vous dans le monde, mon cher mâitre? Je n'ai plus de boeufs ni de brebis; les paiens les ont expédiés, et l'empereur de Trébisonde a mangé mon coq jusqu'a la crète. Je n'ai pour tout bien que notre malle que vous m'avez donnez l'autre jour; et je ne sais pas encore si monsieur le curé ne la voudra pas rafler pour votre enterrement!

> Oh my good lord and my master, he cried, weeping from the bottom of his heart! It is now then that we must separate! We will never see each other again but in the great valley! Ah poor orphans, your father is dead. The princesses will have good reason to cry, no one will go to help them; and knighthood is going to collapse all at once because it has lost the knight who

supported it. Alas, what will I do without you in the world, my dear master. I no longer have oxen nor sheep; the pagans have dispatched them, and the emperor of Trebisonde has eaten my cock, comb and all. I have no goods except our wallet that you gave me the other day; and I don't know yet whether or not the priest will want to carry it off for your burial!

Nouvelles avantures de Don Quichotte X, p. 435

This passage in itself was no small achievement in the first decade of the eighteenth century. Perhaps Le Sage had in mind when he wrote it the closing lines of Molière's *Dom Juan*, where the hero's valet expresses his disturbance at his master's being suddenly swept off to hell only in a lament for his unpaid wages. There is certainly a close relationship between both passages, but Sancho's lament represents a return to the spirit of Cervantes rather than Molière and a new interest in the complexity of character which is represented here by humour rather than reductive comedy.

Le Sage and Robert Challes, writing at the beginning of the eighteenth century, were able to develop a new seriousness in their attitude to contemporary life and a more humane interest in character which demanded expression in the novel rather than romance, *nouvelle* or comic romance. In the process by which they became novelists their study of Cervantes was an important element. It is fair to say that Cervantes' work dominates this period of the novel's history and absorbs the attention of writers who are drawn back to it again and again even though, missing its secret message, they distort it according to their own ideas of fiction. And eventually, in spite of distortion and adaptation, *Don Quixote* had its effect, mediating in the process by which rationalist attitudes of the period were replaced by a new way of looking at fiction and at life.

LES ILLUSTRES FRANCOISES (1713)

Robert Challes' only novel, *Les Illustres francoises*, published at The Hague in 1713, perhaps without his prior knowledge, is the first work of fiction actually to comply with the theory of the *nouvelle*. The novel is a collection of *nouvelles* or 'histoires', joined together within a narrative frame, so it belongs to the fictional genre which also contains Boccaccio's *Decameron*, *The Canterbury Tales*, the *Heptameron*, and, more recently, Segrais' *Les Nouvelles francoises* (1656). *Les Illustres fran-*

coises is unique among these collections of tales, however, in that it shows an integral and complete connection between the tales and the frame which contains them. In Challes' novel he takes care to develop a strong social situation which attracts a good deal of attention in itself and then allows members of the social group to explain their present situation in the group by what has happened to them in the past. By this means he achieves a thorough examination and elaboration of the values which are demonstrated as important in the behaviour of the group. *Les Illustres francoises* is also unusual in its realism, in representing life according to the conditions in which it is lived in contemporary society, in avoiding sensationalism or melodrama, and in fulfilling other conditions outlined in discussions in the court of the Princess Aurélie. Yet at the same time it is a very conservative work from some points of view. Challes maintains considerable distance from his characters and their emotions. His values are fundamentally similar to those of earlier writers, especially Scarron. His work is revolutionary in the way in which it focuses more closely on the texture of experience than earlier fictions, but at the same time it places very heavy stress on the elements which restrain and shape emotional and impulsive elements in the human character.

A good deal of Challes' success derives from his handling of the frame situation which holds his novels together and greatly increases their interest. Our sense of the actuality of the moment of narration rather than the present tense of particular *nouvelles* is never destroyed. Individual *nouvelles* are related in quite complex ways to each other and are made to spring quite naturally from the various social meetings between the group of young people whom the novel concerns. Particularly important, however, is the way in which narration of the separate stories is made to relate to the situation of the most important single character, Des Frans, whose history is especially typical and presents us with the novel's central problem—the tension in human character between conceptual elements and emotional impulses.

The novel begins at the point when Des Frans returns to France after a long absence. Rescued from among the wheels of the many carriages in a Paris street by an old friend, Des Ronais, Des Frans renews old acquaintance and makes new friends in a series of social gatherings where those present tell their own stories or those of other members of the group. Des Frans' own story is among these. He has to explain the circumstances which caused his mysterious exile and his present sadness and misogyny, but important factors in his own story remain unknown to him until they are provided in the closing narrative of his friend, Dupuis. The completion of his history, to the point when he is able to marry again and settle down, brings the novel to an end.

Des Frans is a very prominent member of the group of young people. He is the only unattached male and a very attractive personality, but he is also important because his social position and the moral problems associated with it are of great significance. Des Frans inherits from his father nobility of blood and sentiment and finds it very difficult to adjust to a society which is increasingly money orientated. The various employments offered by his mother's brothers—both successful men of affairs—require that he compromise with his independence and sensitivity. Des Frans gives some detail about the difficulties he encounters in this respect, though he deals with other aspects of his youth and manhood quite briefly. He is a gentleman before he is a man, and also someone who tends to feel conflicting loyalties and claims strongly, resulting in illness and faintness at moments of crisis.

This tendency is confirmed and developed by the central event in Des Frans' life—his relationship with Sylvie, who becomes his wife. Her ambiguous social position, conflicting with his own sense of gentility and his mother's quite justified disapproval, is problematic from the start, but the relationship as it develops causes such a sharp tension in Des Frans that he inclines to fatalism to explain it. He regrets the circumstances which kept him in Paris on the occasion when he first met Sylvie because they led to so much trouble:

Je dis pour mon malheur; car si j'avois été par tout ailleurs, je ne me serois pas perdu par ma propre faute comme j'ai fait, mais comme forcé par une certaine puissance que je ne comprens point; & qui me fait croire, que si nos actions sont tout-à-fait volontaires, du moins peut-on dire que nôtre vie n'est pas toûjours gouvernée par nôtre seule volonté, & que l'Etoile en régle les principaux mouvemens & la disposition. En effet toute la force de ma raison se bornoit à me faire connôitre le péril où je me jettois, & ma propre foiblesse, sans me donner la force de m'en sauver.

I say for my misfortune; because if I had been anywhere else, I would not have been lost through my own fault as I have been, but as if compelled by a certain power that I in no way understand; and which makes me believe, that if our actions are completely voluntary, at least it can be said that our life is not always governed by our will alone, and that the stars rule its principal impulses and its disposition. In fact the whole force of my reason was sufficient only to make me recognise the peril where I was throwing myself and my own weakness, without giving me the power to save myself.

Les Illustres francoises, ed.. F. Deloffre (1959), Biblotèque de la Faculté de Lettres de Lyon, p. 289

The initial difficulty over Sophie's position is made much worse by an anonymous letter which accuses her of being a foundling, of immoral and unseemly behaviour, of theft, and of a cold-blooded attempt to deceive Des Frans as to her real parentage and social position. These assertions are confirmed by what seems hard evidence, including that of the man Sylvie had chosen to be her father, and this time the requirements of honour are supported by those of social respectability and backed up by the powerful arguments of his mother.

Des Frans promises never to see Sylvie again, but he combines the business of buying horses to leave Paris with an attempt to find out more about the affair and is gradually drawn in spite of himself to visit Sylvie once more. Here he feels for the first time what he takes to be the full measure of his weakness. He is persuaded, merely by being with Sylvie, to give her a chance to explain what had happened. Looking back on his behaviour he is quite unable to explain it:

Je lui jurais que c'étoit mon coeur qui parloit par ma bouche; que j'étois prêt de monter à cheval dans l'instant même. Que je ne regarderois de ma vie une si infame créature. Que je ne m'en souviendrois même qu'avec horreur. Enfin je dis tout ce qu'un homme véritablement repentant de ses folies pouvoit dire. Je croyois que c'etoit ma pensée, je l'aurois juré: mais je ne connoissois pas encore tout mon foible: ou plûtôt je ne scavois pas que mon Etoile avoit résolu ma perte, & que j'étois destiné a sçavoir & à connoitre l'horreur du péril qui me menacoit, sans avoir la force de l'éviter.

I swore that I spoke in all sincerity; that I was ready to take horse at that very moment. That I would never in my life see such an infamous creature. That I would not even think of her but with horror. Finally, I said all that a man truly repentant of his follies could say. I thought that I believed it, I would have taken an oath: but I did not then know the extent of my weakness: or rather I did not know that my Star had resolved that I should be lost and that I was doomed to experience and to recognise the horror of the danger which threatened me, without having the power to avoid it.

Les Illustres francoises, p. 306

At this stage the reader is ignorant of the reasons why Des Frans is quite so convinced that his love for Sylvie is weakness rather than an acceptable impulse of affection. In the event Sylvie is able to explain all the accusations away as the result of malice and disappointed spite of a would-be lover, except the attempt to deceive Des Frans as to her parentage. The company agree that this is excusable: 'everyone agreed with Mme de Mongey, that if everything Sylvie had said in her defence were true, she was quite innocent. . . .'[31] Des Frans himself confirms the truth of her explanations, the difficulties are tidied up and the villain disposed of. There follows a secret marriage, during which Sylvie shows herself to be truly generous and motivated by the highest possible principles. At this point Des Frans' problem seems to be solved.

The problem breaks out more seriously again, however, when Des Frans returns to Paris after an absence and finds Sylvie in bed with his friend Gallouin. Outraged, he restrains the impulse to kill them both, removes a necklace from her neck to be used as evidence of his knowledge of her crime, and withdraws. Later he returns publicly to Paris, picks a quarrel with Gallouin and wounds him, leaves town again and orders Sylvie to break up the household and follow him. Then he imprisons her with the utmost severity for three months before he relents enough to give her the choice of living separately or going into a convent. Unable either to deny or to explain her infidelity, Sylvie accepts the arbitrary will of Des Frans almost without complaint and in a way which softens him to the point where the fears that he may take her back. Before going into the convent Sylvie again shows her generosity and affection. Des Frans flees, not trusting himself to stay. Falling desperately ill at Lyons, he is persuaded to repentance and returns to forgive her, only to find her recently dead. He leaves the country, his mood embittered.

Des Frans' major problem arises not from Sylvie's infidelity, but from his own inability to come to terms with it. He is unable to reconcile it with her character, or himself with the strength of feeling which draws him to her in spite of it. Des Frans is in a state of acute and persistent psychological crisis. The problem is eventually solved for him by Dupuis who learned as a result of his intimacy with Gallouin before the latter died, that he had used natural magic to seduce Sylvie, unaware of the secret marriage between her and Des Frans. The

---

[31] '. . . & tout le monde tomba d'accord avec Madame de Mongey, que si tout ce que Sylvie avoit dit pour sa justification etoit vrai, elle etoit fort innocente.' P. 337.

instrument was the very necklace that Des Frans had removed, thus breaking the charm. Now we understand the dreadful situation of Sylvie, unable to explain her own infidelity to herself, let alone to her husband. The use of magic perhaps weakens the case. Sylvie's own explanation is more interesting in psychological terms, and perhaps might have been used—that is, she thinks she has been humiliated because she had too much reliance on her own virtue and her love for Des Frans. But the important point remains the same—neither man nor wife can adjust to reality because they think of it as simpler than it is. It is interesting to compare Challes and Cervantes here. Challes is not prepared to tackle the adultery as a complete psychological fact and so removes Sylvie's moral responsibility, whereas Cervantes had tackled this difficulty directly in 'El Curioso Impertinente'. But on the other hand, where Cervantes ends his story abruptly, with the death of Anselmo, Challes keeps Des Frans alive so that he can study the way in which he responds to his experience.

Des Frans, of course, suffers partly because he is so sensitive to the standards of behaviour which a gentleman will be judged by. In Dupuis, the second most important character in the novel, Challes introduces us to someone who suffers from too little sensitivity of this kind. He makes Dupuis' narrative into a study of *honnêteté* and its relationship with the libertine ethos. Dupuis himself is quite conscious of a purpose in his narration and is often quite explicit in his interpretation of his own history, but the modern reader is likely still to experience difficulty in appreciating his story. It records the process by which Dupuis acquires *honnêteté* and becomes capable of occupying a fixed position in society, but it is not structured so as to show this process from within. Neither Dupuis nor Challes write as if experience or character organise themselves from within. *Honnêteté*, after all, is not a fully internalised concept but a condition the individual arrives at partly in spite of himself, as a result of his social position. So Challes organises his narrative arbitrarily, changing its focus according to the way in which he is preoccupied by various aspects of his subject-matter at different times. The result may remind the English reader of the novels of Defoe, for Dupuis fails to make a consistent relation between his state of mind at the time of narration and that at the time he is describing in much the same way as Moll Flanders and other Defoe characters. But for Challes the important thing is how his narration reflects on the other stories told in his novel, and he is saved from Defoe's dilemma by virtue of the fact that he has provided a narrative frame which is not that of the individual's account of his own life.

Dupuis begins by explaining the background which conditioned his growing up to be completely undisciplined: a fond father, a mother who unfairly favours an older son; resentment and premature independence following his father's death. He shows the development of a personality which is savagely egoistic, impatient of any restraint or insult—in fact, a crude version of the gentleman. The narrative develops through several important incidents—confrontation with a riding-master, an adventure while bathing in the Seine, a duel with his elder brother. His headstrong wildness is seen in a series of early debauches and in his attitude towards women, which is adequately explained by his relationship with his mother and his early sexual experiences with the chance-met mistress of a Knight of Malta between thirteen and sixteen. Gradual maturity causes him to abandon the scene of his early adventures and make new acquaintances and he enters a new phase in which we see him behaving as the traditional libertine, in a series of affairs motivated more by egoism than sexuality.

These adventures show Dupuis as an unstable personality, unable to come to terms with his own impulses or to make a suitable assessment of his own character and motivation. First comes the affair with Sophie, in which his annoyance at having been made use of in her attempt to encourage the lover who later marries her leads him into excesses which are quite unjustified. Having forced her to a hasty marriage by his attempts to ruin her reputation, he then does his best to ruin the marriage by using Gallouin's knowledge to render the husband impotent for the first four months. He then proceeds to take advantage of this himself until he sees that he is in danger of becoming seriously involved with Sophie, who is thinking of obtaining an annulment of the marriage in order to marry him.

Dupuis shows in this first encounter that he is driven on to quite extraordinary lengths by the desire to make himself felt in his relationship with women, even where love or sexual desire are completely absent. This becomes more apparent in the aftermath to his long-standing relationship with Célenie whom he seduces with a promise of marriage and callously abandons after the birth of their first child. Astonishingly, after returning to Paris and finding her engaged to someone else, he exerts himself to win her back. With no love on his side and considerable hatred on hers, he does all he can to prevent the marriage, including appeals to her virtue and good faith! And then, when it is actually consummated, he sends the husband an account of the whole affair.

The final episode in this part of the narrative is designed to show us that if he is not prepared to be deceived himself, he is also unwilling to see his friend deceived, but here it becomes clear that he is not in full possession of the facts about his own motivation. For this story shows a consistently developing urge to project his personality at the expense of women that subsumes his concern for his friend. Attracted to Mlle Récard, the object of his friend Grandpré's affections, he does all he can to seduce her and is only prevented by circumstances and her caution. His warning to his friend when he learns that he intends to marry her is ignored but he learns by chance that Mlle Récard is in the habit of going to the house of a local procuress to satisfy the appetite he has detected in her himself. Consequently he arranges for a meeting without revealing his name and has Grandpré and another woman along as witnesses. The supposed object of this encounter—to reveal her real character and shame her and then to mollify the outraged lover—is obviously a mask for the desire to sexually humiliate someone who has rejected him. The episode which concludes the scene is quite unprecedented in serious fiction for what it tells us about the levels of human motivation:

> Je fis dessein dans le moment d'épuiser toute la colère de Grandpré & de l'obliger a me demander pardon pour elle. Je la fis nüe comme la main; je la visitai par tout le corps, & la fis boire dans cet état à la santé de son amant & à la mienne: enfin j'en fis tout ce qu'un débauché peut faire d'une paillasse de corps de garde, excepté que je ne voulus point en venir au fait. Je la mortifiai & l'humiliai autant que je pus, & tant qu'enfin Grandpré me demanda quartier pour elle, & me pria de la lasser là.

> I made a scheme on the spot of exhausting all Grandpré's anger and of obliging him to ask pardon on her behalf. I stripped her stark naked; I went over her whole body, and I made her drink in that state to her lover's health and to mine; finally I did everything with her that a debauchee can do with a lifeguardsman's mattress, except that I didn't try at all to come to the point. I mortified and humiliated her as much as I could, & so much that in the end Grandpré begged mercy for her and begged me to go no further.
>
> *Les Illustres francoises*, p. 473

We ourselves have to reconcile this sexual aggression with the *honnêteté* which Dupuis goes on to acquire, for he is quite incapable of doing it. As far as he is concerned his treatment of Mlle Récard reveals no discrepancy between actual and professed motive. But our task as readers is made much easier by the fact that the discrepancy is quite consistent. Dupuis's understanding of his own case is partial, but his report is an honest one, and the stability he finally acquires proceeds quite naturally according to a process of development recorded in his story.

The next important phase of action centres around Dupuis' relationship with a rich widow who gives him a good deal of sound affection and the kind of attention he is greatly in need of. The narrative focus at this stage is rather unstable. Challes is clearly concerned to work in a certain amount of material regarding the proper freedom which ought to exist between the sexes and the need to balance social and sexual considerations. But the material is very relevant to Dupuis' situation. What women are taught very early he has to learn himself—that is, that sexual and social factors must be related in all relations. Ironically the central episode here is one in which Dupuis assumes a completely hypocritical rectitude in order to further his affair with his widow. He turns on a man who has basely deserted and publicly mocked a widow who has become pregnant by him as a result of an offer of marriage which cannot be legally enforced because of the pregnancy, and he preaches him an impromptu sermon on the nature of a virtue which he lacks himself. According to Dupuis *honnêteté* is something which no gentleman can live without:

> Je trouve, Monsieur, lui dis-je, qu'elle dépend, non seulement de ne point tromper une femme comme cette demoiselle l'est, mais même de ne point tromper le plus mortel de ses ennemis. L'honnêteté d'un homme, poursuivis-je, git dans sa sincérité, dans sa probité, dans sa bonne foi, dans une vraie compassion pour les malheureux, dans un retour sincère de tendresse pour les gens dont il est aimé, dans la reconnoissance des bontez qu'on a pour lui, & dans une stabilité fixe & inébranlable dans ses promesses.

> I find, Sir, I told him, that it consists not only in not deceiving a woman such as this lady, but even in not deceiving one's most mortal enemy. A man's *honnêteté*, I continued, lies in his sincerity, in his probity, in his good faith, in a true compassion for the unfortunate, in a sincere return of tenderness for people who love him, in the recognition of goodwill towards him, and in a fixed and unbreakable firmness in his promises.

Les Illustres francoises, p. 493

This fine speech has an immediate effect on the man in question who repents almost immediately and marries the woman a few days afterwards. It also works in the favour of Dupuis in advancing his fortunes with his own widow, who is finally brought round by his giving her to think that he possesses the art of preventing conception or of dealing with it after it has taken place.

The most important aspect of the speech, however, is not its hypocrisy, or its effectiveness, but the fact that Dupuis can make it at all, because it proves that he is developing a conception which he showed no awareness of previously. In the long-standing relationship with the widow he changes a good deal, and he begins to be able to approach his own ideal of behaviour. But his character is not finally formed until after this relationship has come to an end and he has learnt what love is in coming to know Mme de Londe. In beginning the story of this relationship he takes us back to an earlier period of his life when he first met her as Gallouin's sister. At this stage he is acting the part of a penitent for no apparent motive, and he is again acting when he meets her years later. He falls on his knees in the gravel and acts a passion which he does not feel. But gradually he becomes serious, firstly because he can make no headway against her, even though he knows that she is attracted by him and even emotionally involved. For the first time he has encountered solid virtue, which he cannot shift, and as a result he begins to develop a serious passion for her. Eventually this leads to delirium and fever and attempted suicide, which is followed by a sort of promise from Mme de Londe that she will satisfy him. At this point the death of her husband makes marriage possible. The subsequent death of Gallouin further postpones this event, but Dupuis shows no impatience at this. It seems that he has at last acquired mental stability and maturity, capable of living according to the idea of *honnêteté* he had previously formulated merely as a form of words.

A good deal of the effect which Dupuis' story has in *Les Illustres francoises* comes from its position as the last in the series of stories. Coming at the end, it makes explicit a lesson which is implicit throughout—that is, that the life of the individual in the settled society which Challes depicts can only proceed satisfactorily if a certain balance is struck between internal impulses and external pressures. Character as Challes sees it is formed at the point when these factors meet, combat each other and combine. Life itself as he presents it is rather like the Paris street from which Des Ronais rescues Des Frans—potentially chaotic and dangerous but capable of being managed by those who are willing to express themselves within the concepts and circumstances allowed them by contemporary society.

The complexity with which human beings actually respond to life is illustrated in the first *nouvelle* in the novel in a very interesting way. It concerns the relationship between Des Ronais and Mlle Dupuis, cousin to the Dupuis whose story closes the series. Their only problem derives from the wilfulness of her father, who refuses them permission to marry before he is dead. His behaviour is completely logical and completely selfish, and also completely infuriating. Consequently Des Ronais, who does all he can to make him change his mind and to circumvent him, has good reason to hate him. But Dupuis treats both his daughter and his son-in-law to be with consideration and respect. He helps Des Ronais twice in serious matters, firstly, to avoid a potentially costly breach of promise case, and secondly to purchase a valuable office. Furthermore Des Ronais finds him amusing and pleasant and cannot help responding to him personally. So he finds himself in a situation where he simply cannot react as he would have expected:

> Enfin, par la suite du tems, je m'étois fait une maniere de vie que je ne comprenois pas moi-même. Je voyois tous les jours un homme, dont la vie me faisoit mourir de chagrin, & que je ne pouvois haïr: Car outre ce qu'il avoit fait pour moi, il me recevoit comme son fils, & me faisoit rire. . . . Tout ce que j'en puis dire, c'est que ne voyant pas jour à réüssir, après avoir tant manqué d'entreprises, le coeur et le corps s'étoient fait une habitude, de se laisser conduire par l'esprit et par la raison, & s'étoient rendus traitables.

> In a word, in the passage of time, I had established a way of life that I didn't understand myself. I saw every day a man whose life made me die of chagrin and whom I could not hate; because apart from what he had done for me, he received me as his son, and made me laugh. . . . All I can say about it is, that not being able to see ahead to a time when I would succeed, after having failed in so many attempts, heart and body had formed a habit, of letting themselves be guided by mind and by reason and had become tractable.

> *Les Illustres francoises*, p. 49

Des Ronais' surprise at himself is paralleled later by our surprise when we have to revise our opinion of the old man in a way which considerably enlarges our understanding of human character as a product of compromise between impulse and attitude, instinct and social prejudice.

From what we know of Dupuis senior in the first instance, he is some kind of a bear, outrageous in his behaviour to his wife, making her the victim of his own fantasy. His later attitude to his daughter's wedding confirms us in this feeling, but as we come to know him better through Des Ronais' narrative, we change our mind. Des Ronais gradually comes to realise that he is a fundamentally honest man whose whole attitude to life is distorted by insecurity and irrational fear, which he describes as 'fear of the future'. His apology to Des Ronais and his daughter as death approaches is honest and touching:

> Je vous demande pardon à l'un & à l'autre, de m'être si long-tems opposé à votre union, mais je suis plus excusable que condamnable, de n'avoir pû vaincre dans mon coeur une foiblesse qui y étoit & que la seule approche de la mort en chasse.

> I ask pardon from both of you for having so long opposed your union, but I am rather excusable than blameable, for not having been able to defeat in my heart a weakness which was there and which only the approach of death drives from it.

> *Les Illustres francoises,* p. 50

This morbid fear of the future is ironically justified by the conduct of Des Ronais himself after the old man's death when he takes it into his head to decide that Mlle Dupuis has been unfaithful to him. In fact, she cannot have been, and when he meets her again at the instigation of Des Frans, he immediately admits that he has been wrong. There is something wilful in his behaviour, and in view of the fact that it only happens when they are free to marry, we can only interpret it as the result of some irrational impulse in Des Ronais, similar to the old man's fear. In the end sense triumphs, joined to the affection between the young people, and they are reconciled. But the episode comes as the fitting climax to a story which stresses throughout the way in which various elements work together in human character, which is beyond the power of the will, but capable of sensible adjustment.

Des Ronais remains an important character in the next *nouvelle* because he is the narrator and is free to intrude his own observations. The story is basically a version of King Cophetua and the beggar maid. Angelique, poor but of gentle birth, is obliged to enter service for her living, is wooed by and eventually marries the wealthy, respectable, Contamine. This is a story of *sagesse*. Both lovers place the idea of honour and reputation above personal gratification. Their problem is how to raise the social position of Angelique sufficiently high to enable them to marry without compromising her reputation. Their mutual affection motivates an extremely cautious management of their emotions and with the help of Angelique's *sagesse*, which includes the idea of chastity but a great deal more besides, they eventually achieve happiness.

Contamine establishes Angelique in a house of her own which she manages so well that she can prove her chastity. The climax of their story comes when she meets by chance the Princesse de Coligny, in whose house she had been in service and whom she had left on pretence of marriage. The Princess asks after her husband, receives an unsatisfactory answer and assumes the worst. From that moment the whole scheme is spoiled, but Angelique, motivated by love for Contamine and respect for herself, goes against his wishes and appeals to the Princess herself. Through Mlle Dupuis she obtains an interview with the Princess and in an extended process of self-justification which includes an illness brought on by the threat to her reputation, she establishes herself as respectable and as a fit wife for Contamine.

Angelique's self-justification is an interesting mixture of self-interest and affection which assumes that emotional and social considerations are inextricably mixed. It is interesting to see the way in which Des Ronais judges her, assuming at first that she is not chaste and becoming convinced only gradually. Des Ronais refuses to judge by appearances. 'She is chaste,' he says at one stage, 'or at least it very much seems as if had she not been, she wouldn't have got where she is.'[32] What convinces him in the end is her ability to act against Contamine's wishes:

> Il n'en put jamais tirer d'autre raison, & cette obstination me fait croire qu'elle avoit véritablement vécu sage avec lui; car s'il avoit eu quelque pié sur elle, elle n'auroit eu garde de faire une démarche de cette conséquence malgré lui.

> He could get no other satisfaction in this, and this obstinacy made me believe that she really had lived chastely with him; because if he had had any hold over her she would not have persisted in taking a step of such consequence in his despite.
>
> *Les Illustres francoises*, p. 105

---

[32] 'Elle est sage, du moins il y a beaucoup d'apparence que si elle ne l'avoit pas été, elle ne serait jamais parvenue où elle est.' P. 100.

The phrase which Des Ronais uses to describe the advantage which
Contamine would have had over Angelique is very revealing—literally
to have one's foot on someone! He does not feel it incompatible with the
affection between them that there should also exist the possibility of
sexual conflict. The reason for this seems to be that he has no idea of
personality being absolute but depending on action and reaction to
external considerations. The best example of such a reaction, which
modern readers might well take as illustrating self-interest, but which
Challes' characters interpret as showing real sensitivity, is when
Angelique waits to kiss her future mother-in-law's hand until the
Princess, her social superior, has left the room. The action charms all
who witness it!

Immediately after the story of Angelique and Contamine we witness
the reconciliation of Des Ronais and Mlle Dupuis and this in turn forms
the introduction of the story of M. de Terny and Mlle de Bernay, which
was involved with their story by chance. The basic situation here is
similar to that of most of the *nouvelles*. How are two consenting lovers
to be brought together in spite of external circumstances and their own
passions? In this case the opposition is provided by a selfish and
spiteful father and worsened by the malice of a younger sister. The
action is close to the typical love story—meeting, love declaration,
opposition, persistence, triumph, dramatic dénouement and assertion
of love. What makes it follow this pattern, however, is the nature of the
actors—passionate, headstrong and inconsiderate on both sides. The
difference is that they are prepared to be careful and to wait for each
other and to support nature with common sense and persistence. The
central theme of the story concerns the repression of nature, threatening violent reaction, and the achievement of the lovers is that they were
able to contain that, in spite of themselves.

The next story—M. de Jussy et Mlle de Fenouil—similarly
threatens tragedy, again has a pronounced romanesque element and
again shows the avoidance of tragedy by sense. The difference is that in
this case the nature of the opposition is more acceptable, the enemy is
the law of the land, and the lower social status of the man. She is young
and headstrong and forces him to act against his better judgement. He
is obliged to act twice in a way which is wrong, in pursuance of the
greater right; and the fact that they put emotional considerations before
social soon redounds on them when they are arrested and he is tried for
his life for abduction. Her intervention shows the persistent control of
circumstances and nature, and turns the tide, and his absence, their
mutual fidelity and caution assures a happy ending for them both.

At this point we come to the central story of M. Des Prez and Mlle de l'Epine, which has elements common to all the others, but differs in that it is tragic in outcome. The most interesting thing about it, however, is Challes' deliberate avoidance of the obvious moral point we might have expected him to make. The schematic moral stated in the Preface suggests that the story proves that you can't rely on anyone other than your husband—we might also say that it proves splendidly the dangers in self-indulgence because it is impatience that precipitates the conclusion and loses her life. But in fact Challes is no moralist, even though he is interested in human behaviour. He throws the emphasis not on tension, but on the sense of loss. The story is put well in the past and is reported at two removes so what we concentrate on in the first instance is the way in which Des Prez is taking the tragic loss of his wife. Then we approach the history itself, wanting to find out the way in which it could have come about. The first factor here, of course, is the tyranny of Des Prez' father and his ability to tyrannise over the lovers through abuse of his social position and legal authority. This is the condition of everything. Then we notice the strong similarity between the meeting and the same event in the story of Angelique and Contamine. The development is without tension or incident. The first stage is the deprivation, followed by their decision to take the chance of a secret marriage. Des Prez makes his arrangements with great caution, and his impetuousness is qualified by the caution of the priest who does all that he can to prevent the anticipated danger. The danger when it comes, however, is of a totally unexpected type—it is not from the separation forced on them by the father—patience and persistence would have forced him to accept or made his acceptance irrelevant because Des Prez was of age and could rely on the income inherited from his mother, and his imprisonment was not justified by the law. What makes the issue tragic, changing this from a story which would have had a greater chance of success than the one before, is the brutality of the mother—that is, a violent reaction from a quarter which was not expected. The brutality which leads to Mlle de l'Epine's unexpected death and introduces an element of tragedy which was not anticipated by the father in his most cruel and headstrong moments.

The effects of this savage, selfish temperament are all the more striking because they had been anticipated before by the lovers when the moment for declaration drew near and worked out in a scene in which the mother is imprisoned in the room after being told about their marriage until she has cooled down. What happens later brings into prominence what human nature is capable of. The moral point still holds firm — their behaviour had laid them open to this kind of insult, and this need for the help of other people. But we are aware of that as a secondary consideration, much more important being our awareness of the way in which crude passion, unrestrained by the expected considerations of reputation, morality and sentiment, can break out to destroy. The lovers are passionate and inconsiderate themselves. The incident with a peasant who discovers them making love in his field proves that beyond dispute; but they do allow for their own character and act with bravery and foresight. It is a cruder aspect of human character which they had not really thought about from animalistic impulse, joined to sordid temperament, and does not involve the highest motives.

As far as Challes is concerned tragedy has little sublimity about it and involves the lower rather than the higher emotions. One of the most striking things about *Les Illustres francoises*, in fact, is the way it avoids either tragedy or comedy and tends to treat human character and human situations straightforwardly, judging them according to their outcome in much the same way as we judge our own situations in everyday life. Because of this and because of the way in which Challes deals with contemporary society, with ordinary people and ordinary emotions, and the way in which he stresses the conditioning factors at work in the lives of his characters, it is tempting to call him a realist. And if Challes may not be called a realist, it is difficult to see what general application the term may have at all! Yet, on the other hand, it is interesting to notice that Challes' popularity was in the eighteenth century, not in the nineteenth, and that even when Champfleury, in his *Réalisme* (1857), tried to revive his work, he showed little appreciation of the actual nature of the novel. In fact, Challes' realism is the realism of 1713 rather than 1857 or 1918. It derives from a society in which individual human beings were appreciated as such only in so far as they could assimilate into their characters criteria reflecting economic and social values. All realist art requires that man adjust to his environment, of course, but the art of the nineteenth century reflects in one way or another the romantic idea that man and the universe share the same spirit. This idea was a long way away in 1713. Challes' realism consequently reflects the nature of his own world, and his fiction incorporates experience within the *nouvelle* and within the social situation which the novel describes rather than letting it take a shape suggested by romantic analogies between the life of man and organic Nature.

L'HISTOIRE DE GIL BLAS DE SANTILANE (1715)

The shape of *Gil Blas* can be seen emerging through Le Sage's adaptation of Avellaneda, which increasingly showed the influence of the first part of *Don Quixote* as it went on. Avellaneda would have been shocked to see how his work could mediate between Cervantes and Le Sage, but this is clearly what happened. The first volume of *Gil Blas*, published in 1715, adopts the basic plan of *Don Quixote* I, which seems to have come naturally to Le Sage as he was re-writing Avellaneda. That is, it incorporates a series of episodic adventures with a love-intrigue, both of which are concluded together. The adventures of Gil Blas become entangled with those of Don Alphonse and Séraphine, just as those of Don Quixote had been worked in with the intrigue concerning the four lovers, and those of Avellaneda's hero were mixed up with the story of Engracie and her brother in the *Nouvelles avantures*. Le Sage, however, introduced a new element into the combination, which transformed it. The influence of Cervantes was counterbalanced by that of the picaresque. Le Sage translated *Guzmán de Alfarache* and imitated the picaresque in his *Estevanille Gonzales* (1734) and assimilated it entirely into *Gil Blas*. So instead of a series of episodes initiated by a madman, his novel reflects the adventures of a young man seeking to establish himself in the world. On the other hand, his presentation of Gil embodies a consistency and logical development which did not exist in the picaresque and which was Le Sage's original contribution. The result of this unique combination of elements was the creation of a flexible and natural fictional pattern. Le Sage's framework was used again and again by later novelists—particularly, of course, by Fielding and Goethe. Indeed, it was so influential as to be in the end positively harmful. Le Sage's influence on Scott and Dickens, at any rate, reinforced by that of Fielding, may well have inhibited their development rather than helped it.

In the perspective created by the classic novels of the nineteenth century *Gil Blas* was a great step forward in the direction of the *Bildungsroman*, and in the process in which novels came to be structured around the internal development of individual characters. It also reflects a new seriousness in its attitude to ordinary human experience, breaking away from the tradition of reductive comedy as we have it in the work of Sorel and Scarron and an important stage in what has been called the *encanaillement* or democratisation of the

novel.[33] So Ferdinand Brunetière, the great exponent of the evolutionary attitude to the history of fiction, called it the first modern novel,
after which the novel would be the representation 'of that which is
human, doubtless, in each of us, but above all, of that which is most
analagous to the ideas, the usages, the manners, and the ways of life
of our time'.[34] This may seem high praise, but it brings with it fundamental criticism, because in *Gil Blas* the narrative is not actually structured around the experience of the hero at all. Furthermore, the novel
almost totally lacks an interest in subjective experience as such. It
treats human passions only by means of inset *nouvelles* or romanesque
intrigue. Gil himself lacks passion and even a complete self-consciousness, frequently fading altogether into the background of his narrative. So in the perspective created by Stendhal and Flaubert, *Gil
Blas* dwindles to the status of a minor achievement, a mere *roman
à tiroirs*.

   Gil Blas, however, is not a nineteenth-century novel, and Le Sage's
failure to develop Gil's character, or even to confine his narrative stance
to the framework of Gil's biography, must be seen in relation to positive
factors which shape his work as a work of art on its own terms. In fact,
this failure might well be considered in conjunction with another
feature of his work which comes out strongly when we compare him
with later novelists. This is his refusal to develop a particular social
context for his characters. It is highly significant that he set his novel in
Spain, which readers in both France and England have traditionally
regarded as the country of the *picaro*, the rootless wanderer. If we
compare him with Challes, so nearly his contemporary, we notice at
once that Le Sage has entirely avoided what the author of *Les Illustres
francoises* took most pride in—the representation of relationships in
contemporary society. Clearly Le Sage was attempting something
different, which is suggested by the quality of his language. The style
of *Gil Blas* entirely lacks the colourfulness and the range of the Spanish
picaresque and the idiomatic bluntness of Challes. He maintains a
consistent distance from the experiences he is describing, carefully
preventing his language register from falling beyond a certain point
and tending rather towards the restricted and elevated vocabulary

[33] See particularly, G. May, in his excellent study, *Le Dilemme du Roman au
xviiie Siècle. Etude sur les rapports du Roman et de la Critique, 1715–1761*
(1963).
[34] '. . . il sera la peinture de ce qu'il y a d'humain, sans doute, en chacun de nous,
mais surtout de ce qu'il y a de plus analogue aux idées, aux usages, aux modes,
et aux façons de vivre de notre temps.' 'Le Roman Francois au xviie siècle,'
Etudes critiques sur l'histoire de la littérature française 4e serie (1891),
pp. 45–6.

associated with the neo-classical drama. Le Sage's stance as a novelist is objective and detached. He is interested in man as object rather than as subject. Though not a determinist, he is preoccupied with the individual's need to protect himself from, and relate himself to, certain forces universally at work. Gil himself exemplifies the situation of all men, constantly balancing between the roles of victim and exploiter, impressionable, gullible, cowardly, but capable also of courage, cleverness and initiative. Man's main problem in the world of *Gil Blas* is himself. Human nature, twisted into a million different shapes by the forces which produce individual temperament, constantly defeats its own aspirations. Human society is a net in the folds of which the individual must struggle to exist and to thrive.

It was because of this vision of the world that Le Sage was obliged to set his novel outside society, in the picaresque world of Spain a generation before his own time and was forced to offset treatment of passion in *nouvelles* and interpolated story. In his plays Le Sage had already shown his sensitivity to the sort of pressures at work in contemporary French society. In *Turcaret* (1709) he produced a satire of the financier which also reflected sharply on the society in which he existed. In *Crispin rival de son maître* (1707), he brought out a comedy which was based on the possibility of the interchange of social roles. A similar theme is developed in *Gil Blas*, in the story of Don Raphael, but there it has been relegated to a subordinate narrative. Gil Blas himself actually has a social status almost as low as that of the French valet and had Le Sage set his novel in France it would have been as a similar figure that his hero would have appeared. It would have been difficult for him to have broken away, in that case, from the tradition set up by Molière and later developed by Beaumarchais and Diderot, of the comically roguish valet. Had he made his hero a gentleman, on the other hand, he would have been confining himself in another way, making it impossible for him to maintain the kind of distance he was trying for and extending the range of experience beyond that of the *nouvelle*. It is difficult, in fact, to imagine how Le Sage would have managed at all to have gone beyond the achievement of Scarron had he set his novel in his own country, and impossible to conceive what social situation he could have chosen which would have allowed him to represent an individual at once socially insecure and capable of serious emotional experience.

Sir Walter Scott, one of Le Sage's most ardent admirers, made the important point that in reading *Gil Blas* we are most charmed by the flow of the narrative. This is largely because Gil Blas as narrator maintains a consistent stance, which is closely related to that of Le Sage himself. Gil's narrative contains nothing that is incompatible with his character or his circumstances, but maintains a quite impersonal distance. Gil is just as much in charge of his own experience, in fact, as he is of the experience of other characters whose life-stories find their way into the pages of his biography. The opening sentences of the novel set a tone of objectivity and control which is maintained throughout. Gil's father and mother enter the novel as objects of our attention quite independent of the fact that they are related to the hero:

> Blas de Santillane, mon pere, après avoir longtems porté les armes pour le service de la Monarchie Espagnole, se retira dans la Ville où il avait pris naissance. Il y éspousa une petite bourgeoise qui n'étoit plus dans sa première jeunesse, et je vins au monde dix mois après leur mariage.

> Blas of Santillana, my father, after having for a long time borne arms in the service of the Spanish monarch, retired to the town where he had been born. There he married a woman of the lower middle classes who was no longer in her first youth, and I came into the world ten months after their marriage.

> *Gil Blas* I, ix, ed. A. Dupouy (1935), p. 7

Having introduced his parents, Gil moves on immediately to his uncle, Gil Perez, who is brought before us with all the economy and vividness we expect from Le Sage and a great deal more objectivity than we have any right to expect from Gil Blas. It is striking too that Gil maintains exactly the same distance from his uncle as from his early self, obliging us from the start to read his account of his adventures not as a process of character development, but as a series of related episodes all of which call equally for the exercise of our judgement. There is an important point being made about Gil and his background at this stage. We are being introduced to a hero who has no help of any kind in starting in the world. His parents are themselves helpless and the education his uncle provides him with is useless in preparing him for what he is to find in the world. But the last thing that Le Sage wishes to do in presenting his hero's entry into the world is to suggest that his inability to deal with experience derives from the way in which he has been brought up. His point is rather that it is Gil's nature—and particularly, his *human* nature—which make him the victim in turn of the begging soldier, the flattering parasite and the innkeeper and the horse-dealer who cheats him.

The same point is being made in Gil's description of the incident in which the lustful muleteer frightens his travel companions with the idea of torture in order to forward his designs on the chastity of the young bride. Gil over-reacts, panicking through ignorance and self-preoccupation, and so finds himself in the hands of the robbers who conduct him to their underground cave. This is the central episode of Book I of the novel and it is very typical of Le Sage in that it has several different functions. With regard to its effect on Gil, it is a test of character, teaching him that self-reliance is important and that he must imitate the virtues of the robbers if he is to regain his freedom. Particularly important is the fact that he must learn to act better than they do if he is to deceive them, which he eventually does. Typical of Le Sage too, of course, is the inset incident in which Gil shows us that if he is sophisticated enough to fool the bandits, he is still gullible enough to be fooled by the priest who leaves him a bag of worthless medals instead of his money. A secondary test is built into this episode also, because Gil has to learn courage in learning to be a bandit, which he does successfully. The individual's capacity to overcome his own temperament, and especially the impulse of self-protection through flight, is something which Le Sage returns to several times, reflecting his preoccupation with the tensions at work in human nature in general.

As far as Gil is concerned the robber's cave has a third function, because it teaches him how important it is to fulfil the simplest human impulses in order to attain happiness. The life in the cave is secure, even luxurious, Gil fits in well and is well treated. But he is unable to respond to the good advice of the old woman and reconcile himself to it, simply because it is a cave. The robbers, however, free to go as they please, are perfectly happy in their habitation, and in making Gil repeat their histories, as he has heard them repeated at table, Le Sage gives the situation another narrative function. Rolando, the captain, has come to banditry through being spoiled, his lieutenant through being bullied, another after making an indiscreet religious profession, another after having lost his proper social station. The variety of motives directs our attention to the one common factor in all the robbers, which is a temperamental inclination to the role. This is how they respond to their situation in the world, giving rein to their appetites and devoting their considerable energies to the task of exploiting others and society in general.

Throughout this episode Le Sage varies the narrative focus constantly, considerably blurring our sense of the time-scale when it suits him. With the introduction into the cave of the captured Donna Mencia he introduces what is in effect an interpolated *nouvelle* which has a quite separate focus and a different narrative tone. Donna Mencia is a woman of probity and honour who tries to raise herself above fortune by force of character, and fails. In the first instance she chooses carefully in love and marries a man whom she knew would make a good husband. Fortune removes him and she is led to believe that he is dead. She lives impeccably in straitened circumstances until chance brings the offer of marriage from an elderly nobleman who admires her character. This refuge is destroyed when her husband returns and she flies with him, only to fall into the hands of the bandits and lose both husband and liberty. Later, in Book II, we learn what happens to her after Gil helps her to escape from the cave. Returning to her second husband and finding him on his deathbed, she retires from the world in order to protect her reputation and herself. We have to read her story of course in the light of what would have happened to her had it not been for Gil Blas. She would have been kept in the cave to satisfy the appetites of her captors until her inevitable death. Le Sage is not concerned to make only this point, however, though it is implicit in the story as he tells it. His concern is with the relationship between character and circumstances in social living rather than with extreme situations.

Book I ends with a repetition of the earlier theme of gulling, though now in a more complex situation. Returning to the world Gil is treated worse by legal authorities than he had ever been by the robbers, and even after being rewarded by Donna Mencia, he is quite unable to protect himself from a combination of flattering friendship and sexual temptation. So he is reduced again and prepared for the new situation opened out in Book II, where he is initiated by his friend Fabrice into the world of service. The theme of exploitation is further developed here. We are introduced to the successful hypocrite in the person of Dame Jacinthe who feathers her own nest while she serves the canon. Gil is fooled here, however, not by her, but by the canon himself, whose legacy of a library shows us that malice and self-interest are not the only motives producing deceit and exploitation of others. The central episode at this stage, however, is the introduction of Dr Sangrado, the physician who murders through an unmitigated regime of blood-letting and water-drinking. At this stage Gil as a character moves into the background and he becomes a means of furthering the satire against medical quackery. The importance of the episode as a whole lies in its capacity to show us how far the quack and his apprentice collaborate in a process of mutual deception, satisfied with their own idea of their function while it is clearly harmful to everyone else concerned.

Interpolated into this episode is the incident in which Gil attempts to recover the valuable ring of which he was gulled after leaving Donna Mencia. Here Gil assumes wolf's clothing and goes with Fabrice and a group of friends to the lodging of Camille, impersonating law officers. Unfortunately they go too far, create suspicion, and are arrested themselves. Once more Gil is stripped of his possessions, his ring finally disappears, and he escapes from prison only as the result of the efforts of Fabrice's employer. Here we are reminded not only that you need a long spoon to sup with the devil, but that acting must be authorised in order to be safe!

Book II also has a long interpolated story which changes the scene and persona completely. Le Sage gets Gil away from Dr Sangrado and the town of Valladolid by introducing the theme of cowardice again in a rather humorous way and lets him meet on the road a talkative barber called Diego, whose story parallels Gil's own. Forced to travel because of the poverty of his home, he is rejected by an uncle who has succeeded in the city as a poet and dramatist, and is now travelling home to rejoin his family. The possession of a family is the factor which makes the difference between Gil and Diego, for it means that the latter actually has somewhere to go; and its importance is stressed when they arrive and find the family in possession of the money of the uncle who had refused him help in Madrid.

Inset into Diego's story is an episode which Le Sage adapted from the Spanish picaresque story, *La Vida del escudero Marcos de Obregon* (1618) and considerably altered. In the Spanish book the story of Donna Mergelina, the surgeon's wife who falls in love with a barber's apprentice, was related by the elderly squire. Le Sage makes the subordinate character of the boy into the narrator, so changing the focus altogether. The central character of Donna Mergelina, however, remains unchanged. What interested Le Sage in her story was how her character altered completely with the change of demeanour urged on her by the squire for social reasons. Wilfulness and impulsiveness, which had previously shown themselves in brusque rejection of the attentions of would-be lovers, now find a different outlet, firstly in infatuation for the barber's boy, secondly in opposition to the duenna her husband chooses for her, and finally in fulfilment of her inclinations in spite of him. The story constantly questions where reality of character lies. The old duenna has a profitable career by seeming strict to husbands but being gentle to wives, and Donna Mergelina herself changes completely, without changing at all.

Similar questions about the nature of human character are raised in Book III. The first master Gil serves in Madrid makes us realise the force of temperament in fixing a man's destiny. Don Bernard de Castil Blazo has formed his whole life in a way which will permit him to be completely lazy, has realised his whole fortune and lives on his capital with a total lack of responsibility to anyone or anything. His relationship with Gil brings out a similar point to that which had been made by Gil's impatience with life in the robbers' cave. Though his situation is a perfect one, Gil's curiosity makes him dissatisfied with it until he becomes worried as to whether his master is a Portuguese spy. Ironically, his master suffers a similar misapprehension. Seeing Gil in company with Rolando, the erstwhile bandit leader, Don Bernard assumes the worst and sacks him. Another interesting element in this episode is the implicit contrast between Don Bernard and Rolando himself, who is now a law officer, having survived the destruction of the gang, but whose inclination is drawing him back again to the life of a bandit. Gil brings out the point in his refusal to join Rolando: 'Everyone has his inclinations, I replied to Rolando; you were born for bold enterprises, and I for a sweet and tranquil life.'[35]

This debate is continued in the novel's next episode, when Gil becomes the valet to Don Mathias, where the question of acting is taken up explicitly for the first time. Gil as valet acts the *précieux* in company with his social equals, rivalling his superiors in affectation and effrontery. We have already begun to think of the relationship between the stage and life itself through meeting the cheerful actor, Zapata, on his way home from Madrid after failing in the theatre of the capital city. Now the question of naturalness in acting and the proper criteria for judging it are canvassed during a discussion between the friends of Don Mathias and Don Pompeyo de Castro. This part of the novel in fact is organised as a complex investigation of the relationship between acting on the stage and in life and its connection with and effect on character itself. The stage is brought into the novel not only through discussion of the theatre but through Gil's meeting Laure and going as intendant to the actress Arsénie. Gil himself, of course, is an actor, not only in aping his master in the society of valets but in dressing in fine clothes and going in search of assignations. More seriously, Don Mathias himself is acting the part of the successful lover, even to the point of fighting a duel in defence of his imaginary reputation and getting himself killed.

There is a close parallel between Don Mathias and Don Pompeyo,

[35] '... chacun a ses inclinations, dis-je alors à Rolando; vous êtes né pour les entreprises hardies, et moi pour une vie douce et tranquile.' P. 180.

who is presented as the ideal gentleman, who knows how to protect his reputation and his character without going to excess. In his inset story we see him in a position where his honour can be maintained only by the most delicate conduct. Savagely beaten by the lackeys of a social superior, Don Pompeyo resolves on revenge at any cost and patiently awaits an opportunity. But when offered the chance of a symbolic restitution, he takes it in so tactful and tolerant a way that he wins the friendship and the niece of the man who had offended him. His achievement consists in so governing his character, the emotional impulses proper to a gentleman and the considerations due to a member of a social hierarchy, that he satisfies all the demands made on him. Don Mathias, on the other hand, through overacting the role of fashionable gentleman, is undermining the financial and social basis of his position, and throwing his life away.

At the end of Book III Gil leaves the actors with whom he has been living comfortably for some time, in spite of, or perhaps because of, the affection he has for the easy-going Laure. The change is dealt with externalistically, actually a change of thematic direction rather than an object of attention in itself. Gil's dissatisfaction with the dissipated life he leads as Arsénie's servant is quite in character, especially when taken in conjunction with his later relationship with Don Alphonse, because he constantly seeks social stability as well as comfort. The actors pretend to a social status higher than that of other people, but in fact have no status at all. However, Gil's temperamental unsuitability for the life they lead is not made much of in his narrative. It is merely part of the psychological substructure which runs through the narrative without carrying the weight of the building.

Book IV begins with an incident demonstrating comedy of character again. Gil misinterprets the attentions of his master's daughter when he is serving Don Vicente de Guzman, and makes a fool of himself. However, this incident is really little more than a medium of transition by which Le Sage introduces us to the central concern of this book. This is the relationship between Donna Aurore and Don Luis Pacheco. His management of this affair is extremely subtle from the narrative point of view. It is introduced firstly as character comedy and then developed through our interest in Gil and his growing determination to settle down and earn his employer's approval. Then, after the death of Donna Aurore's father, it is further developed when she decides to disguise herself as a man and set in motion a plot which will conclude by enabling her to marry the young man she has set her heart on. This plot is basically a *nouvelle* in itself, clearly suggested by Scarron's borrowing from Solorzano, 'A Trompeur, Trompeur et Demy'.[36] But before it properly develops Le Sage introduces an inserted *nouvelle* proper, this time based on historical events, which parallels the story of Donna Aurore in a different narrative tone. 'Le Mariage de Vengeance', suggested in the first instance by a picture showing a tragic scene, is one of Le Sage's rare incursions into tragedy. It takes place at the highest social level, the protagonists being the King-elect of Sicily, his prime minister and the latter's daughter. The characters are motivated either by considerations of love or *gloire*, which suggests an elevated conception of one's own character and reputation as things to which the individual life may fitly be devoted. Enrique, King of Sicily with no more than a tenuous hold on the throne, attempts to manipulate circumstances so as to marry Siffredi's daughter. In the event, however, he is trapped by his position and manipulated by Siffredi for the sake of his own security as king. Siffredi employs the idea of *gloire* both in persuading Enrique to give up Blanche and in persuading Blanche to make a hasty marriage with the Constable of Sicily:

> Cependant, puisque nous ne pouvons aller contre les destinées, faites un généreux effort. Il y va de votre gloire de ne pas laisser voir à tout le Royaume que vous vous êtes flattée d'une espérance frivole.

> In the meantime, as we cannot go against our destinies, make a generous effort: it concerns your *gloire* not to let the whole kingdom see that you have flattered yourself with a vain hope.

Gil Blas IV, iv, p. 268

The effect Siffredi actually produces by his manipulation, however, is disastrous. After Blanche's marriage with the Constable has taken place Enrique returns at night, making use of a secret door to enter her room. The Constable, humiliated by what he has discovered of his wife's loathing for him, and now waking to find another man in his room, acts with the heroism demonstrated by all the characters: 'Nevertheless, though this realisation put him in a situation almost as deplorable as that of Blanche, he had enough control over himself to hide his suspicions.'[37]

This event makes things worse for Enrique and Blanche as well,

[36] See above, p. 63.
[37] 'Neanmoins, quoique cette conoissance le mît dans un situation presque aussi déplorable que celle de Blanche, il eut assez de force sur lui pour cacher ses soupcons.' P. 271.

because he learns in a cruelly abrupt manner that she is married, and she thinks that he has come back only to take advantage of her. Both, however, continue to behave heroically, referring each other to the highest concepts and ideals of conduct. When they meet, Blanche leaves Enrique in no doubt: 'I am the Constable's wife: and to spare me the continuation of an interview which embarrasses my pride, permit me sire, without lacking in the respect I owe you, to leave a prince to whom I am not permitted to listen.'[38] In order to obtain another interview Enrique imprisons the Constable on a charge of treason and goes to see Blanche. The Constable, obtaining his release on parole, also returns, and the scene is set for the final tableaux which initiated interest in the *nouvelle*. Blanche tells Enrique that he must renounce her for ever, for the sake of their characters: 'Farewell sire, fly from me; you owe this effort to your pride and my reputation. . . .'[39] But at this point the chance extinction of the lights causes her to open the door and let in the Constable. The fight that ensues ends with his receiving a mortal wound, but spite and revenge cause him to stab his wife, so they both die, leaving Enrique and Siffredi to draw the inevitable conclusions about the attempt to manipulate human desire and emotion even in the service of the very highest concepts.

Donna Aurore's drama is played out in a very different tone and leads to very different results. The situation differs from that in 'A Trompeur, Trompeur et Demy' in an interesting way, because the protagonists have not actually ever met, which tends to remove something of the emotional charge from their situation so that it makes more of a contrast with 'Le Mariage de Vengeance'. Both stories, however, place equal stress on the importance of appearances in love intrigue. The difference between them is fundamentally the fact that in the one manipulation works in the interest of restraint and conceptualisation, in the other on behalf of natural feeling, where wit and humour support sincerity.

The next episode in Book IV brings Gil to the foreground again, teaching him that honest service requires an honest master if it is to be successful. It also develops the concern with different aspects of character. Gil puts loyalty and truthfulness into the balance against the self-deceitful and self-indulgent love of his master, and loses. Don

[38]'Je suis l'épouse du Connêtable et pour m'épargner la suite d'un entretien qui fait rouger ma gloire, soufrez, Seigneur, que sans manquer au respect que je vous dois, je quitte un Prince qu'il ne m'est plus permis d'écouter.' P. 277.
[39]'Adieu, Seigneur, fuyez-moi. Vous devez cet effort à votre gloire et à ma réputation.' P. 284.

Gonzago is unwilling to sacrifice his love to his honour, even though he has no reason to disbelieve Gil's account of his mistress's disloyalty. Consequently he declares himself satisfied with his mistress's excuses and dismisses Gil, though not unkindly.

Gil goes from Don Gonzago's house to that of the Marquise de Chaves, where another kind of self-deceit is in practice. This phase of the novel has a direct contemporary reference, satirising the salon of the Marquise de Lambert, but also has direct relevance to the pattern of character analysis which is built up within the novel as a whole. The Marquise, above ordinary motives of self-interest, and deceitfulness, still falls well below the elevated world of the *nouvelle*. She is happily gulled through her belief in magic and clairvoyancy.

The Marquise's world, in fact, is dangerously near to that of contemporary reality, and Le Sage is somewhat embarrassed to get Gil Blas out of it and on his travels again. Once again he has recourse to the idea of Gil's cowardice—he has either to leave or face a duel over a woman he has shown some interest in. But now Le Sage introduces Don Alphonse and begins the action which is to conclude the novel and complete the scheme of the book. Gil meets Don Alphonse on the road, warns him that he is being pursued and goes with him off the road in search of shelter from the rain. There, in a hermitage, Don Alphonse tells his story, so introducing a third major love situation into the book. Like Don Pompeyo, Don Alphonse is precipitated into a dangerous situation as a result of a casual love-affair. He fights a duel, kills his man, and flees. By chance he then meets the story's heroine, Séraphine, in circumstances which make it possible for him to fall violently in love with her and for her in turn to take a favourable impression.

It is significant that Don Alphonse shares with the young man Le Sage introduced into *Les Nouvelles avantures* a completely gentleman-ly character and uncertain birth. Consequently he starts with a great disadvantage in any love-affair. Nevertheless, he shows great mag-nanimity and noble feeling, forgetting his own interest completely in his attempt to trace her missing sister. Séraphine herself is an interest-ing character in that she has already been married, and widowed, but had been completely unable to respond to her husband's affection. 'In effect,' she explains, 'at that age I was hardly fitted to appreciate the refinements of such a delicate passion. . . .'[40] Séraphine now shows a refreshing ability to respond to directness and force of feeling, without losing any of the self-control which Don Pompeyo's story had shown to

[40] 'Effectivement, à l'âge que j'avois, je n'étois guère propre à goûter les raffinemens d'une passion si délicate.' P. 339.

be so important.

These qualities are thoroughly tested in the situation which follows their meeting. Don Alphonse returns to tell her that he has been unable to find her sister and also to declare his identity—to the extent that he can! Then they discover that she is actually the sister of the man he has killed, and find themselves plunged into a situation resembling that of the protagonists of Corneille's *Le Cid*. Without the straightforwardness of Rodrigue, Alphonse is nevertheless able to make use of the situation to make a declaration, delicate in terminology but quite positive: '. . . since the death of a brother is not capable of moving you to shed my blood, I want to irritate your hatred by a new crime.'[41] Séraphine's reply shows that she knows how to combine respect for the point of honour with consideration for the object of her emotions: 'This bold avowal', replied the lady, 'would doubtless offend me at another time, but I pardon it because of the trouble which moves you.'[42] The passion of the lovers is beyond dispute—Alphonse actually returns to Toledo after the interview to provoke his fate—but they also have a degree of sound sense which determines the channel in which their passion runs.

Book IV comes to an end with the revelation that the hermit and his assistants are none other than Don Raphael and Ambroise Lamela who had gulled Gil out of his money in Book I. Book V is entirely taken up with the narration of Raphael's adventures which delays the development of Alphonse's adventures and greatly widens the scope of the novel's scheme at an important moment. Raphael is what Le Sage's plan had prevented Gil from being—that is, a finished rogue who can rival any *picaro*—and his story provides a last opportunity for Le Sage to investigate the relationship between character and circumstance. Raphael has been thrown on the world without proper guidance and protection and led astray by his temperamental liking for adventures and his powerful appetite for pleasure. Significantly, he is the son of an actress, who begins life by taking the punishment earned by someone else's misdeed and earns our sympathies in breaking away from his situation and living off his wits. The best example of the way he lives from moment to moment, taking advantage of situations as they arise, is provided by the incident in which he imposes on Jerome de Moyadas as his daughter's intended bridegroom, slipping when challenged into the role of Italian prince travelling incognito and discovered at the end

---

[41] '. . . puisque la mort d'un frere n'est pas capable de vous exciter à répandre mon sang, je veux irriter votre haine par un nouveau crime. . . .' P. 341.
[42] 'Ce téméraire aveu, répliqua la Dame, m'offenseroit sans doute dans un autre tems; mais je le pardonne au trouble qui vous agite.' P. 341.

only by a sharp-eyed Alguazil. Brought by chance into a situation of possible security and wealth, he is plunged again into ill luck by a restless, curious temperament, heedless of warning, and is enslaved by Moorish pirates.

In every situation Raphael is alternatively helped and hindered by his temperament. Taking advantage of the favours of the pasha's favourite wife, he is obliged to turn Turk to escape punishment, and is in this state when he meets his mother, also enslaved. Her story is very significant. Originally an actress, but disgusted by her profession when she discovers that the social consideration it affords her is completely illusory, she seeks stability through a series of marriages. Gradually, however, overmastered by the appetites she has contracted as an actress, she adapts to circumstances so extremely as to lose all trace of moral rectitude or human feeling. She ends by abandoning her faith, outraging family ties and becoming savage and revengeful, showing us how temperamental inclinations can become a 'habit of the soul', changing the character out of recognition and actually destroying it. This becomes plain in Raphael's case, too, when his native tendency to effrontery causes him to act viciously, cruelly and basely. As pander to the Duke of Florence he behaves disgracefully, is gulled himself, but again escapes through decisive action, leaving behind him a husband dead and a virtuous wife forced into a convent.

Raphael brings his adventures up to date by explaining the background to the plot by which Gil was originally robbed, and finally explaining what he is doing disguised as a hermit. Then, before Book IV formally ends, Alphonse has the good fortune to rescue Séraphine and her father from bandits, thus breaking down some of the remaining barriers between them. One more adventure remains to Gil and Alphonse before the lovers can be united, which has several important functions. Firstly it has the effect of reminding Gil and Alphonse of the direction they are travelling in company with Raphael and Ambroise, and determining them to split up and return to respectability. Secondly, it is a reminder that the respectability they seek is a moral as much as a social quality, consisting in behaviour rather than in mere function. Raphael and Ambroise decide to rob the Jew, Simon, by disguising themselves as officers of the Inquisition. The trick works because they behave so badly, acting the parts of even greater rogues than themselves. This is an economical episode, disposing of both the gulled and the gulls and leaving only one path open to the joint heroes — the refusal to manipulate or be manipulated, withdrawal from the race. This is a decision which Gil makes quickly when he has a chance to reflect on the action he is engaged in. Now for the first time he has established a relationship other than that of servant and master. When Don Alphonse falls ill and Gil nurses him back to health this is further developed, so that without actually crossing barriers of class, Gil has found the possibility of social security. This becomes a reality when Don Alphonse returns home, finds his real father and his mistress waiting for him and settles down within an enclosed world on his own estate. The last action of the novel is Gil's returning the money stolen from Simon in the capacity of intendant to Don Alphonse and the book ends on a characteristically satirical quip: 'So I was going to make a restitution. It was beginning the job of intendant where it ought to be ended.'[43]

[43] 'J'allai donc faire une restitution. C'étoit commencer le métier d'Intendant par où l'on devroit le finir.' P. 443.

4 Progress and Compromise: The Novel in England and France, 1715–1758

After 1715 it is easier to trace processes of change and development in the novel because it has moved so much closer to the centre of things and become itself the medium through which cultural change takes place. In the middle years of the eighteenth century the novel is prominent among literary forms, no longer merely a potential, but something available to a large number of writers practised in other literary forms. But at the same time the rise of the novel in England introduces a new element of complexity. From this point on it is necessary to take account of two distinct and separately developing traditions in England and France.

The development of the English novel in the period from 1720 to 1750 was sufficiently dramatic to have attracted attention in its own right, and at the same time it was to a large extent an independent movement, a specifically English event. This has encouraged critics in the English-speaking world to consider it in isolation, and even to apply criteria derived from a specifically English conception of the novel to the novel in general in Europe and America. There is some justification for this approach. It is easy to dismiss the translation and imitation of French fiction which took place in the period immediately prior to 1720 because it had little clear influence on what followed. What occurred in the middle decades of the century in England was a shift of sensibility resulting in the assimilation of several different modes of writing into the range of the novel. The predecessors of eighteenth-century novelists are to be found among the writers of Puritan allegory and biography, Anglican and Methodist preachers, in the journalistic work of Addison and Steele, and in the comic and tragic drama of the period. In explaining the timing of the event social and economic factors are important, as they have been clearly identified by many writers working in the field marked out by Ian Watt. Behind every literary movement, at some distance or another, is a social event, and without risking the naïveté of a reference to the specifically middle classes, a term the eighteenth century found it quite easy to do without, we can clearly recognise that a widening in the social classes involved in cultural activity and a consequent breakdown of attitudes associated with higher social groups is a major factor in the novel's rise to respectability in mid-eighteenth-century England.

Yet even if we were to identify the nature of this connection far more carefully than has yet been done in English criticism, we should still be obliged to emphasise the fact that what actually took place, in so far as it affected the writing of novels, was a cultural event rather than a social event. Samuel Richardson, for example, by far the most important writer concerned, brought to the business of writing novels religious and cultural attitudes which were attributable directly to his class, but the process by which he became a writer appealing to all educated classes, was one by which he assimilated existing cultural standards which were originally determined by a wide range of social and political considerations. It is significant that Henry Fielding, who was conscious that he belonged to the gentry rather than to the trading classes, and who drew not a little ridicule upon himself on this account, shares with Richardson many basic attitudes and values. This should help us to remember the extent to which it is possible to see both English and French fiction as part of a common, European tradition, in spite of the differences between them.

This is not to minimise those differences which are apparent at first glance. The comparison between two novels such as Tobias Smollett's *Roderick Random* (1748) and Claude-Prosper Jolyot de Crébillon's *Les Egarements du coeur et de l'esprit* (1736) is extreme but typical. Smollett's novel is relatively formless, episodic, introducing a wide range of characters from many social ranks and several nations. At its centre is the relationship between Roderick, the hero, and his friend, Strap, a relationship ultimately derived from *Don Quixote,* but original in so far as it tends to blur differences based on social rank. The hero's love-affair is a prominent element in the novel, but it is treated in a rather perfunctory way, clearly not an important element in itself. In Crébillon's work the focus is much narrower, as is the social range and range of characters. Crébillon is concerned with the study of character in a given social milieu, which is that of the polite world. His medium is sexual intrigue and his values are worked out entirely in terms of the manners of this society. A prominent part of his work is the style in which it is written. Witty and polished, it tends to obtrude itself on the reader's attention as an element in itself rather than as a means to an end.

This contrast is of longer standing than the eighteenth century, of course. At least since the middle of the previous century it had been developing. In England, since Shakespeare's *Henry IV* at least, there had been a tendency to oppose the values of the down-to-earth, plain-speaking provincial with the mincing affectations of the 'certain lord, neat, trimly dressed', who angers Hotspur on the battlefield at Holmedon. In France something very like the opposite process had been at work. So it is not difficult to see the contrast between the English novel and the French novel in the eighteenth century in terms of political and social history. We might say that while England was benefiting from the social and political changes which manifested themselves in the Glorious Revolution of 1688 and prepared the way increasingly for the early development of heavy industry and capitalism a century later, France was suffering the effects of the over-centralisation which had taken place during the previous hundred years.

But to put it in this way would be to obscure at least one important factor. The fact is that the French novel and the English novel at this time are complementary and not in competition. It is true, as Georges May has pointed out, that there were certain factors at work in French culture preventing the development of the 'sympathetic imagination' which motivated the great expansion in the English novel. May identifies these as a feeling of repugnance for extremes, the taste for abstraction, and a continuing respect for the reader's sense of *bienséance*.[44] We must also note that there are aspects of reality commonly available to even the lesser French writers of the period, such as Crébillon or Charles Duclos, which are beyond the reach of their English counterparts. More important still, the great novelists of the period tend to approach one another very closely. Allowing for differences of language and manners, the same people inhabit the novels of Marivaux and Richardson. Beyond this, we may say that as novelists they share the same fundamental problems and preoccupations. They

[44] G. May, *Le Dilemme du roman au xviiie Siècle* (1963), 195 ff. May attributes the sympathetic imagination primarily to Fielding, but in contrast with the French writers it is clearly applicable to other contemporary English novelists.

are brought to the novel by similar pressures and affected by the novel itself in similar ways.

What brought the novel farther to the forefront of things in Europe in the middle of the eighteenth century than it had ever been was a substantial shift in the way in which people thought of the relationship between different elements in contemporary life. This shift was more sudden and more clearly marked in England than in France. From *The Dunciad* (1728 and 1742) to Richardson's *Pamela* (1740) is not very far in terms of chronology but a good way in certain other respects. Richardson's novel embodies a spirit fundamentally different from that of Pope's mock-heroic assault on Dullness. Indeed, Richardson might well have qualified for a place in *The Dunciad* in view of the fact that his fiction reflects just such a lack of proportion, just that tendency to take seriously those things which appeared most trivial in the light shed by the masterpieces of classic literature, as offended against the poet's sense of order and dignity. It is striking that Pope and his ally Swift both use the weapons of the party they are attacking in their onslaught against the unreason and disproportion of modern life. The change which occurs between their work and that of Richardson and Fielding is one of emphasis rather than manner, a change which amounts to an inclination to take life as it is more seriously. Its consequence, apart from the increase of interest in the novel as a form, was an increasing tendency to reflect certain developing tendencies in modern life: a greater moral seriousness, interest in sexual and personal relationships, a greater sense of society as a whole and as a context for the individual human being.

These changes are as clearly apparent in the French novel of the mid-eighteenth century as the English, in spite of the steadier and more gradual development of the novel in France. Together they make up a progressive tendency which brought new demands in terms of narrative material and techniques. But the special characteristic of the novel of the period in Europe as a whole is not merely a result of their presence but of their presence in conjunction with other elements inherited from the past. Amidst all the different pressures at work in contemporary life at this time, several of the strongest worked towards the establishment and maintenance of social, religious and intellectual orthodoxy. In France the battles between these forces and those of the modern party centred around the conflict between Voltaire and the Encyclopedists and the Church Establishment, especially the Jesuits. The latter were particularly bitter opponents of the novel as a literary form in eighteenth-century France and their case was sufficiently strong in its appeal to the administrative powers to effect the temporary banning of the novel in Paris in 1737. In England opposition to the novel was also strong and testifies to a similar inclination to suspect it of subversive tendencies. What is important here is not, however, the presence of opposition to the novel, but the fact that there continued unchecked in contemporary life a tendency towards enclosed systems of thought. The period from 1715 to 1760 might well be called the Age of Ortho-doxy. It is the period which saw the composition of Pope's *Essay on Man* (1732–4), of Voltaire's *Discours sur l'homme* (1736). Whether we look at England, where social and intellectual complacency were universal, or at France, where rationalist reductivism opposed Jesuit obscurantism, we see that progressive tendencies were cramped within authoritarian systems of thought. Nowhere could they be allowed to take on their natural form or lead to their logical consequences.

Had the situation been otherwise, of course, the novel itself might not have benefited at all. The novel is not the primary medium of those who seek social revolution, give full reign to their interest in passions or explore the individual's relationship with his Maker. It was the desire to compromise between these interests and others that brought the novel to the fore in the first place. But at the same time it stamped the narrative art of the time with a particular quality and presented those who employed it with a particular difficulty. The subject matter of the novel in this period was the representation of modern life with a new urgency and seriousness, its purpose was to reconcile conflicting elements within it. And this was effected by technical means, often by purely mechanical devices. So there was a constant tendency towards manipulation. In the absence of an aesthetic which demanded that the subject should be allowed to develop its own momentum and find its own way to a close, and in spite of the dominance of Aristotelian ideas about the unity of action, very few novelists were able to avoid short-circuiting the tensions embedded in their material, and those few only rarely, at a price.

LE SAGE'S 'FURTHER ADVENTURES'; THE FAILURE OF *GIL BLAS*

In 1724 Le Sage continued Gil's adventures with a further three volumes and followed these nine years later with a final three, so that in the revised publication of 1747 they appeared as a sequence of twelve books, though composed over a period of twenty years.

The continuation has never attracted much favour among readers and though complaints have been largely directed against the tone and relative lack of liveliness of the later books, the basic reason can clearly be seen to be that Le Sage was reflecting and failing to deal with the sort of change of sensibility we have been referring to above. The earlier volume is based on a romance structure combined with a loosely picaresque form and the combination brilliantly adapted to Le Sage's world view at that time. His method in this first volume perfectly corresponds to a world which is structured according to certain permanent laws and in which the individual—himself affected sensibly by those laws in his growth and development—had to achieve a primarily social adjustment. In the later volumes Le Sage's vision has changed. He has become more serious, more preoccupied with the texture of living, and more concerned with major moral problems. The personal, affective dimension, which does not enter into the first *Gil Blas*, except through the *nouvelles* which treat romantic love and revenge, comes to be central to the story of Gil himself. But Le Sage is unable to adjust the fiction to allow for this adjustment of world view, and the result is that he impoverishes it. Gil himself becomes dull and unconvincing, in spite of the fact that from the point of view of satire several incidents represent an improvement over the early volume and have justly become immortal.

Le Sage's first problem, of course, was how to manage the continuation at all, having settled Gil, apparently permanently, at the end of the first volume. He solves this by means of an incident which is effectively self-contained. Gil becomes involved with a duenna called Lorenca Séphora. Discovering, as a result of his jealousy, that she has a cancer in the back, he withdraws, insulting her and giving rise to hatred which ends in his having to leave the house to keep the peace. Gil's behaviour here is in character, though his decision to leave is weakly motivated. The most important thing about the incident is its inner, satiric content. From this point on we get accustomed to feeling that this is so, and gradually the fictional factor becomes weaker and weaker. This is unfortunate because the only way in which Le Sage can continue at all is to develop the personal dimension of Gil's adventures.

So the rest of this 1724 continuation is taken up with Gil's adventures with the Archbishop (Chapters 3–5), his encounter with Laure as an actress among the troop at Granada, including her history since their parting (Chapters 6–11); Gil's return to Madrid, with events centring on other characters, meeting with Fabrice and his service with the Count Galiano, ending with his desertion in illness and recovery

(Chapters 12–16).

Book VIII begins with the machinery through which Gil is inserted in the household of the Duke of Lerma, which Le Sage makes use of to tell a famous anecdote about Ninon Lenclos, and continues with his behaviour as a private secretary. The basic method continues to be that of inserting histories of other people, and *nouvelle*-type stories, but increasing strain is felt between the satirical and personal dimension because these are supposedly located in Gil himself. If the satiric issue is to be centred on Gil, it becomes moral. The objectivity necessary to satire is destroyed by the degree of involvement which the narrative process centred on an individual character brings with it.

This strain increases with Book IX, the last of this phase of the novel. The introduction and development of Scipion, who acts in relation to Gil as Gil had to Don Alphonse, is the main feature of interest. The story continues with Gil's ambition, his fall from power, imprisonment, repentance and decision to retire. The most notable feature of this part is the perfunctory way in which the central psychological event—his conversion—is effected. Typical is the insertion in a closely textured part of the novel, immediately after his imprisonment when we have just been given reflections on his state of mind, of the story of Don Gaston de Cogollos, a *nouvelle*-type story suggesting how love can transcend its own romanesque elements and triumph over circumstances.

The 1724 continuation ends in mid-air, at the point when Gil has returned to Madrid but before he implements his decision to retire. The last phase of his adventures covers his retirement, marriage, death of his wife, return to court as the secretary to Lerma's successor, the latter's death, his final retirement and second marriage. Most significant perhaps, apart from the perfunctory way in which the wife is disposed of, and the second wife acquired, is the visit to the parents, which represents Le Sage's attempt to follow out the development of Gil as a moral entity. It fails entirely, showing the impossibility of Le Sage's ever combating the tendency to turn each event into a self-contained satiric unit. Gil's change of heart is given far too little attention to become convincing. And when he gets onto the scene, to find his father dying, he is made to behave in a quite uncharacteristic way in order to furnish his author with an opportunity for reflection on the idea of the prodigal's return to his native place. The rest of the volume reflects Le Sage's continuing skill as a writer in some respects. It shows a deepening seriousness and an inclination to reflect on many of the problems of contemporary experience, but always at a high level of abstraction totally out of keeping with the structural framework which the development of the original picaresque-type story had provided. In effect Le Sage marks the end of an era in the history of the novel and points the direction in which later writers were likely to find most difficulty—combining particularity and generalisation—finding an appropriate type of fiction to permit the balance of external and internal factors.

THE EARLY MARIVAUX; EXPERIMENTS IN MODERNISM, 1712–1715

Without the early work of Marivaux it would be much more difficult to trace the factors affecting the development of fiction in the period immediately after the appearance of the first part of *Gil Blas*. The gap between that novel and the work of the English and French writers who were publishing between 1735 and 1760 would be very difficult to fill with anything but generalisation and hypothesis. But at the very beginning of his career as a writer Pierre Carlet de Chamblain de Marivaux, born in 1688, twenty years after Le Sage but only one year before Samuel Richardson, produced a series of fictions which are not only important in themselves, but embody very clearly the dilemma of the novelist in that period.

These early works are *Les Aventures de *** ou les Effets surprenants de la sympathie, La Voiture embourbée, Pharsamon ou les Nouvelles folies romanesques* and *Le Télémaque travesti*, which were published at various times but all composed or partly composed, in the three years before the appearance of *Gil Blas*. It is interesting to notice that in some ways they are more revolutionary than anything Marivaux published during his mature period, but that they are also in some other respects very retrograde, showing the uncertainty of a young author working in isolation and without any clear sense of direction. The special problem for Marivaux was finding actions which would correspond to his disposition as a writer. Significantly, he preoccupied himself with the forms inherited from the immediate past, and especially with burlesque and parody which have always been close to the novel's critical spirit. But equally important, he filled these old bottles with very new wine. Perhaps it was the destructive effect that turned him decidedly towards the theatre for the next fifteen years.

In these early novels Marivaux appears as the direct heir of Scarron and Cervantes. Like none of his contemporaries or immediate predecessors, he inherits the dual awareness of fiction's role in representing the substance of human motivation and behaviour and analysing its form, and the relationship between the two. And he does this within a completely new framework of reference. He is deeply interested in the reality of human motivation, but also in the external forms of human behaviour, and the relationship between the two. At the same time he is drawn towards the critical and burlesque forms his predecessors used. But because he is interested in the texture of personal experience and in the reality of human situations in a new way, he is able to come much closer to vitalising these forms than Le Sage.

The 'Avis au Lecteur' in *Les Aventures de **** is a daring progressive statement that puts Marivaux's position clearly and boldly. He is dissatisfied with contemporary *nouvelle*-type fiction and complains about the directness and naïveté which had been the innovation of the previous period, calling them 'simple adventures hastily narrated' and 'spiritless masses of action'.[45] He would prefer to replace these fictions with works such as the one he is supposedly editing for the benefit of his readers, which would 'inspire grand sentiments' and 'elevate the soul' rather in the manner of the old romance. The originality of his argument consists in the stress he places on studying the emotional reactions of his characters and awakening the emotional response of his readers. Because of this he rejects neo-classical rationalist criticism entirely, appealing to instinct—'that internal feeling almost always noble and tender'—which is possessed by women rather than academic critics. This feeling is to be trusted farther than reason itself:

> C'est au goût et à ce sentiment secret, indépendant des lois stériles de l'art, que l'auteur a tâché de conformer le langage et les actions de ses personnages. . . . Pour y réussir, il a tâché de copier la nature, et l'a prise pour règle. Il est vrai qu'avec elle on s'égare; eh! qu'importe, si ces égarements sont vrais? Plus on la corrige, moins elle est parfaite; la raison, en la réformant, ne peut remplacer les beautés qu'elle lui ôte. Mais, dira-t-on, la règle qu'on lui donne rend avec usure à l'esprit les plaisirs qu'elle retranche au coeur, et qui deviendraient fades. Étrange prudence, qui en ménageant à l'esprit des plaisirs souvent faux, et toujours rares, prive le coeur d'un plaisir doux et sûr, et interrompt les douceurs du sentiment, qui sont les plus touchantes!

[45] '. . . simples aventures racontées avec une hâte'; '. . . un amas . . . d'actions sans ame. . . .' *Oeuvres de jeunesse*, ed. F. Deloffre (1972), p. 9.

It is to the taste and to this secret feeling, independent of the sterile laws of art, that the author has endeavoured to make the language and the actions of his characters conform. . . . To succeed in this he has tried to copy nature, and has taken her for a rule. It is true that with her one errs; but oh! what does it matter if these errors are true? The more she is corrected, the less perfect she is; reason, in reforming her, cannot replace the beauties which it takes away. But, it will be said, the rule which is imposed repays the mind with interest the pleasures of which the heart has been deprived, and which would have become insipid. Strange prudence, which in eking out to the mind pleasures often false, and always rare, deprives the heart of a sweet and certain pleasure and interrupts the sweetnesses of feeling, which are the most affecting.

*Les Aventures de ****; Oeuvres de jeunesse,*
ed. F. Deloffre (1972), p. 3

This passage provides the basis for a whole new approach to criticism and composition of the novel, replacing the traditional rules with the inspiration of the writer and the reader's response, appealing to nature as the final resource of judgement and giving a new independence to fiction. Marivaux was not alone in objecting to the application of neo-classical rules to the novel. De Charnes, in particular, had preceded him in this. But he goes much beyond De Charnes and all his contemporaries in projecting a new function for the novel. Not only in this one work, but in all the early fictions, he constantly appeals to nature as the novelist's model and aim, arguing that it demanded its own methods and its own criteria of judgement. So in *Pharsamon*, he tells us: 'Everything in the smallness of its subject is susceptible of beauties, of embellishments; there is only the species of difference. . . .'[46] What he was projecting here, in fact, was a kind of literary Protestantism which would ultimately overturn not only rules and judgement but also barriers of style and characterisation, and social barriers themselves.

This progressive theory, however, is unmatched in Marivaux's practice. In *Les Aventures de **** Marivaux makes use of the outworn techniques of the Heliodoran romance, with impossibly wire-drawn coincidences and terribly inter-involved narratives, in spite of his realistic imitation of manners. *Pharsamon* is more interesting to read

---

[46] '. . . chaque chose dans la petitesse de son sujet est susceptible de beautées, d'agremens: il n'y a plus que l'espece de difference. . . .' *Oeuvres de jeunesse,* p. 602.

and is also more revealing of the way Marivaux's sensibility seems to have been governing his intellect. Here he produces a version of the Don Quixote theme. A young man brought up in the country by his uncle reads too many romances and decides to assume a new character. He persuades his peasant companion to follow him and together they take to the countryside with new names and find adventures which they manage to distort to fit the pattern of romance procedure. Most important, they find two young women of corresponding inclinations and fall in love. The story ends with their restoration to complete sanity and acceptance of normality.

What is interesting about *Pharsamon* is the way in which Marivaux pours completely new material into the old form, outgrowing the satiric pattern altogether. His interest in the psychology of his characters and his determination to locate their adventures in contemporary reality overcomes the satiric element. Both Pharsamon and Cliton are involved in burlesque adventures, and there is a good deal of the farce we would expect after a course of Cervantes continuations, but we can neverthe-less see that Marivaux is constantly coming closer to his material than is compatible with the satiric stance. But at the same time, it is also clear that he is developing no steady sense of direction. He protests at one time, in one of his many Cervantean interjections, that his work will not preserve the unity of tone required by the rationalist critic: 'Doesn't it seem after all to Monsieur the critic, that because he has laughed at one part, I should be obliged to furnish him with matter for laughter all the time?'[47] He claims the right to change the tone of his narrative, and his claim is consistent with his whole position, but its basis here is merely the professed whimsicality of the comic writer: 'Let him dispense with it if he likes; a little variegation amuses me. Follow me, dear reader; to tell the truth, I don't really know where I am going; but it is for the sake of the pleasure of the voyage.'[48]

This statement is typical of Marivaux at this stage in his career. The central characteristic of this early work is its unevenness and inconsis-tency. Marivaux is adventurous and experimental; above all, he is drawn closer and closer to experience itself; but at the same time is unable to find a literary mode or pattern within which he can develop.

[47] 'Ne semble-t-il pas après tout à monsieur le critique que parce qu'il a ri quelque part, on soit obligé de lui fournir toujours de quoi rire.' *Oeuvres de jeunesse*, p. 457.
[48] 'Qu'il s'en passe s'il lui plait; un peu de bigarrure me divertit. Suivez-moi, mon cher lecteur, à vous dire le vrai, je ne sais pas bien où je vais; mais c'est le plaisir du voyage.' *Oeuvres de jeunesse*, p. 457.

This comes over very clearly in *Le Télémaque travesti* where a similarly burlesque purpose is constantly being overcome by Marivaux's growing interest in what we can only call the reality of contemporary experience. Though Marivaux does keep within the basic frame of the *Don Quixote*-type of parody as interpreted by the writers who preceded him, he still generates a degree of interest in contemporary experience and in the way in which individuals actually relate to contemporary events of seriousness and personal events of seriousness for them, such as disappointments in love. Most striking of all, for the first time since Cervantes, he introduces into his work contemporary political events. He is carried by the travesty into a treatment of recent anti-government rebellion in the Provinces and though this is nominally so that he can justify the hero's delusion, what actually happens is that the deluded hero takes his place against the background of real events, directly and strongly narrated, so that the parodic purpose is judged itself in so far as it can throw light on the experience of contemporary society.

The result is our confirmation in the rejection of the code of judgement which the parodic frame implies—that in which reason, expressed in terms of social normality, dominates and orders individual experience. The sheer reality of characters such as Pymon, who is completely real and completely outside the boundaries set up and recognised by contemporary culture, confirms our mistrust of the parodic impulse. Pymon and the many characters like him are foreshadowings of Squire Western. It is even true to say that the rebel leader Araste is a version of Scott's Balfour of Burleigh. Marivaux at times does seem in this work, on the very edge of a new vision of reality.

This position, of course, could not be held. It was only reached because of uncertainty about the appropriate frames for experience. In Marivaux we have no social rebel but rather a young author looking for a way to adjust to contemporary culture. Perhaps his position can be most clearly seen in a passage from *Pharsamon* which foreshadows his turning to the theatre and perhaps to his later development as a novelist. This comes when Pharsamon and Cliton are being shown by a peasant *fermier* round a strange château, shortly after they have lost touch with their respective mistresses. Suddenly, while they are in the picture gallery, a door opens and the two girls appear. Transfixed, the lovers stare at one another; Cidalise faints, Pharsamon, miming his delighted astonishment, falls and hits his head, but before he has set the situation out, as it were, dramatically, Marivaux's interest in the actual nature of their reactions draws him to comment on the likely combination of *mouvements* in people whose states of mind were complicated by a mixture of love and romanesque delusion. His sense that he has gone beyond his brief in turn draws from him a typical comic digression in the form of a discussion with an imaginary critic; and this in turn is followed by a step by step analytic description of the physical disposition of the lovers which yet returns again into a novelistic analysis of the characters' reaction to their situation:

Etrange extrémité pour Cidalise, que sa faiblesse n'étourdit point assez, pour qu'elle ne voie pas son amant à terre! L'état où elle est, faux ou vrai, est une expression vive et tendre du plaisir qu'elle a eu en retrouvant son amant; ce plaisir a épuisé ses forces: sa faiblesse est un demi-évanouissement, et cette faiblesse ne semblerait plus qu'une feinte, si elle se levait pour secourir Pharsamon. La satisfaction de remplir romanesquement l'aventure, lui paraît préférable au plaisir de porter du secours au chevalier, qui, de son côté, ressent vivement le coup qu'il s'est donné, et qui résiste à sa douleur par scrupule pour le faiblesse mutuelle.

Strange extremity for Cidalise, that her weakness did not daze her enough for her not to see her lover on the ground! The state she is in, true or false, is a lively and tender expression of the pleasure which she has had in finding her lover again; this pleasure has exhausted her energies; her weakness is a semi-faint, and it will seem no more than a feinte if she gets up to help Pharsamon. The satisfaction of completing the adventure romantically seemed preferable to her to the pleasure of bringing help to the chevalier, who, for his part vividly feels the blow which he has given himself and who restrains his grief out of respect for their mutual weakness.

Pharsamon ou les Nouvelles folies romanesques; Oeuvres de Jeunesse, ed. F. Deloffre (1972), p. 531

It is difficult to imagine how these characters would ever have got themselves out of their situation at all, had not Marivaux drawn in the peasant-guide, with typical dramatic skill, to unravel the situation with his laughter, even though he ends it finally with a comment in his capacity as satirist: 'Strange effect of fortune! the finest adventures exposed to the grossness of a rustic.'[49]

The years between *Pharsamon* and *La Vie de Marianne* (1731–42) are those in which Le Sage was publishing the later volumes of *Gil Blas*

[49]'Etrange effet du hasard! l'avanture la plus belle, exposée a la grossiéreté d'un rustre!' *Oeuvres de jeunesse*, p. 532.

and a number of imitations or translations of Spanish picaresque tales of a hundred years before. It is a period when, in spite of the superficially democratic tendencies of the *nouvelle*, and greatly increased interest in travel, secret *histoires*, memoirs and biographies, little true development of the novel took place. Marivaux's case perhaps suggests the reason why. His interest in sentiment stimulated an almost revolutionary development in his early attitude to fiction and the early works which resulted from this were no mere false start to a career as a dramatist. They revealed an astonishing talent and a strong impulse towards the representation of areas and levels of experience which would require a new type of realism, a new seriousness in fiction. The withdrawal from fiction is an admission of defeat by the medium he was employing. Marivaux was advancing rapidly towards an art which would directly represent areas of contemporary reality which had never yet fallen within the scope of prose fiction. To have gone farther than he did he would have needed no stronger impulse but rather patterns of action and reaction which he could imitate. And his constant return to the patterns of the past, to burlesque, comic romance and satire, tell us as clearly as anything could, that they simply did not exist. The choice of drama rather than fiction was a decision to abandon the attempt to structure a complete world view and to concentrate rather on working out the relationships between certain aspects of the world view. It was a decision also to keep within a narrower social range and a narrower register of experience than fiction offered. And when he turned again to the novel, in spite of his great originality, the effects of that decision are still visible. And even then, as a mature writer, he was still unable to solve the structural problems his art presented.

BETWEEN TRUTH AND LIE; THE PROBLEMATIC CASE OF DEFOE

Daniel Defoe's position in the history of the English novel is secure and unchallenged. If not quite, perhaps, the first English novelist, he plays an important part in the development of fiction and the techniques of realistic representation which are generally regarded by English critics as essential to the existence of the novel as a form. His place in European tradition is much more problematic. Between Cervantes on the one hand and Marivaux on the other he can hardly be thought of as a progenitor of the novel. But even in this kind of company his case is as interesting and instructive as ever. Defoe came from a different social class from the majority of contemporary novelists; he wrote for a different audience; and he showed no interest in the themes and preoccupations we think of as typical of the fiction of the period. He approached the business of fiction-writing from a unique point of view, not attempting to write novels but fraudulent biographies which would impose themselves on his readers as literally true. His work proceeded from a sensibility moulded by the principles of religious Dissent, which at once pushed him towards fiction and drew him away from it. The result was a deep-rooted confusion in his mind, reflecting itself in confusion and inconsistency in his work. Ironically, these are the basis of his achievement and his place in the history of the novel.

Defoe professed contempt for the novel. Of the two sorts of writing he thought were useless to everyone except the stationers, the novel was one, which he scorns because of its evident fictionality:

> One of these are *Novels*, in which the Author sits down and invents Characters that never were in Nature: He frames a long Story or Intrigue full of Events and Incidents, like the Turns in a Comedy; and if he can but surprize and delight you enough to lead you on to the End of his Book, he is not so unreasonable to expect you should believe it to be true; no, he has no Design of imposing upon Mankind: His only Aims are to divert the Publick and to get a little Money to pay his Taylor.
> *A Collection of Miscellany Letters, Selected Out of Mist's Weekly Journal* IV, Letter XXII (1727), pp. 124–5

For 'Novel' in this passage, of course, we ought to read *nouvelle*, which is what Defoe has in mind, but the important point of the passage is unaffected by this. Defoe is objecting to fictionality as such and this objection is present in all the prefaces to his own fictions, where he habitually denies that he is writing 'Novels and Romances' and claims to be producing 'private history'.

There is nothing unusual in this, of course. Everybody did it in the period between 1700 and 1740. 'To distinguish this,' wrote Eliza Haywood in the preface to *The Fair Hebrew* . . . (1729), 'I am obliged to inform my Reader, that I have not inserted one Incident which was not related to me by a Person nearly concerned in the Family of that unfortunate Gentleman. . . .' But most of these claims were purely formal. Defoe's are different, firstly because he took such very great care to validate them in the body of his works, and met with such a great success in doing so, and secondly because they are so urgent and confusing. So far as I know, at least, no one ever bothered Eliza Haywood by assertions that her 'real Matters of Fact' were actually fictions, but they did bother Defoe, precisely because of his success in persuading a wide public that his stories were literally true. *The Disguis'd Prince: or, the Beautiful Parisian* (1733) belied its subtitle—'A True History . . .'—in its matter and its manner and even if it were to be read as a moral tale, its morality could not be thought to depend on its literal truthfulness. But *Robinson Crusoe* not only seemed to be true, it wrapped up its claims to be true with its claims to be moral in a very confusing way. The Preface to *Robinson Crusoe* (1719) concluded with a sentence which makes no real sense at all:

> The Editor believes the thing to be a just History of Fact; neither is there any Appearance of Fiction in it: And however thinks, because all such things are dispatch'd, that the Improvement of it, as well to the Diversion, as to the Instruction of the Reader, will be the same; and as such, he thinks, without farther Compliment to the World, he does them a great Service in the Publication.

Later statements are less confusing perhaps, but no less ambiguous, although in the Preface to *The Farther Adventures of Robinson Crusoe* (1719) there is what seems to be a clear hint that the story is actually a fiction which the writer believes to be justified by its morality: 'The just Application of every Incident, the religious and useful Inferences drawn from every Part, are so many Testimonies to the good Design of making it publick, and must legitimate all the Part that may be call'd Invention, or Parable in the Story.'

There is nothing new in this claim either. Mateo Alemán's *Guzmán de Alfarache* (1599–1604) is comprised of fictional elements in a context of moral analysis and debate. But in Defoe's case the moral commentary itself is part of the fiction—or the history. His narratives are first-person accounts of their adventures by supposedly religiously-minded penitents and although they may allure the unsuspecting reader with their appearance of truthfulness, they are very far from being consistent or coherent representations of a religious point of view. This was immediately apparent to Defoe's contemporaries and is the basis of the swingeing attacks of Charles Gildon in his *Epistle to Daniel Defoe* (1719). Gildon takes Defoe's claims literally and shows that they are inconsistent and absurd. He begins a process of close analysis and reasoned examination of the texture of Defoe's narratives which continued up to the time of Ian Watt, who produced what we may think of as the authoritative demolition of Defoe's own claims to truthfulness and coherence. Gildon descends on the passage in Defoe's Preface where he claims 'legitimation' by his Design:

> I think we may justly say that the Design of the Publication of this Book was not sufficient to justify and make Truth of what you allow to be Fiction and Fable; what you mean by *Legitimating, Invention* and *Parable*, I know not; unless you would have us think, that the Manner of your telling a Lie will make it a Truth.
>
> *Postscript* to *An Epistle to Daniel Defoe* . . . (1719); *Novel and Romance, 1700–1800*, ed. I. Williams (1970), pp. 67 8

Defoe laid himself wide open to Gildon's attack in what must have seemed a quite wilful way. He could have claimed merely that his fictions were parables, and have dispensed with the element of moral commentary. This argument satisfied Bunyan as a defence of *The Pilgrim's Progress* (1678) and if put forward with tact and respect for the scriptural parallel, is difficult to assail. His actual position was extremely weak. It could only have been maintained if Defoe had managed to create a completely consistent relationship between a mature, penitent view of the individual's experiences and the representation of those experiences. Failing to do this, he laid himself open to charges of hypocrisy or naïveté, and undermined the status of his own fictions as such. In the final analysis it is impossible to read Defoe's works as novels at all, except, as Ian Watt puts it, by positing 'a kind of limited liability' for the novelist.[50]

The problem posed by this failure has attracted the attention of many critics of Defoe, including, of course, those who have tried to explain it in terms of irony. It is all the more acute because it arises in the case of a writer whose primary claim to importance is precisely that he did bring the experience of the individual into the foreground in a way that had never been done before. Comparing Defoe's fictional biographies with the more nearly historical accounts of Tristan l'Hermite, Courtilz and Count Hamilton, mentioned in an earlier chapter, it is striking that his work reads as if it were true whereas theirs does not. In the first place Defoe uses the individual life as a framework for his fictions. Secondly he creates a narrative style which reads completely naturally. This is only partly a matter of the so-called 'circumstantial detail', which other writers have mastered with a greater economy than Defoe. At least equally important is the fact that Defoe's own view of the nature of the

[50] I. Watt, *The Rise of the Novel* (1957), p. 115.

world corresponds with the character of his narrators and to the kind of experience which they relate. Another important factor is the correspondence between the episodic structure of the fictions and the psychology of his characters, hampered by circumstances, almost overmastered by them, and never achieving more than a partial self-consciousness or self-control.

Factors such as these lie behind the widespread tendency to identify Defoe himself with his characters and to explain away the inconsistency between promise and performance as the result of the kind of naïveté actually shown by characters like Moll Flanders and Robinson Crusoe, who in real life are only too likely to demonstrate the same kind of inconsistency and constitutional hypocrisy as they show in fiction. This is basically Ian Watt's position. He argues that Defoe's allegiance to Puritanism was purely formal. 'His spiritual intentions were probably quite sincere,' Watt suggests, 'but they have the weakness of all "Sunday religion" and manifest themselves in somewhat unconvincing periodical tributes to the transcendent . . . Puritanism made the editorial policy unalterable, but it was usually satisfied by a purely formal adherence.'[51] For Watt, it seems, Defoe is fundamentally the same sort as Moll, playing at Bo-Peep with the Almighty: 'From the sentence and the incident to the fundamental ethical structure of the whole book, his moral attitude to his creation is as shallow and devious and easily deflected as his heroine's.'[52]

Defoe, however, was not Moll Flanders, and though it may be difficult to defend him in actual life against charges of shiftiness and hypocrisy, it is not sufficient merely to dismiss his adherence to Dissent as purely formal. Defoe's prefaces are written against a very definite background of discussion regarding the nature of fiction and its claim to historicity. It is true to say that he quite obviously goes out of his way not to take the easy way out provided by the terminology of this debate. In fact, he was completely sincere in his claims regarding the moral benefit to be gained from his books and quite unable to do anything but claim that they were literally true. It was his allegiance to Dissent that brought him to fiction and governed his whole stance as a writer. From this his virtues and his faults arose.

It is instructive to compare Defoe with John Bunyan. Quite clearly they belong to different phases of the movement. Bunyan is writing for the converted, for members of the Dissenting sects—for the godly rather than the worldly-wise. His idea of religion implies an abandon-

[51] Op. cit., p. 84.
[52] Op. cit., p. 130.

ment of the world, as *The Pilgrim's Progress* (1678) shows. When he produces an account of his spiritual history, as in *Grace Abounding to the Chief of Sinners . . .* (1666), it lacks climactic development and is intended as a document where those who have experienced similar conversion can find material which will strengthen and encourage them in the Way of Righteousness. Defoe, in sharp contrast, lives in the world, in a generation when the Dissenting churches are losing a lot of their original impetus and beginning to adjust to a new function. But in spite of this the Dissenter had not lost his fundamental tendency to look on the world as an evil place and on the life of the individual as a unique opportunity to prepare himself for the operation of Grace. An example of what conversion means to Defoe is provided by his characterisation of the tutor in *Colonel Jack* (1722), who thanks God daily for the circumstance of his condemnation and transportation because it was the occasion of his conversion. He carries with him a copy of verses which embody his attitude to life and to suffering:

> Lord! whatsoever Sorrows Rack my Breast,
> Till Crime removes too, let me find no Rest;
> How Dark so e'er my State, or sharp my Pain,
> Oh! let not Troubles Cease, and Sin Remain,
> For Jesus sake, remove not my Distress,
> Till free Triumphant Grace shall Repossess
> The Vacant Throne, from whence my Sins Depart,
> And make a willing Captive of my Heart;
> Till Grace Compleatly shall my Soul Subdue,
> Thy Conquest full, and my subjection True.

The History and Remarkable Life of . . . Colonel Jack (1722);
ed. S. H. Monk (1970), p. 163

This conversion, from highwayman to transported penitent, is completely sincere, Jack informs us, and leaves the tutor's character and bearing permanently affected. It is interesting, though, that it involves no permanent separation from worldly interests. The tutor later proposes marriage to Jack's recently rediscovered first wife, divorced from him many years before, and he is not above feeling that he has been badly done by when Jack remarries her himself.

The tutor has a problem Bunyan's pilgrim escaped, which arises when you have to live with your conversion to a state of mind which regards the world as a fundamentally evil or, at best, completely meaningless, place. Even Bunyan himself experienced something of this problem in his continuation of *Pilgrim's Progress*, which relates the adventures of Christiana and her children. Problems of time and place tend to interfere with the straightforward narrative development inherited from the earlier volume. For Defoe the problem was more complex and more acute. The first-person mode demanded that he should endow his hero-narrators with a consistent attitude which would govern their presentation of events. But his whole idea of conversion, the only mental event which would justify the presentation of fiction at all, prevented this development. A person who has gone through the process of conversion as Defoe understands it does not regard human experience as capable of consistent interpretation except in terms of Providence, which is knowable only through inward knowledge and by its very nature incapable of being traced in its external manifestations. An awareness of the working of Providence in his own life is an important factor not only in the tutor's conversion, but also in Colonel Jack's, which brings the volume to a close:

> There remain many things in the Course of this unhappy Life of mine, tho' I have left so little a part of it to speak of that are worth giving a large, and distinct Account of, and which give Room for just Reflections of a Kind which I have not made yet; particularly, I think it just to add how, in collecting the various Changes and Turns of my Affairs, I saw clearer than ever I had done before, how an invisible over-ruling Power, a Hand influenced from above, Governs all our Actions of every Kind, limits all our Designs, and orders the Events of every Thing relating to us.
>
> And from this Observation it necessarily occur'd to me, how just it was, that we should pay the homage of all Events to him; that as he guided, and had even made the Chain of Causes and Consequences, which Nature in general strictly obey'd, so to him should be given the Honour of all Events, the Consequences of those Causes, as the first Mover, and Maker of all Things.
>
> I who had hitherto liv'd, as might truly be said, *without God in the World*, began now to see farther into all those Things, than I had ever yet been capable of before, and this brought me at last to look with shame and blushes upon such a Course of Wickedness, as I had gone through in the World.
>
> *Colonel Jack . . . ,* p. 307–8

External evidence for the existence of Providence as a force guiding our affairs is available in Scripture; internal evidence presents itself to each individual in fleeting glimpses. Providence as a whole cannot be known because it amounts to the manifestation of the divine will in every individual instance.

Nor, if it cannot be known, can it be the basis of a fiction. In place of the providential design, Defoe develops the idea of improvement, which itself derives from his position as a Dissenter. Colonel Jack refers to his experiences as giving room 'for just reflections'. In the Preface to his adventures the editor describes them 'as capable of so many improvements, that it would employ a book as large as itself to make improvements suitable to the vast variety of the subject. . . .' The Preface to *Roxana* (1724) informs us: 'The Advantages of the present Work are so great, and the Virtuous Reader has room for so much Improvement, that we make no Question, the Story . . . will . . . be read both with Profit and Delight.' This idea relates to life as well as to literature and reflects the Dissenter's stance in a world where he must feel himself a stranger. Without expecting to find in experience itself any essential unity or any meaning other than that given by Providence, he regards it as the material of moral reflections. He regards it not as something which may be studied for its own sake but rather as something which can be made to illustrate meaning derived from elsewhere — something which can be *improved*, in fact. This is how Defoe wishes his fiction to be read. As he tells us in the preface to *Moll Flanders* (1722): 'This Work is chiefly recommended to those who know how to read it, and how to make the good Uses of it, which the Story all along recommends to them. . . .' The hero-narrators of his fictions are themselves such readers of their own experience, not seeking to organise it in terms of any coherent overall pattern, but rather making what good of it they can in its crude state.

Of course, the basis of the idea of improvement is that the raw material concerned should actually be true. Defoe could hardly have recommended his virtuous readers to exercise their improving reflections on material which was merely imagined. Consequently he is driven to attempt the kind of fiction which can most readily be accepted as true, the personal memoir, or private history, which itself has a respectable history in the context of Puritan writing. He is also obliged to make the kind of deliberately misleading claims which make his Prefaces such difficult reading. Yet the same factor actually prevents him from trying to provide the kind of consistent, overall view which would alone have enabled readers like Gildon to have accepted his fictions. It is interesting to compare Defoe with a later Dissenter like Joseph Priestley, who differed from his predecessor in possessing a rigorously intellectual attitude to his own faith. Priestley's major intellectual problem was in reconciling the ideas of Providence, free will and necessity, and he developed a special doctrine which enabled him to do it. Defoe, by contrast, avoided the implicit contradictions in his own thinking, not because he was less honest or more worldly than Priestley, but because he was less secular. Defoe did not feel that his religious criteria could be measured by intellectual criteria, or should be reconciled with them. It is ironical that the result of his work, as far as the modern reader is concerned, is a complete demolition of his central convictions, precisely because they are not validated by the experiences he depicts. What his fictions show us is a series of characters who are unable to maintain consistent moral and religious attitudes and who actually demonstrate to us that those attitudes are irreconcilable with the facts of human nature and the human condition. The only consistent way of reading Defoe, in fact, is as a kind of anti-Defoe.

There is no other eighteenth-century novelist of which we could say such a thing. Defoe stands out among them most sharply with regard to the nature of his inspiration as a writer and the particular combination of success and failure he achieved. Yet in one important respect he belongs with his contemporaries in both France and England, that is, with writers whose company he would have scorned precisely because they sought to establish an impression of fictionality. He is typical in that his problems as a writer derive most fundamentally from a lack of commitment to the secular—to life as an integral whole—and yet that he was drawn to fiction itself by the very elements in his sensibility which prevented the development of such a commitment.

ENLIGHTENMENT AND ABSURDITY; PRÉVOST'S LE PHILOSOPHE ANGLAIS

If the lack of inner coherence in his stories were ever to make us wish that we could have had Defoe rather more an intellectual, the case of Antoine Prévost is likely to serve as a useful corrective. For Prévost, whose work is equally strikingly similar and dissimilar to that of Defoe, adventured widely in those very areas of consciousness and literary endeavour which Defoe ignored, and came away with a very great deal less to show in terms of literary achievement. Leaving aside his *nouvelle*-length tale of the adventures of the Chevalier des Grieux and Manon Lescaut, we can take his novels as vivid examples of the absurdities which could come about when the novel was twisted to fit the frame of progressive rationalism in the 1730s.

Prévost was like Defoe in being something of a projector, in his liking for exotic incident and his reliance on travel through strange and distant parts of the world. Like Defoe, too, he cared about the appearance of truth, even though he was quite unable to achieve the convincingness of the English writer. He was unlike Defoe in being something of a *philosophe*, in setting out to give a coherent account of human society and in trying to make the novel a fitting vehicle for such an account. Going from Le Sage or Defoe on the one hand to Prévost one is aware that one is moving forward in some respects. He is taking a significant step towards increasing the range of the novel and the importance of its structure, towards changing its cultural role and function. Yet at the same time one is aware that it is a step which Prévost himself is quite unable to take smoothly, but which involves him in strains and tensions which undermine the effectiveness of his work and reduce it to levels of absurdity which neither Le Sage nor Defoe ever reaches.

Prévost's *Le Philosophe anglais ou Histoire de M. Cleveland* (1732–9), presents an initial absurdity to the modern reader which would not have affected the contemporary and which tends to obscure certain important elements in the work. The absurdity derives from the fact that the hero is supposed to be the illegitimate son of Oliver Cromwell, whose wickedness extends from political to personal life and who is supposed to go to any lengths to prevent the disclosure of his evil sexual habits. In fact, in a period when very little was known about the actual Cromwell, a good deal before his nineteenth-century revaluation, there was nothing intrinsically absurd about this idea to a French reader, especially because it satisfied the inclination to connect political disorder with moral corruption. What is important is that Cleveland's background indicates from the first Prévost's political prejudice and suggests that this goes hand in hand with social conservatism and a dislike of all solvent pressures in society. This is the more important because the whole basis of the novel is towards the criticism of what might be called the theological idea of human society and its replacement by a secular, rational and 'humane' view, Prévost's own. This substitution involves no social change, merely a change in attitude. Prévost's work is written on behalf of the Enlightenment but sustains the same class in power.

In this respect, of course, Prévost's position is ironical in that he was advancing views which were eventually to wreck the society which he was a part of. But 1789 was a long way ahead of 1732, when *Le Philosophe anglais* began to appear, and what is more interesting for the present is the fact that his position involved a basic tension which helped to ruin the aesthetic coherence of his work. Prévost's whole scheme depended on an investigation of human nature, which in turn demanded the presentation of internal experience, passions, faculties, etc. At the same time it also involved a pronounced degree of generalisation and abstract assertion of principle, which no such action would coherently permit. So he was involved in two difficulties at once, both of which were insoluble. He had first to find an action which would be convincing on the individual level and would sustain his quite arbitrary social and philosophical compromise: secondly he had to devise an aesthetic form which combined the individual elements with wideranging material which sustained and developed his view of life as a whole.

These two difficulties governed the whole shape and substance of *Le Philosophe anglais*. They dictated the nature of the individual action and the shape of the whole novel, in both cases with disastrous effect. It is clear that Prévost had a much more advanced idea of the possibilities of the theme of education of the individual by life than Le Sage or Defoe. He designs the whole story as the reflections on his experiences of a sophisticated, highly sensitive individual who sees his own life as a coherent whole and is able to make appropriate reflections. His schematic approach to the business of laying the foundations of human character involves him in the initial mild absurdity of having his hero brought up in a vast complex of caves in the region of Wookey Hole, where another illegitimate son of Cromwell had previously sheltered, but this is not too disastrous in view of the difficulties involved. Much more important is the fact that Cleveland sees his whole life as centred around the dreadful consequences which follow from his wife's irrational jealousy of him. Apart from the fact that it proved quite impossible in the event to manage this, it becomes palpably clear that this derives only from Prévost's determination to make Cleveland's experience teach him that a life made meaningful by human companionship and love can only be made securely happy by the attainment of religious conviction. This in itself, perhaps, would be easy enough to prove but not in conjunction with his other aims.

At one point Cleveland himself seems aware of some of the difficulties which face Prévost. Reflecting on the chain of miseries which his life has made up, he laments the fact that he cannot present them to the reader in an appropriate way and apologises for the fact that he is obliged to play the part of the commenting narrator as well as the actor of his own story:

Je ne sais quel triste plaisir je trouve, à mesure que j'avance dans cette histoire, à m'interrompre aussi moi-même, et à prévenir, comme je fais, mes lecteurs sur ce qui me reste à leur raconter. Chaque événement de ma vie n'a-t-il pas de quoi les attacher par des singularités touchantes; et l'un a-t-il besoin du secours de l'autre pour se faire lire avec quelque attention? Non; mais c'est la situation de mon ame que je consulte bien plus que les règles de la narration et que les devoirs de l'historien. En quelque nombre que soient mes infortunes, et quelle que soit leur diversité, elles agissent toutes à-la-fois sur mon coeur; le sentiment qui m'en reste n'a point la variété de sa cause; ce n'est plus, si j'ose parler ainsi, qu'une masse uniforme de douleur, dont le poids me presse et m'accable incessa-ment. Je voudrois donc, si cela étoit possible à mon plume, réunir dans un seul trait toutes mes tristes aventures, comme leur effet se réunit dans le fond de mon ame. On jugeroit bien mieux de ce qui s'y passe. L'ordre me gêne; et ne pouvant représenter tous mes malheurs à-la-fois les plus grands sont ceux qui s'offrent le plus vivement à ma mémoire, et que je souhaiterois du-moins de pouvoir exposer les premiers.

I do not know what sad pleasure I find in thus interrupting myself in proportion as I advance in this story, and forewarning my readers about what remains for me to relate. Is not each incident of my life able to attract the reader's attention by touching singularities; and do they need to borrow support from each other to be read with attention? No; but I consult the condition of my soul much more than the rules of narration or the duties of the historian. However numer-ous and diverse my misfortunes may be, they act together on my heart; the sensation which remains with me has nothing of the variety of its cause; this is nothing, if I dare speak in such a way, but a uniform mass of grief, the weight of which incessantly presses on me and overwhelms me. So I would wish, if it were possible to my pen, to reunite in one stroke all my sad adventures, as their effect is united in the depth of my soul. Then the reader would better judge what is happening there. Order constricts me; and not being able to represent all my misfortunes at one time, the greatest are those which offer themselves most vividly to my memory and which I would wish to expose first at least.

Le Philosophe anglais ou Histoire de M. Cleveland (1732–9); *Oeuvres Choisies de Prévost* V (1810), pp. 267–8

In fact, of course, there is nothing preventing Cleveland from doing this, except for the fact that the presentation of his misfortunes, as such, is not very high on the author's list of priorities. They give way so often so consistently that not only is any radical departure from the historian's mode of narration impossible but Cleveland has to keep harping on them to remind us that they are important at all. Particularly it is true to say that his wife's jealousy as a motive in the action is so unprepared for in terms of the representation of her character, and so circumscribed in its effects, that nothing but Cleveland's rather melodramatic presentation of it could have convinced us that we were meant to take it seriously at all.

Fanny's jealousy is badly prepared for and weakly effected. But more important, its weakness as a motive draws our attention to the fact that there is no single coherent principle which ties the whole narrative together. There is a constant digressive tendency, resulting in a weakening of the story line to the point of inanition. One major episode is narrated indirectly and is completely separate from the rest of the story. Typically Prévost falls into the trap of his seventeenth-century predecessors and relies on indirect narration in order to broaden the basis of his story. The most basic point in his criticism of society is an opposition to systems founded on superstition or arbitrary authority of any kind. One way of getting this over is by introducing various villainous Jesuits here and there in the story and of making various other secular villains turn Jesuit in order to escape the consequences of their crimes. The central figure here is Gelin, originally introduced as a friend of Bridge, Cleveland's step-brother. He falls in love with Cleveland's jealous wife, Fanny, foments her jealousy and encourages her to elope with him. When he is reproved by Bridge he attacks and kills him and is left seemingly dead himself. He later turns up in France after Cleveland has relocated his wife and just before he is reunited with her after discovering that she has remained chaste after all. At this point Gelin tries to kill Cleveland, is prevented, arrested and tried for his life. Found guilty and condemned, he escapes by conversion to Catholicism, becomes a Jesuit and later turns up again in England as the notorious Captain Blood, the murderer of Cleveland's younger son and again a would-be assassin.

The second most villainous Jesuit in the plot is the one who arrests and attempts to rape the Protestant Cecilia whom Cleveland had intended to marry before his reconciliation with Fanny. This Jesuit later appears in London, an important figure in the Popish plot, and Cleveland encourages the king to have him poisoned in prison. A third perhaps worth mention figures briefly, deceiving a friend's wife into sleeping with him, leading to her suicide and the husband's disconsolate death.

These Jesuits are paralleled by a Protestant minister who effects as much harm as all three. Prévost introduces him via the adventures of Bridge who joins a secret Protestant colony which has taken refuge after the fall of their town in an isolated part of the island of St Helena. This colony gives Prévost an opportunity to sketch out the ideal, isolated community and to argue that it would fall into confusion of its own accord if organised on anything but the principles of reason and humanity. His Protestant minister, though not an evil man, is corrupted by the exercise of the priestly authority. Power has made him arbitrary, and so he opposes the natural and legitimate preference of the young men brought to the colony to make good the deficiency of males. Eventually he is prepared to go to any lengths in this opposition, finds support among the old men of the colony, is able to use the Church to make his case good and succeeds in achieving their exile. When Bridge and his two friends eventually succeed in finding their way back they find the colony in disarray. Shortly afterwards it falls apart.

The novel presents us with another self-contained society. In America Cleveland meets Fanny and her father Lord Axminster who are naked and destitute in the wilderness, having recently escaped from hostile Indians. Cleveland goes with them to friendly Indians, the tribe of his companion Igiou, with whom he has established a friendship similar to that which Robinson Crusoe strikes up with Friday. With these Indians, the Abaquis, we get an opportunity of studying a primitive society and Cleveland gets a chance to organise a society on the principles of reason and humanity. Cleveland accepts some of the Abaquis' manners, including their summer nakedness, but decides to reform their morals, religion, and social organisation. His basic principle is that the rational human soul recognises the need for authority as the central social principle and that social forms ought to be organised in a way that would make this possible. He is not particular about religious form, dispenses with marriage himself, accepting the father's authority in his union with Fanny and making sure that no element of superstition or mystery remains in the new deistic religion he fashions for the Indians. The root of social organisation is the father's authority, which is based on natural affection but leads eventually to a recognition of the authority of God:

Je leur fis comprendre que s'ils étoient obligés de s'aimer les unes les autres, parce qu'ils étoient citoyens d'un même lieu, et unis par les mêmes intérêts, ils devoient quelque chose de plus particulier à ceux qui les touchoient encore de plus près par le bienfait de la naissance et de l'éducation . . . qu'en croissant même et en avancant en âge, ils n'acquéroient point de droits qui pussent diminuer ceux de leurs pères, puisque la force et la santé portoient toujours sur la vie qu'ils avoient recue d'eux, comme sur leur principe; qu'ils ne devoient rien trouver de genant dans un devoir rien trouver de genant dans un devoir dont l'exécution ne s'exigeoit jamais avec dureté et avec rigueur; que le temps viendroit d'ailleurs où les enfants auroient leur tour, et qu'après avoir respecté leurs pères, et leur avoir rendu leur obéissance, ils auroient aussi des enfants dont ils se feroient obéir et respecter.

I made them understand that if they were obliged to love one another because they were inhabitants of the same place and united by the same interests, they owed something more particular to those who concerned them yet more on account of the benefit of birth and education . . . that even in growing up and advancing in age, they would acquire no rights which would diminish those of their parents, since strength and health depended on the life they had received from them, as their origin; that they should find nothing constricting in a duty the execution of which demanded nothing from them in the way of hardness and rigour; that the time would besides come when children would have their turn and that after having respected their parents, and having given them their obedience, they would also have children whom they would make obey and respect them.

Le Philosophe anglais ou Histoire de M. Cleveland V, pp. 132—3

Cleveland's reasonings are not quite adequate to sway the hard core of Indian opposition. A primitive hand-grenade let down through the roof of their conference room is required before the principles of nature and reason completely prevail! But before long he obtains complete ascendancy and sets up a society based ultimately on his own authority but which is organised on the basis of seniority. When he has done this he is able to persuade them to accept his own idea of a suitable religion, reflecting the same principles:

Au-lieu qu'en leur faisant envisager tout l'univers comme un temple magnifique que Dieu s'est fabriqué de ses propres mains, et Dieu lui-même assis au-dessus des nues comme sur un trône, où il est prêt sans cesse à écouter nos voeux et à recevoir nos adorations, il me sembla qu'une si noble et si respectable idée seroit capable de fixer leur attention, et de s'imprimer dans leurs cerveaux grossiers d'une manière ineffaçable.

Whereas in making them envisage all the universe as a magnificent temple that God has made himself with his own hands, and God himself seated above the clouds as on a throne, where he is ready incessantly to hear our supplications and receive our adorations, it seemed to me that such a noble and respectable idea would be capable of fixing their attention and of imprinting itself on their heavy brains in an ineffaceable manner.

Le Philosophe anglais ou Histoire de M. Cleveland V, p. 165

Cleveland's final observation on his system, having explained how he has arranged for them to assemble religiously twice a week and recite a set prayer there and every day in their families, makes explicit the reference of the Abaquis reforms to corrupt and superstitious Europe: 'Humanity has nothing to do with whatever clashes with reason, or goes beyond it; and in this sense, we should, perhaps, find as many savages and barbarians in Europe, as in America. . . .'[53]

A similar function is served by the later section of the novel when Cleveland is made to play an important part at the court of Charles II. Designed primarily for French readers, Prévost made this section of his hero's adventures reflect on the effects of Jesuit intrigue in undermining good government in England, and by implication, France too. Unfortunately, coming after Cleveland's adventures are virtually over and not arising convincingly from anything in his character or situation, it is the weakest and least effective part of the whole.

That whole, however, is not greatly effective at all, mainly because the personal dimension is almost totally lacking. Cleveland is present in the novel almost as a disembodied voice, unable to relate effectively or interestingly to his own past experiences. His language is the language of abstraction, his own life far too distanced from the present of narration, in spite of his frequent laments on the griefs and miseries he has endured. He writes, in fact, as a philosopher, but it is difficult to see that, apart from the early sections when he is in the cave, his experiences have contributed to this state of mind. Change is dealt with, in a

[53] '. . . tout ce qui est opposé à la raison, ou qui s'en écarte par quelques excès, n'appartient point à l'humanité; et, dans ce sens, l'on trouveroit peutêtre autant de Sauvages et de barbares en Europe qu'en Amérique. . . .' P. 172.

completely mechanical way, by the influence of other people, and is reported rather than shown. Prévost is unable to get inside his hero. The moving principle in the story is always outside the hero; he reacts to motives of other characters, who are often brought in only to provide this motivation. Primary here are Mrs Lallin and Mrs Bridges who exist in the novel only as motivating phenomena rather than as people. Both are eventually disposed of in ways which impact on us separately, as if they were told by missionaries in a Sunday service. Mrs Bridges, because she is old and fat, is burnt alive and eaten by Indians, together with Cleveland's infant daughter; Mrs Lallin, having served Prévost faithfully, is captured by pirates, threatened with dishonour by the captain (this has happened to her before; though she is the cause of Fanny's jealousy, she is attractive to everyone except Cleveland), rescued by and married to the mate, forced to sleep with the wicked Jesuit. Her suicide is a happy escape for the reader if not for her!

The centre of *Le Philosophe anglais* is in fact not where it should be. It should lie with the narrator and his experiences, governing the selection and narration of his life. It actually lies with Prévost's didactic purpose. Prévost had gone far enough to feel the need for validation of social principles according to human nature, and was drawn to the novel instinctively as the natural expression of a completely secular and humane view of the world. But he had not gone far enough in this direction to allow the experience of an individual to shape his didactic statement. This is not merely because he was not a good novelist. His view of the novel is more advanced than that of his predecessors, his talents great, and in *Manon Lescaut*, where he was not under the pressures at work in his larger fictions, he produced a masterpiece where the action expands according to its own law and takes the natural shape dictated by the logic arising from character and circumstance. In *Le Philosophe anglais*, however, he was putting over a view of life which depended on a compromise as arbitrary and superstitious as any he was attacking. His rationalism short-circuited experience and involved him necessarily in gross manipulation and consequent absurdity. Defoe might also have fallen into the trap, had his idea of the novel and his idea of human life been somewhat more elevated and consistent. Prévost, it is true to some extent to say, fell into it because of his finest intellectual virtues.

LA VIE DE MARIANNE: THE NOVEL AS PORTRAIT

The originality of Marivaux's later fiction is generally held to consist in

the fact that it extended the novel's social range, went a good way
towards breaking the tyranny of the levels of style, and developed the
epistolary mode. All this is important, but Marivaux's achievement
involved one factor more fundamentally important than this. He may
be said to have introduced a new idea of the novel as such and to have
taken a fundamental step forward, in itself the basis of a great
achievement and of great historical significance.

In *La Vie de Marianne* (1731–42) Marivaux takes up a position
which was extremely common in the eighteenth century but which is
much more important than it seems at this distance. He claims to be
merely editing the collection of letters which follows and defends this
claim by arguing that if they had been fictional they would have shown
more action and fewer of the comments and exclamations with which
the narrator-heroine is constantly breaking into the course of action and
which betray her naïve character. In itself this is not unusual, or
original—the fictional editor/author founds the historicity of his fiction
on its truth to life. Marivaux expands his case, however, to argue that
La Vie de Marianne is something entirely new, neither history, nor
fiction, but the result of Marianne's attempt to relate her own life, not as
a list of events but as a complex web of thoughts, actions and reactions.
As he says, in the editor's voice, Marianne: 'n'a point songé à faire un
roman . . .':

> Marianne n'a aucune forme d'ouvrage présente à l'esprit. Ce n'est
> point un auteur, c'est une femme qui pense . . . voilà sur quel ton le
> prend Marianne. Ce n'est, si vous voulez, ni celui du roman, ni celui
> de l'histoire, mais c'est le sien. . . .

> Marianne has no form of a work present in her thoughts. This is not
> an author, it is a woman who thinks . . . this is how Marianne
> speaks. It is neither, if you wish, the tone of the novel, nor that of
> history, but it is her own. . . .
> *La Vie de Marianne ou les aventures de Madame la comtesse de ****
>   (1731–42); ed. F. Deloffre, 'Avertissement', II (1963), pp. 55–6

This seems simple and fair enough—a reasonable claim that the work
should be allowed to establish its own stylistic criteria. In fact it
remains this only while we take it quite literally. When we remember
how the novel actually was published, in separate parts during a period
of eleven years, while all the periodicals were referring to it as the work
of Marivaux, we realise that it would have been impossible even for
contemporaries to take it literally. No one could have read *La Vie de*

Marianne as anything other than fiction; and read as such it must be seen to be making a quite revolutionary demand which goes quite beyond the limits of style. Neither history, nor novel, *La Vie de Marianne* claimed to be a new kind of fiction, justified neither on the grounds of truth, nor entertainment, with its own kind of truth, involving the accurate representation of human character and circumstance. This is a revolutionary departure, which brings us back at one step to the terms of Cervantes, in an atmosphere radically different.

Behind this conception of fiction is a radically new conception of character which breaks clear away from anything previously attempted in fiction and informs the whole structure of his work. Marivaux's idea is that character cannot simply be known or represented. Marianne speaks for him here when she comments on her own attempt to give a characterisation of Mme Miran:

> Quand je dis que je vais vous faire le portrait de ces deux dames, j'entends que je vous en donnerai quelques traits. On ne saurai rendre en entier ce que sont les personnes; du moins cela ne me serait pas possible; je connais bien mieux les gens avec qui je vis que je ne les définirais; il y a des choses en eux que je ne saisis point assez pour les dire, et que je n'aperçois que pour moi, et non pas pour les autres; ou si je les disais, je les dirais mal. Ce sont des objets de sentiment si compliqués et d'une netteté si délicate qu'ils se brouillent dès que ma réflexion s'en mêle; je ne sais plus par où les prendre pour les exprimer: de sorte qu'ils sont en moi, et non pas à moi.

> When I say that I am going to present a portrait of these two ladies, I mean that I will give you certain characteristics. One cannot present what people are in their entirety; at least I could not do it; I know the people with whom I live better than I could define them; there are things in them that I don't grasp clearly enough to say, and which I perceive only in myself, not so as to describe them to others; or such as if I were to express them I would express them badly. These are objects of sensations so complicated and of so delicate an outline that they become confused the moment my reflection begins to concern itself with them; I do not know how to take them in order to express them: the problem is that they are in me, but not in my possession.

La Vie de Marianne, p. 166

We have in this passage a development of the ideas which Marivaux originally put forward in the 'Avis au Lecteur' which preceded *Les Aventures de ****. It contains two important points which are ultimately connected—firstly, that character is not monolithic or fixed; secondly, that perception is more subtle than consciousness. Both points together suggest that human beings exist on a level of consciousness quite beyond the reach of the reasoning process presented in conventional description, that what we need in order to refine our knowledge is a refinement of what he calls 'sentiment' rather than reason, and, by implication, that a literary mode which develops sentiment by presenting human character directly has sufficient justification in itself, transcending other criteria.

The novel as a whole expands and develops the conception of character Marianne hints at in this passage. Action and commentary combine to present something which is at once more subtle and more secular than anything which the novel had contained before. It is interesting, for example, to compare Marivaux with Challes in this respect. It is clear that *La Vie de Marianne* is to some extent indebted to the story of Angelique and Contamine in *Les Illustres francoises*, but the two fictions contrast sharply. Challes is interested only in that aspect of character which is susceptible of control and assessment by a social group. The social group remains very important to Marivaux, and it is still true to say that character expresses itself only against the social background. But his whole fiction depends on the fact that character is self-defining rather than defined.

One of Marivaux's most important points is that the factor which determines character is itself absolute, an inherent principle that often finds expression in vanity and pride. Marianne herself admits to vanity without being much ashamed of it. She reports the vanity of her behaviour at church when she consciously rivals the other women in seeking male attention; and again, even in a moment of great strain and anxiety, on her way to the crucial interview with the minister, she admits to a coquettish awareness:

> Je baissai les yeux, et je détournai la tête; mais ce fut toujours une petite douceur que je ne négligeai point de goûter chemin faisant, et qui n'interrompit point mes tristes pensées.
>
> Il en est de cela comme d'une fleur agréable dont on sent l'odeur en passant.

> I lowered my eyes and I turned my head away; but this was still a little pleasure which I did not at all neglect to enjoy as I was going

along and which did not at all interrupt my sad thoughts.

Such incidents are like beautiful flowers whose odour one smells as one passes them.

La Vie de Marianne, p. 313

In order to understand this passage we ought to look at it in the context of an earlier remark which Marianne makes shortly after reporting the scene of confrontation with her hypocritical would-be seducer, M. Climal.

L'objet qui m'occupa d'abord, vous allez croire que ce fut la malheureuse situation où je restais; non, cette situation ne regardait que ma vie, et ce qui m'occupa me regardait, moi.

Vous direz que je rêve de distinguer cela. Point du tout: notre vie, pour ainsi dire, nous est moins chère que nous, que nos passions. A voir quelquefois ce qui se passe dans notre instinct là-dessus, on dirait que, pour être, il n'est pas nécessaire de vivre; que ce n'est que par accident que nous vivons, mais que c'est naturellement que nous sommes.

You are going to think that the subject which first occupied my thoughts was the unfortunate situation in which I found myself; no, this situation concerned only my life, and that which preoccupied me concerned me myself.

You will say that I am dreaming in making this distinction. Not at all: our life, so to speak, is less dear than ourselves, than our passions. Seeing sometimes what happens in this respect, one would say that in order to be, it is not necessary to live; that living is not essential to us, but that we exist in ourselves quite naturally.

La Vie de Marianne, p. 129

This passage perhaps derives from Descartes, but it goes a good deal farther than anything Descartes said. It is clear that Marianne thinks of herself as comprising different levels of identity. She says elsewhere that pride is previous in date and nearer to the centre of being than virtue; no matter how virtuous we are, virtue itself cannot rival pride, the instinct for self-consideration as a motive of action.

Taken to its logical extreme this idea might lead to the abandonment of external considerations and classifications such as virtue altogether, but Marivaux's perception functions only within a clear group of ideas relating to society, cultural and moral values. The idea of the soul as presented by Descartes is developed so as to allow him to reconcile his rather subversive perception with social and moral values. The individual is born with a more or less elevated soul, that is, more or less capable of responding to elevated ideas. And the natural response of the soul is to relate to the self and to seek control over the passions, imposing a pattern of conduct which will bring ultimate satisfaction. The Paris crowd, at the lowest social and cultural level, seek only vicarious gratification, having no capacity to relate themselves as individuals to what they see and hear around them. Somewhat higher in the scale, Mme Dutour, good-natured but weak, is incapable of maintaining a steady pose. Insulted by the coachman whose fare she has refused, she falls back on undignified flyting in order to maintain her dignity and becomes an object of amusement to the crowd. Later, seeing that Climal has bought Marianne's linen elsewhere than in her own boutique, she again becomes enraged and attacks Marianne quite unjustifiedly. Marianne comments after narrating this scene:

> Mme Dutour, comme je crois l'avoir déjà dit, était une bonne femme dans le fond, se fâchant souvent au delà de ce qu'elle était fâchée; c'est-à-dire que de toute la colère qu'elle montrait dans l'ocasion il y en avait bien le moitié dont elle aurait pu se passer, et qui n'était là que pour représenter. C'est qu'elle s'imaginait que plus on se fâchait, plus on faisait figure, et d'ailleurs elle s'animait elle-même du bruit de sa voix: son ton quand il était brusque, engageait son esprit à l'être.

> Mme Dutour, as I think I have already said, was basically a good woman, often making herself more angry than she actually was; that is to say that of all the anger she showed in the event, she could have easily done without more than half, which was only there for show. The point is that she imagined that the more anger one showed, the better appearance one made, and besides she animated herself with the noise of her own voice; when her tone was brusque it drew her spirit on to be so also.

> *La Vie de Marianne*, pp. 98–9

Marianne herself frequently flies into passions at moments of crisis, but for very different reasons. We can fairly say, in fact, that her ability to become extremely distraught is one of her main characteristics. It happens when she appeals for help from Father Vincent, when Valville visits her to find Climal at her feet, when Mme Dutour accuses her of encouraging Climal's evil intentions and when Mme Dutour greets her in the company of Mlle de Fare.

In these moments of great emotion, not to say passion, Marianne is at the mercy of her 'âme', which Marivaux seems to think of as a faculty which may dominate all others, translating their demands into its own terms and bringing the whole personality under its subjection. Certainly Marianne thinks of her soul as something which governs her whole demeanour and her reaction to others, and she thinks that this is true for other people. So she explains her favourable response to the kindness and generosity of Mme Climal in terms of her soul's gratitude for the attention which flatters it:

C'est que notre âme est haute, et que tout ce qui a un air de respect pour sa dignité la pénètre et l'enchante—aussi notre orgeuil ne fut-il jamais ingrat.

It is that our soul is elevated, and that everything that has an air of respect for its dignity captures and enchants it—also our pride was never ungrateful.

La Vie de Marianne, p. 155

It is interesting to see 'âme' and 'orgeuil' closely connected here because the one does seem to come over as a highly refined version of the other. In Marianne's case the refinement has been taken very far. When her reputation is threatened she is beside herself, and rather ironically starts to tear off her clothes in Climal's presence. Passionate resentment of an affront to her pride stimulates the soul to throw aside all considerations but those which will re-establish the reputation.

Non, lui dis-je, ou plutôt lui criai-je, il ne me resterai rien. . . .

Et pendant que je lui tenais ce discours, vous remarquerez que je détachais mes épingles, et que je me décoiffais, parce que la cornette que je portais venait de lui, de façon qu'en un moment elle fut otée, et que je restai nu-tête avec ces beaux cheveux dont je vous ai parlé, et qui me descendaient jusqu'à la ceinture.

Ce spectacle le démonta; j'étais dans un transport étourdi qui ne ménageait rien; j'élevais ma voix, j'étais échevelée, et le tout ensemble jetait dans cette scène un fracas, une indécence qui l'alarmait, et qui aurait pu dégénérer en avanie pour lui.

No, I said, or rather shouted at him, nothing will stay with me. . . .

And while I delivered this speech at him, you notice that I was undoing my pins and taking off my head-dress, because the coif I was wearing came from him, so that in a moment it was off and I remained bare-headed with that beautiful hair I have spoken to you about and which descended right to my waist.

This scene shook him; I was in a blind passion and had no respect for circumstances; I raised my voice, I was dishevelled, everything together gave the scene a din, an indecency which alarmed him, and which could have ended up in humiliation for him.

La Vie de Marianne, p. 124

This tendency to go to any lengths in the defence of her reputation is something which gives Marianne a good deal of power over those around her—it certainly frightens Climal and Mme Dutour. It is also something which the more respectable characters respond to as indicating the possession of a soul of a high order.

Marianne reflects on her own position at one time in words which read rather quaintly but give us a good idea of her creator's own attitudes:

Je n'étais rien, je n'avais rien qui pût me faire considérer, mais à ceux qui n'ont ni rang, ni richesses qui en imposent, il leur reste une âme, et c'est beaucoup; c'est quelquefois plus que le rang et la richesse, elle peut faire face à tout.

I was nothing, I had nothing which could earn me consideration; but to those who have neither rank nor riches to impose respect for them, there remains a soul, and it is a great deal; sometimes it is more than rank or riches, it can face anything out.

La Vie de Marianne, p. 178

We see it working in her favour in her relationship with Mme Miran and impressing Mme Dorsin in her favour. It is the reason why she repeatedly suggests or states that Mme Miran means more to her than Valville, in spite of the fact that she does sincerely love him. Her love for the son belongs to areas of her character less central than her response to Mme Miran's more instinctive and less self-interested recognition of her. Mme Miran utters the classic defence of her position in defending at the Minister's her right to social consideration, educing breeding from behaviour. Marianne herself carries the case farther. The argument of the Minister is unanswerable in social terms, but Marianne simply transcends it. In a magnificent gesture of self-sacrifice she abandons Mme Miran and Valville for their own sake, but even more importantly, for her own.

It is interesting that her reaction to Valville's inconstancy shows her to be not quite so unselfconscious or undemanding as this scene would suggest. In the first place she is overwhelmed by the fact that he has been making love to Mlle Varthon while she has been ill, but once she recovers from this her reaction is surprisingly hard-headed:

Eh quoi! avec de la vertu, avec de la raison, avec un caractère et des sentiments qu'on estime, avec ma jeunesse et les agréments qu'on dit que j'ai, j'aurais la lâcheté de périr d'une douleur qu'on croira peut-être intéressée, et qui entretiendra encore la vanité d'un homme qui en use si indignement!

Cette dernière réflexion releva mon courage; elle avait quelque chose de noble qui m'y attacha, et qui m'inspira des résolutions qui me transquillisèrent. . . .

En un mot, je me proposai une conduite qui était fière, modeste, décente, digne de cette Marianne dont on faisait tant de cas. . . .

And what! with virtue, with reason, with a character and sentiments which were estimated, with my youth and the charms which I was said to have, I would have the cowardice to perish from a grief which perhaps would be thought interested, and which would further flatter the vanity of a man who was using me so shamefully!

This last reflection raised up my courage again; it had something of nobility which attracted me and which inspired me with resolutions which quieted me. . . .

In a word, I proposed for myself a conduct which would be proud, modest, decent, worthy of that Marianne who was valued so highly.

La Vie de Marianne, p. 386

This passage suggests an essential self almost beyond the reach of attack on any front other than that of the reputation, which she knows well how to defend. The essential Marianne it seems exists in apposition to and dependent on the Marianne 'dont on faisait tant de cas'. She seems quite literally to *possess* virtue and reason, character, sentiments, youth and she can think of herself as guilty of cowardice in letting herself be unnecessarily overwhelmed.

The self-possession suggested here comes across strongly in the marvellous scene in which she brings Valville to admit and accept the position they have reached and at the same time brings him back to heel. The scene represents an astonishing achievement on the part of both Marianne and Marivaux. By dint of combining verbal self-immolation with actual humiliation of her opponent Marianne entirely defeats him and sets the manipulations of the less subtle and less conscientiously honest Varthon at nought. Having declared herself completely devoted to his interest and willing to do anything he wishes in furtherance of his interest, Marianne has the pleasure of seeing him almost literally annihilated: 'my generosity overwhelmed him, annihilated him before me. . . .' She leaves him characteristically pleased with herself:

> Pour moi, je revenais toute émue de ma petite expédition, mais je dis agréablement émue: cette dignité de sentiments que je venais de montrer à mon infidèle, cette honte et cette humiliation que je laissais dans son coeur, cet étonnement où il devait être de la noblesse de mon procédé, enfin cette supériorité que mon âme venait de prendre sur la sienne, supériorité plus attendrissante que facheuse, plus aimable que superbe, tout cela me remuait intérieurement d'un sentiment doux et flatteur; je me trouvais trop respectable pour n'être pas regrettée.

> As for me, I returned thoroughly moved from my little expedition, but agreeably moved: that dignity of sentiment which I had just shown to my unfaithful lover, that shame and humiliation I had left in his heart, that astonishment which he must have felt at the nobility of my proceeding, and in fact that superiority that my soul had just acquired over his, a superiority more affecting than annoying, more amiable than proud, all that moved me internally with a sweet and flattering feeling; I found myself too worthy of respect not to be regretted.

La Vie de Marianne, p. 407

Marianne's enemies, if any remained to her at this point in the novel, might perhaps find some sympathy from the reader if they accused her of being more concerned with herself in the last instance than with anyone else. This is quite literally so. Marianne as a centre of consciousness represents only one part of the total character, and the consciousness is no more than a medium whereby that total self finds scope for development. When the consciousness is inadequate to express or defeat it, it is swept away. The total self, incapable of expression in simple straightforward terms even by Marianne herself, dominates the novel.

This is why Marivaux's method of narration is so important. If individuals cannot be simply known except by areas of perception outside the control of the reason and even of the conscious mind, the novel, as the means by which they may be projected and allowed to define themselves freely, is particularly useful as a form. But the epistolary novel especially so, because it permits the heroine and narrator, nominally one self, to develop as different aspects of a complex self, and so to make the process of narration greatly deepen the effectiveness of the work as a whole.

Marianne as narrator is fifty years old, living in retirement, having lost little of her vanity and nothing of her wit. She reports the events of thirty-five years before, and presents her fifteen year old self through the veil of her own reflections. What she is showing us in the first instance is the story of a young girl coming to terms with the world and coming to possession of herself and control of her environment. But in the second instance we see the narrative as the result of the older woman's attempt at self-exploration and self-definition. Inevitably the two dimensions fade into one another—her constant comments keep her in the front of our minds as narrator, but the drama of the events and vividness of Marianne's feelings and reflection at the time of the events bring her to the front. So the action is constantly a movement between the one and the other. If they related consistently this would not be important, but in fact they do not. It is often difficult to say what the relationship is between the later consciousness and the actions of the earlier heroine—especially in the matter of vanity, and the complicated intermittent references to the intervening years. The very fact that we know nothing about this period casts a large area of doubt over the status of the later Marianne as narrator—is she disillusioned, self-satisfied? Has she married Valville and survived him, married someone else, or what? Each of the possibilities would affect our interpretation of her comments and make the novel seem substantially different. As it is the relationship remains confused and shifting, and this means that we are creatively and actively in search of the heroine—not just the fifteen year old as she felt at the time, nor as she is later reported to have been, but also the total Marianne, which we can dimly feel motivating both women and shaping the structure of the whole novel.

Looked at in this way La Vie de Marianne is a masterpiece which marks a milestone in the history of European fiction, but like its companion novel, Le Paysan parvenu, it remains unfinished. The later part, in fact, argues a weakness in Marivaux's basic plan. He promises us at various times the history of a sympathetic nun who befriends

Marianne in the convent and eventually gives it to us as the last three books—IX–XI. The nun's story is narrated directly and is dull and lifeless in comparison with Marianne's. Briefly, she suffers from the indifference of her mother, is rejected by her family and helped by friends; almost seduced into a convent but helped by the confession of a friendly nun; prevented from marrying by the trickery of her would-be husband's heir; rescued by an elderly relative but persuaded to make over the fortune she is left to the proper heirs after falling in love with the young man in the case, only to be deserted at the instigation of his mother; she returns to Paris, finds her mother deserted by a favoured son who despises her because of her originally low condition.

At this point the story breaks off and is never resumed. It is difficult to see how Marivaux could have brought himself to touch it farther, in view of the complete lack of consonance between the two halves. But that he introduced the story in the first place, instead of going on with Marianne's, is deeply significant. Clearly the nun's story is a foil to Marianne's. She fails to sustain her position and impose herself on her circumstances not through any fault of her own but simply because she is not heroic in self-assertion as Marianne is. Her essential goodness and nobility of feeling make her the victim of circumstances while Marianne's more active personality allows her to overcome difficulties equally great. Theoretically it expands the scope of the principal fiction and especially the idea of character as destiny. It fails precisely because it does not dramatise the conception of character as Marianne's story does and lacks the dimension given by the epistolary mode. The point, after all, is not one which can be made in reported action. Why it was included, in spite of the fact that it involved a change of mode and broke across Marianne's story, is probably because Marivaux was aware that he could not finish that story in a way which would develop and complete what he had already done. In a sense that is completed with the interview between Valville and Marianne. After that nothing can happen to Marianne which will shake her self-possession. Her character is formed. But the action she is involved in, her whole conception, depends on the rather romanesque situation which opens the novel—Marianne has to be an orphan, of noble birth. Anything else would have involved a democratic rejection of existing social values which would have undermined the compromise of values which enabled Marivaux to do what he did. He marks the transition from the merely social to the purely moral as a method of assessing character. An ending which restored Marianne to her family and set the seal on her nobility in this way, though it was the only one open, would have undermined the point Marivaux was making. Marianne no longer needs the protection this implies, but has found her place in the wider society and maintains it because of integral nobility. On the other hand, Marivaux was not prepared to reject the association of nobility of character and nobility of blood. The compromise is clear in the confrontation at the Minister's, where the social case is transcended but never answered. That compromise was fruitful in Marivaux's mind. It is fair to say that it made the whole novel possible, but it also prevented Marivaux from finishing it. Had he done so Rousseau's achievement would have been anticipated by twenty years.

THE HISTORY OF CLARISSA HARLOWE: THE TRIUMPH OF FICTION

There are a number of similarities between Richardson's *chef d'oeuvre*, *Clarissa Harlowe*, and Marivaux's *La Vie de Marianne*, which have caused many critics to raise the question of Richardson's possible indebtedness to the French novelist. Both works centre on defenceless young girls who are the victims of sexual intrigue; they both undermine traditional attitudes regarding the style and the tone proper to serious fiction; they are both presented in the form of letters. But these similarities are overshadowed by important dissimilarities of tone, texture and purpose. One might well be tempted to take Marivaux and Richardson as typical of French and English attitudes in this period. Certainly it is true to say that they are the products respectively of Catholic and Protestant countries. *Marianne* is not an unserious book by any means, even in terms of its subject matter. Marianne and her patron, Mme Miran, are sincere and devout. But in spite of this the novel as a whole leaves one with the impression that their religion does not extend far enough from the Church itself to affect their daily thoughts and relations with other characters. This is not to say that prudery and puritanism were not powerful in the society in which Marivaux wrote, of course, but rather that they had not affected the idea of what was serious in literature.

In England this was not the case and if Richardson himself had a great effect in furthering the tendency to assimilate moral and literary values, the reception of his work indicates the extent to which the process was already well advanced when he began to write. Religious seriousness pervades *Clarissa Harlowe* to such an extent that we can say that the purpose of the novel is not literary at all, but moral.

Richardson intended his representation of Clarissa's sad history to have a direct effect on the disposition and behaviour of his readers. That is, he sought to make them more moral and more religious. His book made a contribution to the debate concerning human character which dominated eighteenth-century literature. *Clarissa Harlowe* is set against those works, from Montaigne's *Essais*, through Molière's *Dom Juan* to Voltaire's *Candide*, which seek to undermine the basis of idealist views of human character. Clarissa is presented as a Christian who achieves something very little short of perfection, her moral will achieving total victory over other elements in her nature. Clarissa herself says that her experiences have been important in so far as they have modified her character and humbled her pride, but much more important to us is the extent to which she has mastered them and brought them to serve the interests of her leading characteristic.

As it happens, there is more than one way of looking at Clarissa's character, and the novel eventually escapes from Richardson's control. But this was very much in spite of his efforts to make it a coherent statement of Protestant orthodoxy. It is customary to refer his emergence as a writer, his characteristic style and purpose, and the enormous success of his novels, to social causes, and especially to what is referred to as the rise of the middle classes. Richardson's class origin is obviously important. It is difficult to imagine anyone who had been at either of the two universities in England at this time moving anything like so far away from the dominant literary conventions as Richardson. On the other hand, it is important to notice that Richardson was in no way socially progressive. His achievement indicates the existence of a very strong trend in eighteenth-century society, one condition of which was the social flexibility which had been developing for some time and the resultant tendency for class divisions to become blurred. In relation to literary culture, what was happening in the mid-eighteenth century was the development of the strong tendency to assimilate different social groups into a wider cultured class. This involved, of course, fundamental change in the dominant cultural standards and especially a turn towards sentiment and sensibility, a trend towards greater moral seriousness, and increasing respect for individual integrity.

These are tendencies which were first developed within what we might call the Dissenting classes and it is perfectly fair to associate them with the trading classes in general rather than with the landed gentry. But we need to remember that in eighteenth-century England they were increasingly present as conscious elements in literary culture and in the work of writers who had no allegiance to these classes. A general change was taking place in English culture at this time which had a social dimension, but also political, economic and religious implications. Behind it all we should probably be right in discovering the economic developments of the period, especially increasing preoccupation with international trade. The struggle for expansion overseas was linked to the religious issue partly by virtue of the fact that Spain and France were Catholic countries, but perhaps more strongly through recent political history and its continuing existence in the Jacobite threat. The period saw a steady increase in consciousness of the nation as a whole which was often linked to acceptance of the Hanoverian dynasty. The latter was also increasingly associated with the preservation of specially English liberties. The Anglican Establishment, with its characteristic avoidance of theology, its encouragement of practical charity and education as almost the only spheres in which active Christianity was possible, played an increasingly important part in this process, not least because it could claim to be a specifically English Church. It is an interesting symptom that Methodism, which produced an astonishingly fertile effect in Wales in literary terms, was little more than the object for coarse satire to mid-century English writers. The spirit of Methodism affected English letters only through the Evangelican movement later, within the Anglican Church and very much socially approved.

In this whole movement, as is so often the case in England, there was a pronounced element of anti-intellectualism, directed against materialist views of human character and against deism and free-thinking in general. And this was no doubt beneficial in so far as it tended to increase consciousness of the individual as a whole. It was particularly important in so far as it helped to make the connection between Protestant religious attitudes and interest in sentiment and the emotions in general. Corresponding to this in the realm of aesthetics was a stronger inclination towards nature.

Richardson's fiction was at the very centre of this process, which was to some extent taking place in other Protestant countries in Europe. It is interesting to notice that he was very successful in Holland, where the battle between Protestantism and Catholicism was being very actively fought in his day. From the Protestant point of view this was a battle 'for the rights of liberty of conscience and religion' as Richardson's Dutch translator put it,[54] against the encroachments of the Jesuits. In

[54] J. Stinstra, a letter to Richardson, 24 December 1753; quoted here from I. Williams, *Novel and Romance 1700–1800* (1970), p. 213

France the latter were amongst the greatest enemies of the novel and the firmest advocates of classical ideas about the maintenance of style and *bienséance* in fiction and literature in general. Richardson himself said little about literature outside his own prefaces, where he displays a crudely moralist attitude not dissimilar to Defoe's. From his friend and eulogist, Aaron Hill, we get profusely enthusiastic praise of his power to raise the passions through representation of Nature, and very little else. From Bishop Warburton we have a preface to Volume II of *Clarissa Harlowe* which registers no awareness of its originality at all. Significantly, one of the most perceptive comments came from Albrecht von Haller, the Swiss poet and scientist. Von Haller's remarks were published in the *Gentleman's Magazine* for 1749 and may be said to have Richardson's own approval in view of the fact that he read them before publication and appended his corrections and replies. Von Haller obviously thought of the novel as a distinctively Protestant statement and brought this out in a comparison with *La Vie de Marianne:*

> . . . Marianne speaks like a girl of wit, who loves a kind of general virtue, which consists in preferring her honour to the gratification of her tenderest wishes. But the particulars which constitute a virtuous life are not exhibited; there is no representation of the minutiae of *Virtue,* no example of *her* conduct to those by whom *she* is surrounded as equals, superiors, or inferiors. *Marianne* is a kind of chronicle, in which some memorable adventures are well described. *Clarissa* is an history, where the events of her life follow each other in an uninterrupted succession. *Marianne* is a young lady of quality, who knows neither the duty of managing or educating children, nor the employments which fill the life of a person of merit; whenever she appears she is loaded with ornament, either to please her benefactress, or her lover. — *Clarissa* is a very different person: she is a lady of quality, who at once knows and fulfills her duty: she mentions, in the most minute and particular manner, her duties towards God (never found in *French* romances), her parents, her relations, her friends, her servants, and herself; the duties peculiar to every hour of a life of perfect virtue are there delineated. The reflections and remarks which are interspersed in her letters are the result of great knowledge of mankind; yet the whole is within the reach of every capacity, and is calculated to make every reader both the wiser and the better. *Marianne* amuses, *Clarissa* not only amuses, but instructs; and the more effectually, as the writer paints nature and

nature alone.

Gentleman's Magazine, XIX, June and July 1749; *Novel and Romance, 1700–1800*, ed. I. Williams (1970), p. 132

Mild though it may appear at first glance, this passage is quite surprising in the way it turns traditional ideas upside down and presents a completely new approach. The comparison between chronicle and history had often been used in criticism of the *nouvelle*. History there implied a report of a completed action rather than the inconsequential sequence of the chronicle and encourages association of history and fiction as two forms of poetry. Here on the other hand we see for the first time the idea of history which was to predominate in the next century—that is, history as the presentation of an uninterrupted sequence of events, involving emphasis on the texture of daily life rather than concern with large-scale actions. In Haller's theory, as in Richardson's practice, this conception is inseparable from the Protestant idea of virtue as governing every relation, every detail of daily life. It is interesting, too, to notice the stress here on naturalness rather than formality and artifice. *Clarissa Harlowe* instructs by virtue of its historicity—a novel adaptation of the Horatian idea—'the duties peculiar to every hour of a life of perfect virtue'; but it is effective only in so far as it paints nature. This connection between virtue and nature is essential to Richardson's novel. Lovelace, of course, denied it, but Clarissa proved him wrong.

Richardson's purpose in *Clarissa Harlowe* was essentially to prove that perfect virtue is perfectly natural, that concept and character can be completely identified. He sets out to prove this by showing us a young girl brought up in a sheltered situation, who has aimed at the practice of perfect virtue as he apprehends it—that is, the complete subjugation of the lower faculties to the higher and a determined application of Christian principles within a given social framework. His heroine is oppressed by selfish and insensitive relatives and elopes, unintentionally, with her rakish lover, himself the occasion and the instigator of the oppression. In his power she is wooed and persecuted by turns and manipulated by means of the moral and emotional sensitivity which prevents her from making a direct appeal to him. Every device and intrigue is used against her without success until she is finally drugged and raped. From this point on, almost her lowest, she begins to reassert control of herself. Gradually, under the influence of new persecutions designed to humble her, she reduces her will to live. She eats less and prays more, and without making any design on her health or her life, she gradually fades away. Richardson stresses the fact that she is pleased at the symptoms of approaching dissolution, which is the answer to her problems. It provides her with the only way of recovering her self-respect after the initial act of weakness in leaving home with Lovelace.

When they are trying to force her to obey them and marry against her inclinations, Clarissa's family use a very crude logic against her. If she is obedient, she will obey; if she does not obey, she is not obedient, and therefore is not the person she claimed to be and the person who had previously earned their respect and affection. The only motive strong enough to overcome her training, and the tendencies of her previous life, they argue, must be an unworthy attachment to the rake Lovelace, her family's professed enemy, and she must be protected against this. By running away with Lovelace Clarissa seems to justify this logic and the harsh treatment which accompanied it. By dying she proves herself to have been modest beyond any imputation. She answers her family, in fact, with their own type of logic; and indeed, in answering them, she is answering herself. Clarissa's conception of virtue does not allow of the possibility of an unresolved tension between lower and higher elements of motivation. It is tempting for the modern reader to apply the terms of post-Freudian psychology to her case, which certainly allows it. So critics have argued that Clarissa actually wanted Lovelace to rape her, that she invited violence as the only form of sexual experience open to her. Others have thrown the clear light of clinical analysis on the workings of Lovelace's mind. Certainly, the way in which Lovelace himself makes constant reference to his relationship with his mother as a kind of terminal point invites further inquiry. And farther in the background stands brother James, whose vicious violence to his younger sister is perhaps to be explained in the light of his immediate and quite unjustified tendency to attribute her behaviour to over-developed sexuality rather than to his financial greed and love of power. It would be unfair to say that such interpretations are superfluous to the novel because it does invite them, but they are basically irrelevant. The origin of the impulses which make up motivation in *Clarissa Harlowe* is not really important. What really matters is the tendency of motivation. The innermost tension in the novel is not affected by analysis of impulses, but rather derives from the struggle to impose will on impulse, heightened by the struggle between individuals to impose will on each other.

It is interesting to compare *Clarissa Harlowe* with Cervantes' *nouvelle*, 'El Curioso Impertinente'. In Cervantes' story we have the history of someone who is tormented by doubts about the relationship between concept and actuality of character. Anselmo is a Lovelace who tests his wife *after* marriage rather than before. Cervantes, the great idealist in matters of character, brings home the reality by showing how the connection between character and concept may be broken down. But he continues beyond this to show how when that happens, character itself begins to break down. No method could be farther removed from the economy of the *nouvelle* than the epistolary mode as Richardson practises it, building up reality of presentation through abundance of detail of time and place, giving space for every impulse of character to reveal itself and develop through the spontaneous effusiveness of the letter-writing process. But of course, Richardson's realism is the means by which he asserts an idealist position. It is not unfair to say that Lovelace is no more than his catspaw, through whom Richardson himself plays the part of Anselmo, testing Clarissa. And of course, this Anselmo finds his Camila absolutely chaste. The event, however, is the same in both cases — that is, the death of the heroine, in the one story read as the sordid result of a mad experiment, in the other a victory over the flesh.

All the major characters in the novel share Richardson's and Clarissa's idea of virtue, and it might be said that they conspire together to make us believe it too. This is especially true of Lovelace. The rake dominates the action, takes a diabolical delight in his ability to control the actions and even the motives of other characters, and yet not only fails to control Clarissa but proves himself to have been totally dependent on her, capable of acting only on her initiative. Lovelace confesses to Belford that his principal aim is to test the virtue of Clarissa. This may seem a rather carelessly worn cloak for his sexual ambitions, but how often does Lovelace not declare his lack of interest in the physical consummation of his intrigues? Sexual satisfaction is not his aim, but rather he is set in motion by the idea of female chastity. The refusal of his advance is his *raison d'être*. He exists only by virtue of his own success in proving that women are not chaste. The woman who proves him wrong will win the honour of a hand which he is yet unable to give. Giving it, he would have no further motive for existence. His letter to Belford, shortly after the elopement, reveals his dependence on Clarissa:

And what! (methinks thou askest with surprize): Dost thou question this most admirable of women? — The Virtue of a CLARISSA dost thou question?

I do not, I dare not question it. My reverence for her will not let me *directly* question it. But let me, in my turn, ask thee—Is not, may not, her Virtue be founded rather in *Pride* than in *Principle*? Whose Daughter is she? And is she not a *Daughter*? If impeccable, how came she by her impeccability? The pride of setting an Example to her Sex has run away with her hitherto, and may have made her till *now* invincible. But is not that pride abated? What may not both *men* and *women* be brought to do in a *mortified state*? What mind is superior to calamity? Pride is perhaps the principal bulwark of female virtue. Humble a woman, and may she not be *effectually* humbled? . . .

As to my CLARISSA, I own, that I hardly think there ever was such an angel of a woman. But has she not, as above, already taken steps, which she herself condemns? Steps, which the world and her own family did not think her *capable* of taking? And for which her own family will not forgive her?

Nor think it strange, that I refuse to hear any-thing pleaded in behalf of a standard virtue from *high provocations*. 'Are not provocations and temptations the Tests of Virtue? A standard Virtue must not be allowed to be provoked to destroy or annihilate itself.

'May not then the Success of him, who could carry her *thus far*, be allowed to be an encouragement for him to try to carry her *farther*?' 'Tis but to try. Who will be afraid of a trial for this divine creature? . . .

I must assure thee, that I have a prodigious high opinion of Virtue. . . .

And now, to put an end to this sober argumentation, wilt thou not thyself . . . allow me to try, if I cannot awaken the *woman* in her? To try if she, with all that glowing symmetry of parts, and that full bloom of vernal graces, by which she attracts every eye, be really inflexible as to the grand article? . . .

Now, Belford, all is out. The Lady is mine; shall be *more* mine. Marriage, I see, is in my power, now *she* is so. Else perhaps it had not. If I can have her *without* marriage, who can blame me for trying? If *not*, great will be her glory, and my future confidence. And well will she merit the sacrifice I shall make her of my liberty; and from all her Sex Honours next to divine, for giving a proof, 'that there was once a woman whose Virtue no trials, no stratagems, no temptations, even from the man she hated not, could overpower'.

The History of Clarissa Harlowe (1747–48); 1751 ed. VII, pp. 344–54

Against this passage we might well place one of equal extremism, describing Clarissa's death: her beauty not gone, but her 'vernal graces' reduced to pallor and languor, her physical strength so reduced as scarcely to permit speech, but her presence of mind and calm confidence in a future life unimpaired:

> Bless—bless—bless—you All—And now—And now—[holding up her almost lifeless hands for the last time] Come—O come—Blessed Lord—Jesus!

> And with these words, the last but half-pronounced, expired: Such a smile, such a charming serenity over spreading her sweet face at the instant, as seemed to manifest her eternal happiness already begun.

The History of Clarissa Harlowe II, p. 89

Richardson's own reading of this passage is dependent on his literal acceptance of the fact that Clarissa was dying a completely Christian death and was about to be rewarded accordingly. For those not so convinced he built into the novel the other deathbed scenes and scattered delicate implications among Clarissa's last paragraphs: 'O dear, *dear* gentlemen, said she, you know not what *foretastes*—what *assurances*—And there she again stopt, and looked up, as if in a thankful rapture, sweetly smiling.'[55] We are intended to interpret these remarks in the same way as the repentant Belford. Richardson cannot actually go beyond Clarissa's death, but there is no doubt that he would have if he had been able to. The novel is not in fact designed merely to present an image of virtue, but to present that image in such a way as to bring with it a certain kind of conviction. *Clarissa Harlowe* is in fact, a sermon before it is a novel and becomes a novel only in so far as it fails to be completely effective as a sermon.

Richardson works hard throughout the fiction to maintain control over his reader's reactions. He does this partly through crude devices like the description of Mrs Sinclair's dreadful deathbed, surrounded by the raddled harlots of a thousand sermons. More important is the digressive tendency he develops, which seems to reflect an absolute determination to cover all possible sides of the debate and to anticipate all possible criticisms. This is carried so far sometimes as to distract attention from the central action and to develop subordinate actions which are quite self-contained. The most obvious example of this is the section of the novel which deals with Lovelace's reception by his own family after the rape. This is drawn out to proportions which threaten

[55]VII, p. 87.

the integrity of the central action, but it obviously derives very directly from Richardson's own concern for the way in which the central action should be regarded by the reader. The fact that Lovelace can bring round to grudging acceptance, and eventually humorous tolerance, a family at first outraged by his actions, indicates the extent to which their disapproval is shallowly based on conventional morality. It also builds up our appreciation of Lovelace as a character of great subtlety, patience and charm, and therefore goes a long way towards easing the strain of our acceptance of certain parts of the central action. A similar episode, though less lengthy, is that which takes place at the house where Clarissa is staying while she is driving round London to avoid the visit she fears. From the theatrical viewpoint this is one of Richardson's best scenes. Its basic purpose is to show how the world—even the middle-class, down-to-earth, trading world, equipped with simple good nature and sound sense—can be won over in its own stronghold, the home and the shop, by a person of Lovelace's charm and address. By such scenes Richardson forestalls his reader's tendency to fall into the same error and extends the range of debate concerning the nature of morality beyond the range of the relationship between Lovelace and Clarissa.

These two episodes are so long drawn out as to threaten the reader's tolerance of the epistolary mode of narration. Normally, though, the letter remains firmly under Richardson's control and is one of the principal means by which he manipulates the narrative and the reader's response to it. The letter form is essential to him in several ways. Firstly, there are several fundamental weaknesses in the dramatic structure of the novel. There are some strained coincidences and manipulations. Belford is kept away from London and Clarissa by the illness and death not only of his uncle, but also of Belton. We notice too that there are moments when the supposed alliance between Belford and Lovelace as members of a confraternity of rakes is subjected to too much strain. Anna Howe's non-interference at an important moment is ensured only by making her pay a visit to the Isle of Wight and by subjecting her mother to a conveniently dangerous illness. Clarissa's behaviour in allowing herself to be lured back into Lovelace's power after she has actually escaped is itself strained, bearing in mind what she had already learned about him and the relative weakness of the motive which prevented her from appealing for help to her friends. Nor have there been wanting critics to throw doubt on the truth to life of central characters themselves. Yet all these potential dangers to the novel's success are prevented from developing to a serious extent by the letter form, which throws emphasis on the texture of reaction and presents a triumphant reality in detail to overcome doubts about the shape of the whole scheme. The letter form also dulls the edge of a good deal of merciless moralising which takes place in the later part of the novel as we follow Clarissa's hearse homewards and watch the reactions of her grief-stricken relatives. On the whole it is impossible to imagine how Richardson could have even set his fiction in motion without it, let alone have brought it so near complete success.

Yet in the final analysis, Richardson does not succeed in doing what he attempted to do. A different kind of success transforms his perfect sermon in to a novel which is imperfect only in so far as it exists within the larger unit, unable to break free from it. This too was a result of his use of the epistolary form. For his use of the letter has the ultimate effect of reducing his own control and leaving the way open for the development of the tensions implicit in the situation which he had conceived and hoped to manipulate. It is interesting to see this happening even at those points in the action when he is most consciously working towards a given end. For example, in the letters between Clarissa and Anna and Lovelace and Belford which follow Clarissa's elopement, Richardson creates a complex web of reference and cross reference through which action is built up. He is very concerned at this point to justify Clarissa by showing how her actions were the result of Lovelace's machinations rather than her own weakness of will. At the same time he wants to maintain our concentration on his heroine's reaction to events as they occur. The actual result, though he certainly achieves his purpose, is the creation of a strong sense of the action as emerging only through the complex series of apprehensions, experiences and reports that is building up before our eyes. In effect what happens in the novel as a whole is that character and event come to us in a way which undermines Richardson's own contentions. Clarissa, for example, presents herself to us as someone who exists precisely *as* a certain conformation of characteristics, impulses, habitual reactions, and not as a total character. And the actions of the novel, including the rape itself, come over to us as having their own integrity, of which the motives of the protagonists form a part. The effect of this is to undermine the basis of morality as Richardson was presenting it to us — something which there were a few contemporary readers sharp enough, or sceptical enough to understand.

This does not happen in Richardson's third and last novel, *Sir Charles Grandison*, because he fails there to generate the kind of tension that exists in *Clarissa Harlowe*. This should remind us that the effect achieved in the earlier novel was nothing implicit in the letter form. If anything Richardson's use of the letter is more controlled and more confident in range in *Sir Charles Grandison* than it had been in *Clarissa Harlowe*. What was important was the relationship between the letter as a medium and the central tension within individuals and relationships between conflicting pressures and impulses. In his last novel Richardson failed to create a sufficient action. His aim was to represent a good man in all his essential characteristics as basically in control of his character and his own circumstances. Unfortunately Sir Charles was not susceptible to rape by Lady Clementina or her Italian relations, and failing this, Richardson was not able to develop an action in which the supposed tension in Sir Charles could be dramatised. Consequently the self-probing, self-revealing medium of the letter lacks justification. *Sir Charles Grandison* is polished and effective in detail, but almost endlessly dull.

With *Clarissa Harlowe* Richardson had succeeded in more than one way, to an almost unprecedented degree. He was received with enormous acclaim in England, Holland and Switzerland on the basis of his success in turning the novel into a sermon. *Clarissa Harlowe* as sermon/novel fitted neatly into a slot which had been prepared for it in eighteenth-century England for some time and formed the centre piece in a conservative cultural display which lasted up to the end of the century. On the other hand *Clarissa Harlowe* as we read it now—that is, as novel struggling to escape from sermon, succeeding in spite of its author—takes a prominent place in the European tradition of fiction. But for our present purpose, even more important than this, *Clarissa Harlowe* succeeded as an instrument of revolution. In the special circumstances which Richardson had set up in order to justify the pretensions of orthodox morality, the personality of his central characters developed in a way which undermined orthodoxy itself. In the final analysis, after all, Clarissa died to justify *herself* and in doing so implicitly laid a claim for the integrity of the personality which Rousseau and Diderot, and after them the writers of a whole generation, were to take up.

HENRY FIELDING'S 'NEW PROVINCE': REALISM AND COMPROMISE

It is interesting that the relationship between Fielding and Richardson is rather similar to that between Thackeray and Dickens. Like Thackeray, Fielding became a novelist at least partly because of the way in which he responded to the work of his popular rival. Like Thackeray, too, he responded in a critical way, demonstrating inherited rationalist attitudes and tending to fall back on neo-classic critical values. So the opposition between Fielding and Richardson, like that between their successors, is partly the opposition of the head and the heart. But of course this opposition should not conceal the fact that both pairs of novelists shared many attitudes and values, the differences between them being basically matters of degree and arrangement. Fielding's reaction to Richardson was in fact a confused and ambiguous one which brought to light certain tensions in his own sensibility. The appearance of Richardson's fiction, it seems, was one of the most important factors in the process by which these tensions resolved themselves in a new attitude to fiction and enabled him to develop from a dramatist and journalist into a novelist.

In contrast to Richardson, Fielding is a representative of neo-classic values, a rationalist who turns naturally to the weapons of wit and humour as means of maintaining cultural standards. He sees himself in the tradition of the great classic humorists, Aristophanes and Lucian. He uses the techniques of the Scriblerus Club—parody, pastiche, mock-heroic, burlesque—and he shares many of the attitudes of Pope and his confederates, especially in defending sanity and order against the inroads of the army of Grub Street. But it is interesting that when he comes to praise Dean Swift, it is not on the satire and irony of the Irish writer that he lays emphasis, but rather on the purpose to which he put them:

A few days since died in Ireland Dr Jonathan Swift, Dean of St Patricks in Dublin. A Genius who deserves to be ranked among the first whom the World ever saw. He possessed the Talents of a Lucian, a Rabelais, and a Cervantes, and in his Works exceeded them all. He employed his Wit to the noblest Purposes, in ridiculing as well Superstition in Religion as Infidelity, and the several Errors and Immoralities which sprung up from time to time in his Age; and lastly, in the defence of his Country, against several pernicious Schemes of wicked Politicians. Nor was he only a Genius and a Patriot; he was in private life a good and charitable Man, and frequently lent Sums of Money without Interest to the Poor and Industrious.

The True Patriot, No 1, Tuesday, 5 November 1745

This passage identifies Fielding clearly as a Protestant moralist, and even more particularly, an English patriot of the mid-eighteenth century. For all his wit, humour, light-hearted banter, satire and burlesque, this is what he was. There is perhaps an increasing tone of seriousness as he grows older, but his basic standards never change, and he is always capable of showing a strong tendency towards pedestrian moralism and even pedantry in matters affecting the language, social intercourse and political standards.

Fielding was also something of a sentimentalist, in spite of his consistent emphasis on the importance of judgement, as we see in his enthusiastic response to Richardson's *Clarissa Harlowe*. He welcomes it first in the form of a letter in his *Jacobite's Journal*: 'Sure this Mr *Richardson* is Master of all that Art which Horace compares to Witchcraft. . . .' Then, after he had read the fifth volume of *Clarissa Harlowe* he wrote direct to Richardson in terms which must have satisfied even him:

What shall I say of holding up the Licence? I will say a finer Picture was never imagined. He must be a Glorious Painter who can do it Justice on Canvas, and a most wretched one indeed who could not do much on such a Subject. The Circumstance of the Fragments is Great and Terrible; but her Letter to Lovelace is beyond anything I have ever read. God forbid that the Man who reads this with dry Eyes should be alone with my Daughter when she hath no Assistance within Call. Here my Terror ends and my Grief begins which the Cause of all my Tumultuous Passions soon changes into Raptures of Admiration and Astonishment by a Behaviour the most Elevated I can possibly conceive, and what is at the same time most Gentle and most natural.

The Criticism of Henry Fielding, ed. I. Williams (1970), p. 189

On the other hand, Fielding's total response to Richardson was ambiguous. Even in this letter of praise he makes a pointed distinction between his head and his heart and says that he is writing in the interests of the latter. Some time before this, after Richardson's *Pamela, or Virtue Rewarded* (1740) had been published anonymously, Fielding had followed it with his own anonymous *Shamela* (1741), which supposed that Richardson's work propagated an entirely false view of the character of its actually lustful and self-seeking heroine. What most annoyed him at the time, it seems, was the eulogic prefatory matter which Richardson published with his novel, but it is already clear in *Shamela* that he was being impelled, by Richardson's idealistic view of human nature, to develop a new realism of his own.

Richardson's own response to Fielding's work was less ambiguous. In his correspondence he takes every opportunity to denigrate his rival's achievement, partly through jealousy, and partly because he felt a sincere dislike for what he regarded as the lowness of Fielding's view of the world. In the Concluding Note to *Sir Charles Grandison* (1753–54) this disapproval found public expression when he wrote:

> It has been said, on behalf of many modern fictitious pieces, in which authors have given success (and *happiness*, as it is called) to their heroes of vitious, if not profligate characters, that they have exhibited human nature as it *is*. Its corruption may, indeed, be exhibited in the faulty character; but need pictures of this be held out in books? Is not vice crowned with success, triumphant, and rewarded, and, perhaps, set off with wit and spirit, a dangerous representation? And is it not made even *more* dangerous by the hasty reformation introduced, in contradiction to all probability, for the sake of patching up what is called a happy ending?

If this remark had a particular reference, it is most likely to have been Smollett's *Ferdinand Count Fathom* (1753), but Fielding might well have felt justified in applying it to *Tom Jones* and *Amelia*. If he did this might well explain the timing of his attack on Richardson in the Preface to *The Journal of a Voyage to Lisbon* (1755), almost the last thing that he wrote:

> If entertainment, as Mr Richardson observes, be but a secondary consideration in a romance; with which Mr Addison I think agrees, affirming the use of the pastrycook to be the first; if this, I say, be true of a mere work of invention, sure it may well be so considered in a work founded, like this, on truth; and where the political reflections form so distinguishing a part.
>
> But perhaps I may hear, from some critic of the most saturnine complexion, that my vanity must have made a horrid dupe of my judgement, if it hath flattered me with an expectation of having anything here seen in a grave light, or of conveying any useful instruction to the public, or to their guardians. I answer with the great man, whom I have just now quoted, that my purpose is to convey instruction in the vehicle of entertainment; and so to bring about at once, like the revolution in *The Rehearsal*, a perfect reforma-

tion of the laws relating to our maritime affairs: an undertaking, I will not say more modest, but surely more feasible, than that of reforming a whole people, by making use of a vehicular story, to wheel in among them worse manners than their own.

Preface to *The Journal of a Voyage to Lisbon* (1755); *The Criticism of Henry Fielding*, p. 145

In its place in the Preface, where Fielding is arguing for a more sombre and literal-minded view of history than he had ever presented before, there is something surprising about this sharply barbed reflection on Richardson. It stands out against the general run of the argument. But even if it had some purely casual inspiration, such as the publication of Richardson's own Concluding Note, it reveals the extent to which Fielding was prepared to react against his rival's crude conception of morality in fictional art. In the Preface Fielding argues against the whole idea of fiction as such, as distinct from history, going so far as to accuse Homer and Hesiod of confusing 'the records of antiquity', which is certainly a development beyond the position he had taken up in *Tom Jones*. His attitude to Richardson is one of the stable elements in his thinking.

Fielding's own attitude to fiction in the earlier part of his career is best illustrated in *Joseph Andrews*. The original impulse behind this book was the desire to ridicule *Pamela*, as had been the case with *Shamela*. Fielding imagines a brother for the virtuous serving-girl and puts him in the ridiculous position of having to defend his chastity against the attacks of his attractive mistress, aunt to Richardson's Mr B, here expanded to Booby. No sooner has he set up this situation, however, and begun to develop it, than his interest shifts from Joseph and his comic dilemma to the dilemma of the woman, who is struggling to overcome an unworthy, and worse—an unsuccessful, passion. Even within this situation he moves a long way from the original parodic impulse, which is soon entirely lost, but he is quite unable to develop it beyond a certain point. Very soon he moves Joseph out of Lady Booby's house and sends him on the journey home around which the action of the whole novel is constructed. The novel as a whole becomes congenitally episodic, suggesting a strong influence from Scarron's *Le Romant comique*, or perhaps the first volume of *Gil Blas*. But in their different ways, of course, both Scarron and Le Sage take the action of their novels seriously. This is not true of Fielding at this stage in his career. The journey of Joseph, with Fanny and Parson Adams, has something of the mock-heroic about it and is certainly far from developing any interest in itself, conceived as an action.

Joseph Andrews contains several explicit and expansive comments on the business of writing fiction as Fielding saw it at the time, which are very revealing. In the first instance Fielding puts forward what by then had become the traditional statement that fiction was capable of a truer truth than history. Orthodox historians, he suggests, should rather be called topographers or chorographers, who deal with the mere externals rather than the inner truth. But to this traditional statement he appends a more innovative claim that his fiction/history should rather be called biography.

> Now, thou, whoever thou art, whether a Muse, or by what other name soever thou chusest to be called, who presidest over Biography, and hast inspired all the Writers of Lives in these our Times; thou who didst infuse such wonderful Humour into the Pen of immortal *Gulliver*; who hast carefully guided the Judgement whilst thou hast exalted the nervous manly Style of thy *Mallet*: Thou who hadst no Hand in that Dedication and Preface, or the Translations, which thou wouldst willingly have struck out of the Life of *Cicero*: Lastly, Thou who, without the Assistance of the least Spice of Literature, and even against his Inclination, hast, in some Pages of his Book, forced *Colley Cibber* to write *English*; do thou assist me in what I find myself unequal to.
>
> *The History of the Adventures of Joseph Andrews* . . . III, i (1742);
> ed. M. Battestin (1967), p. 186

This passage is extremely difficult to interpret because of the mock-heroic style in which it is written and the combination in it of names like that of Swift, whom Fielding respected so highly, and Cibber, whom he so often mocked. It can only be read, however, as a fundamental approval of biography as a mode of private history, though it is clear that Fielding is uneasy about his own attitude to it. His preoccupation with Cibber alone would suggest this, because he gives him a degree of attention throughout his work, from the early papers in *The Champion* on, which cannot be explained by Cibber's intrinsic importance as an object of satire.

What this would suggest, superficially, is that Fielding is moving in the same direction as Richardson, which is towards a closer and closer association of fictional action with the forms of contemporary social life. In fact, though, as the merest glance at any of his novels will show, this was not so. Fielding failed to move in this direction at all, as further passages in *Joseph Andrews* explain. For he goes on to talk of biography in a way that shows he had translated it back to mean something very close to what we mean by 'novel'. His biographers are Cervantes, Le Sage, and Marivaux, the 'classic' novelists, rather than Defoe and Richardson, who might be classed as fictional biographers. And the most important quality of biography/novel he mentions is in fact that previously mentioned characteristic of fiction/history—that is, its ability to represent inner truth, independent of mere facts of time and place. In biography:

> . . . the Facts we deliver may be relied on, tho' we often mistake the Age and Country wherein they happened: For tho' it may be worth the Examination of Critics, whether the shepherd *Chrysostom*, who, as Cervantes informs us, died for love of the fair *Marcella*, who hated him, was ever in *Spain*, will any one doubt but that such a silly Fellow hath really existed? Is there in the World such a Sceptic as to disbelieve the Madness of *Cardenio*, the perfidy of *Ferdinand*, the impertinent Curiosity of *Anselmo*, the weakness of *Camilla*, the irresolute Friendship of *Lothario*; though perhaps as to the Time and Place where those several Persons lived, that good historian may be deplorably deficient. . . .
>
> *The History . . . of Joseph Andrews . . .* III, vix, pp. 238–9

Under this heading, Fielding takes care to point out, he does not include 'those Persons of surprising Genius, the Authors of immense Romances, or the modern Novel and *Atlantis* Writers; who without any Assistance from Nature of History, record Persons who never were or will be. . . .' But in this too, of course, he is associating himself with French neo-classic critics, and with Le Sage and Marivaux rather than with any particularly modern position.

Yet of course *Joseph Andrews* does represent a distinctive contribution to the tradition of the novel, not in terms of theory, or in terms of action, but rather with regard to the representation of character in specific social circumstances. Fielding's famous defence of his technique—that the lawyer he represents: 'is not only alive, but hath been so these 4000 Years'[56]—might well have been made by Le Sage. But this obscures the fact that Fielding's method is actually very different from that of Le Sage, and even from that of Marivaux. What Fielding actually produced was human nature particularised to such a degree that it seems to dictate the terms of its own presentation. The

[56] P. 189.

structure of *Joseph Andrews* is quite episodic, and develops no overall sense of the relationship between human character and the conditions which affect its various manifestations. But within separate episodes the character of individuals is allowed to develop itself to such an extent that this essential relationship becomes clear. In the scene which produced his famous comment about the lawyer, Fielding was presenting a version of the Good Samaritan story, each one of the characters apart from the postilion demonstrating different aspects of selfishness in dealing with the proposition that the naked hero should be allowed to enter the coach. The scene, however, develops a complexity and a solidity which quite transcends this schematic function, and other scenes of the novel have a similar quality, so that the total effect, in spite of its episodic structure, is that of a unified and strikingly realistic vision of human society in a specific place and time.

In the character of Abraham Adams we have a parallel development leading in the same direction, which amounts to an important step in the progress through the work of Sterne to Sir Walter Scott and the nineteenth century. Fielding's idea of humour takes the theories of Addison and Steele a step farther. Parson Adams is a living embodiment of his conviction that the individual becomes humorous and ridiculous through the excessive development of any part of his character. Even virtue, he informs us, may, like patriotism, honesty, loyalty, etc., degenerate into humour and make the character ridiculous. But what is important about Adams is not so much the fact that he becomes ridiculous at times through vanity, pomposity or naïveté, which might happen to any character, but that he is not ridiculous in the massive grotesqueness of his whole character. Fielding's earnestness and sentimentalism here had taken him a step farther than his predecessors towards letting the individual have free run.

In *Tom Jones* (1749), however, this aspect of characterisation is firmly under control and no individual is allowed to develop in the way that Adams developed in *Joseph Andrews*. The most humorous character, in fact, Squire Western, is firmly fixed within a neo-classic framework, reinforced by political considerations which damn his irrational Toryism. And this indicates the extent to which *Tom Jones* represents a further stage in Fielding's thinking—that is, one which involves a great deal more systematisation of his ideas than *Joseph Andrews*. His literary theory in the later work is more consistently developed and more consciously elaborated around the idea of the comic epic, representing an effort to fill out the neo-classic genres which had been going on in French criticism for generations. The

Archbishop of Cambrai's *Télemaque* (1699) reflects a similar preoccupation. The assimilation of the idea of the epic with the idea of the novel, of course, had one beneficial effect in so far as it tended to raise the status of the novel. The origin of this association, however, was a long way in the past and from the point of view of eighteenth-century ideas about the novel, rather disreputable. What Fielding says about the novel as epic, after all, is not very different from what had been said by Mme de Scudéry in her discussions of the romance. In fact the development of the theory of the comic epic might well be thought of as indicating the strengthening of two factors which worked against the development of the novel—that is, it encouraged Fielding to think of the action of his fictions as purely mechanical and arbitrary, and also tended to increase the distance between the author and his material.

Fielding's increased tendency to systematise his thinking was also dangerous in another respect. In this major work he was setting out to give a whole view of contemporary life. His overt purpose in the novel is disappointingly vague—to produce a speaking picture of virtue, to convince men that their true interest lay in pursuing it and 'Lastly . . . to inculcate, that Virtue and Innocence can scarce ever be injured but by Indiscretion. . . .'[57] Fortunately for us his actual emphasis fell in another direction, however. The moral scheme on which the novel is based rests on a rather uneasy combination of different elements. Fielding attempted to reconcile social interests, a rationalist view of human character and a critical assessment of human motivation with an orthodox Protestant morality. The result was good enough for his journalism, where the emphasis is always on the application rather than the theory, but it will not stand the strain imposed when it is stretched out to cover the plot of *Tom Jones*. The element through which the reconciliation of these different interests was to be achieved was his reinterpretation of the Christian view of charity so as to give it social and intellectual value. The great rule of conduct extracted from the Sermon on the Mount became the primary rule governing all human intercourse—do unto others as you would they should do unto you. In Fielding's reading of human character two elements took precedence—good-nature and judgement. Without good-nature charity itself was inconceivable. It was even, he argued, a prerequisite of Christianity itself—the 'amiable quality, which, like the Sun, gilds over all our other Virtues';

It is (as Shakespeare calls it) the Milk, or rather the Cream of Human

[57] *The History of Tom Jones*, ed. M. Battestin and F. Bowers (1974), p. 7.

Nature, and whoever is possessed of this Perfection should be pitied, not hated for the want of any other. Whereas all other Virtues without some Tincture of this, may be well called *Splendida Peccata*. . . .

> *The Champion*, No 58, Thursday, 27 March 1740

Judgement, however, was essential to good-nature. This was the 'distinguishing faculty' which enabled men to maintain mental balance, to distinguish truth from falsehood and to maintain that moderation in all things without which the individual declined into a figure of humour, his virtues merely splendid faults:

. . . Good-Nature requires a distinguishing Faculty, which is another Word for Judgement, and is perhaps the sole Boundary between Wisdom and Folly; it is impossible for a Fool, who hath no distinguishing Faculty, to be good-natured.

As there was never a better Rule for the Conduct of Human Life than what is convey'd in that excellent short Sentence—Ne quid nimis, so there is none so seldom observed. . . . Men often become ridiculous or odious by over-acting even a laudable part: for Virtue itself, by growing too exuberant, and (if I may be allowed a Metaphor) by running to Seed changes its very Nature, and becomes a most pernicious Weed of a most beautiful Flower.

> *The Champion*, No 58, Thursday, 27 March 1740 and No 53, Saturday, 15 March 1740

This amounts to an attempt to make all forms of human activity and intercourse dependent on Lockean psychology and Protestant morality and was associated closely with the dominant political and social conservatism of mid-eighteenth-century England which Fielding enthusiastically shared. Its weakness as a moral system derives from the fact that it presents evil merely as something which is irrational or impolite and virtue either as the result of unthinking good-nature or something to be followed out of self-interest: 'the virtuous and temperate Man only', Fielding tells us, 'hath Inclination, hath Strength; and, (if I may be indulged in the Expression) hath Opportunity to enjoy all his Passions.'[58] It has equal weakness as a view of contemporary life because it restricts Fielding's scope and prevents him from following out lines of consequence which are built into his material. In *Tom Jones* only a series of manipulations and coincidences prevents the reader

[58] *The Champion*, No.30, Thursday, 24 January, 1739–40.

from coming face to face with a whole range of social and philosophical questions which would destroy his interest in the narrative.

Tom Jones survives in spite of these weaknesses by virtue of Fielding's adoption of the Cervantesque device of developing the relationship between the narrator and the reader. Apart from the fact that it has a simple biographical frame, prevented from developing to any serious extent by Fielding's maintenance of epic distance, the structure of Tom Jones is not notably different from that of Joseph Andrews. It has two dimensions—that concerning the fate of the hero and heroine, worked out through the central plot; and the smaller-scale, more closely textured series of confrontations, conversations and brawls which primarily involve the novel's many minor characters. The novel's main emphasis, however, falls on neither of these. Increasingly as we read our way into it we become aware of Fielding's narrator, himself a great humorous character and at the same time we come to think of the action as in his control and at his disposal. Because of his manipulation of us—the first and major one concerning Tom's birth, of course—we gradually acquire ourselves an idea of the importance of judgement as a condition of living with our fellow men at all. The primary question becomes not whether Allworthy was wise or just in his treatment of Tom, but whether we are wise or just in our view of Allworthy. Fielding's main concern was with human motivation rather than with questions of good or evil. In the final analysis he leaves us as squarely as Richardson with God Almighty. Only He can judge the future of Lawyer Dowling who ends the novel as we knew he would, with unblemished reputation and secure material position. The closing chapters of Tom Jones are clearly its weakest part. As the elements of tension in our relationship with the narrator become relaxed, so we are left in more and more direct contemplation of the situation of Tom Jones, whose complete and quite undeserved prosperity together with Fielding's evident satisfaction in narrating it, give us serious doubts as to his sensitivity. But in spite of this—and various other doubts the reader may have from time to time—the novel remains a great novel because Fielding succeeds in dramatising the major tension between experience and apprehension and, in doing so, validating his own values. Good-nature and judgement together, after all, we have to have if we are to read Tom Jones at all without making fools of ourselves at every important stage.

This great success of Tom Jones ensured the initial success of Fielding's third and last novel, Amelia, but readers who rushed to buy it in 1751 were sadly disappointed. In contrast to Tom Jones, Amelia lacks humour and incurred the criticism of being 'low', and then, because of Fielding's unfortunate error of judgement in producing a heroine with a damaged nose, it became the object of humour in others. The development from *Tom Jones* to *Amelia* is frequently attributed to the growing seriousness of Fielding in his later years, when experience as a London magistrate, the loss of wife and child, brought him fewer and fewer reasons for the gaiety which marks his earlier works. But it is as well to remember that *Amelia* is very much the logical result of tendencies which were implicit in Fielding's whole career. If, as has often been observed, he was coming in his later years closer and closer to the position occupied by Richardson, it was not as the result of any fundamental change in his thinking—and of course, his attitude to Richardson did not change. On the other hand, we should not under-estimate the originality of *Amelia*. Of all the novels of the eighteenth century, including those of Jane Austen, *Amelia* was fittest to serve as a pattern to Dickens and Thackeray. Their later realism owed a good deal to Fielding's achievement in this last novel.

Fielding had always had a sharp awareness of the society he lived in. Like Cervantes he thought in terms of the nation as a whole and was concerned for the interpenetration of all aspects of its life. This spirit motivates all his journalism and is especially prominent in the pages of a journal like the *Jacobite's Journal*. But Fielding also had what Cervantes lacked, and that was a sense of contemporary society as a medium through which individual character expressed itself and as a web or texture of conditions and factors which affected the whole shape of his life. In *Amelia* this sense is especially strong. In *Amelia* he looks more closely at the consequences than he had done before. In effect he takes Tom out of Paradise Hall once again, this time encumbered with a wife and children, and leaves him free to wander through the world. His theme remains the same—he wants to show how judgement and stability of character are essential to happiness and how their lack exposes us to misery and wretchedness.

In Chapter I of *Amelia*—'Containing the exordium'—Fielding shows that he has gone a good way, certainly farther than any previous writer, towards thinking of human life as an integral unit and of the integral fiction as an apt representation of it:

Life may as properly be called an art as any other; and the great incidents in it are no more to be considered as mere accidents than the several members of a fine statue or a noble poem. The critics in all these are not content with seeing anything to be great without

knowing why and how it came to be so. By examining carefully the
several gradations which conduce to bring every model to perfection,
we learn truly to know that science in which the model is formed: as
histories of this kind, therefore, may properly be called models of
HUMAN LIFE, so, by observing minutely the several incidents
which tend to the catastrophe or completion of the whole, and the
minute causes whence those incidents are produced, we shall best be
instructed in this most useful of all arts, which I call the ART OF
LIFE.

> *Amelia* I, i (1751); ed. G. Saintsbury (1930), I, p. 4

The implications of this passage are revolutionary, but Fielding himself was quite incapable of drawing them out. In the first instance,
he was unwilling to abandon the satirical aspect of the novel, and
frequently bends his plot so as to permit particular attacks on aspects of
the English judicial or legal system. But more important than this, he
provides his novel with nothing but a mechanical structure which is
completely unable to bear the moral weight that he wants the story to
have.

Fielding's basic failure here derives from his inability to centre the
novel in the experience of his hero. As a result of this his heroine is the
uninterestingly passive victim of events and his hero something very
like what used to be called a cad. In order to do this, of course, he would
have had to abandon his whole position. The novel rests firmly on the
assumption that truth awaits acceptance rather than discovery. Life as
Fielding saw it was not an integral, organic thing, but rather a series of
mechanically related events, quite meaningless without reference to
Scripture. The modern reader of *Amelia* must be struck immediately by
the fact that although Fielding opens his novel with an exposure of an
unfairness and ineffectiveness of the English judiciary system, he is not
at all disturbed by the general implications of this failure. Among the
prisoners brought before the dreadful Justice Thrasher is an Irishman
unfairly found guilty of assault, an innocent servant sent to Bridewell
for a month as a prostitute, an honest witness committed for perjury on
the word of a whore and Fielding's own hero, imprisoned for an assault
he has not committed. Fielding ends this horrific scene, and his chapter,
with a brief statement: 'The delinquents were then all dispatched to
prison under a guard of watchmen, and the justice and the constable
adjourned to a neighbouring alehouse to take their morning repast.'[59]
The next chapter, which begins the action of the novel proper, describes

[59] I, p. 11.

Booth's reception in prison. The fate of the others is disposed of within a parenthesis: '(for we shall not trouble you with the rest)'. And this is typical of Fielding's method throughout the novel. In effect it does not occur to him to require that life itself should provide its own balance between justice and injustice, though in practical terms no man ever worked harder to ensure that it should.

This attitude explains the structure of the novel, which has traditionally been held to relate to Homer's *Odyssey* as *Tom Jones* relates to the *Aeneid*. Fielding thought it quite adequate to structure his novel according to an arbitrary principle, just as he felt it quite appropriate to insert material which had no essential connection with the history of Amelia and Booth. And then, when the time comes to bring the action to an end, he also thinks it permissible to announce that an action has taken place which effects an alteration in the hero's character and so ensures his future happiness. Visited in a sponging house by Dr Harrison, who has good cause to be annoyed with him, Booth informs the Doctor that he has undergone a kind of conversion:

> Booth at last began himself in the following manner: 'Doctor, I am really ashamed to see you; and, if you knew the confusion of my soul on this occasion, I am sure you would pity rather than upbraid me; and yet I can say with great sincerity I rejoice in this last instance of my shame, since I am like to reap the most solid advantage from it.' The doctor stared at this, and Booth thus proceeded: 'Since I have been in this wretched place I have employed my time almost entirely in reading over a series of sermons which are contained in that book (meaning Dr. Barrow's works, which then lay on the table before him) in proof of the Christian religion; and so good an effect have they had upon me, that I shall, I believe, be the better man for them as long as I live. I have not a doubt (for I own I have had such) which remains now unsatisfied. If ever an angel might be thought to guide the pen of a writer, surely the pen of that great and good man had such an assistant.' . . . 'Very well,' answered the doctor, 'though I have conversed, I find, with a false brother hitherto, I am glad you are reconciled to truth at last, and I hope your future faith will have some influence on your future life.' 'I need not tell you sir,' replied Booth, 'that will always be the case where faith is sincere, as I assure you mine is. Indeed, I never was a rash disbeliever; my chief doubt was founded on this—that, as men appeared to me to act entirely from their passions, their actions could have neither merit nor demerit.' 'A very worthy conclusion truly!' cries the doctor; 'but if

men act, as I believe they do, from their passions, it would be fair to
conclude that religion to be true which applies immediately to the
strongest of these passions, hope and fear; choosing rather to rely on
its rewards and punishments than on that native beauty of virtue
which some of the ancient philosophers thought proper to recom-
mend to their disciples. . . .'

Amelia II, p. 287

Strictly speaking this conversion should end the action of the novel, but
Fielding adds to it the discovery of the plot which has kept Amelia and
Booth from the rightful inheritance so as to allow them to end in
happiness and prosperity. In this way he perhaps satisfied his natural
sense of justice, but fatally weakened the structure of his novel. The
whole of *Amelia* depends, in fact, on the assertion of values and
convictions which are never embodied in the novel itself. Unlike *Tom
Jones*, *Amelia* merely asserts rather than dramatises. The process by
which Booth changed should have been at the centre of the novel, but
Fielding simply did not have the sense of internal process as a means of
structuring a fiction which was meant to comment on the art of life.

Had he done so there is no doubt that he could have made out of
Amelia a great novel and one which would have revolutionised European fiction. The achievement, though, was impossible in 1751 — or for
many years after that. His problem was basically similar to that of
many other novelists in the period. Half-way, but only half-way,
towards freedom from the old authoritarian conceptions of truth,
committed to social stability and a reconciliation of social and moral
values. This it was that brought them to the novel and enabled them to
develop it so signally, but just as their social position required a
compromise, so their attitude to fiction involved a compromise, and
that did not permit development beyond a certain point. In the final
analysis fiction remained subservient to a framework of ideas which
limited its development. Success was still possible within this
framework — Le Sage, Marivaux, Richardson and Fielding all demonstrate this, but this success depended on the individual's happening to
develop a standpoint within an individual work which allowed the
dramatisation of his central ideas. This in turn was possible only to the
greatest writers of the period and only to those whose 'realism' was
most incisive and persistent. Only they could avoid the dangers
attendant on the temptation to compromise on the level of action and to
have recourse to manipulation and unreality. This the novel cannot
stand any more than the pedestrian assertiveness of *Amelia*. But the

problem we are dealing with here is not a simple one, nor one which could be solved merely on the level of fiction. It was a problem which derived from the state of society and culture in the middle of the eighteenth century, from the fact that different elements were held in uneasy compromise not only in literature but in society and in individual character. Advance towards the modern position required a radical development, new forms of thinking, of feeling, and even new forms of being, as well as changes in the outer conditions which govern human lives. These when they came were foreshadowed and perhaps affected more than is almost credible by the work of one man—Jean Jacques Rousseau, who is typical of his period perhaps in the blend of success and failure his work achieves, but completely unique and revolutionary in the sensibility and the values which it embodies. *La Nouvelle Héloise* marks the beginning of a new period just as Fielding's *Amelia* stands at the end of the old.

5 The Age of Rousseau, 1760–1800

Before finding the vision which was missing from Fielding's *Amelia* we have to wait for the appearance of the novels of Sir Walter Scott. Scott's work is interfused with a particular spirit, recognised by contemporaries and successors as equally original and important. He saw human life as a whole, as the point of union between forces dramatically opposed and yet essentially unified, and developed a standpoint fundamentally different and yet strikingly similar to that of the great Renaissance writers. There is a scene in *Rob Roy* (1817) which demonstrates this perhaps more clearly than any other. In the Highland fastness of Rob Roy, having recently destroyed a troop of infantry sent in search of him and learned that he has been captured by the treachery of the gauger Morris, Roy's wife condemns the latter to immediate death:

> She gave a brief command in Gaelic to her attendants, two of whom seized upon the prostrate suppliant, and hurried him to the brink of a cliff which overhung the flood. He set up the most piercing and dreadful cries that fear ever uttered—I may well term them dreadful, for they haunted my sleep for years afterwards. . . .
>
> I was so much moved by this horrid spectacle, that, although in momentary expectation of sharing his fate, I did attempt to speak in his behalf, but, as might have been expected, my interference was sternly disregarded. The victim was held fast by some, while others, binding a large heavy stone in a plaid, tied it round his neck, and others again eagerly stripped him of some part of his dress. Half-naked, and thus manacled, they hurled him into the lake, there about twelve feet deep, with a loud halloo of vindictive triumph—above which, however, his last death-shriek, the yell of mortal agony, was

distinctly heard. The heavy burden splashed in the dark-blue waters, and the Highlanders, with their poleaxes and swords, watched an instant to guard, lest, extricating himself from the load to which he was attached, the victim might have struggled to retain the shore. But the knot had been securely bound—the wretched man sunk without effort; the waters which his fall had disturbed, settled calmly over him, and the unit of that life for which he had pleaded so strongly, was for ever withdrawn from the sum of human existence.

    Rob Roy, Chapter xxxii; The Waverley Novels (1890), IV,
pp. 357–8

We may compare Scott as author of this passage with Cervantes and with Fielding. The first thing we notice is that his work embodies a concern for the individual human being as an end in himself which is missing from theirs. The death of Morris contrasts strikingly with the sentencing of the innocent offenders in Justice Thrasher's court; and if we turn to the final part of *Don Quixote II* we see at once that Scott has a care for the individual no matter how unimportant which is totally lacking from the scenes dealing with Roque Guinart or the incident of the galleys. This is clearly a matter of sentiment. The civilised Francis Osbaldistone is shocked by the murder because he responds to Morris as a human being like himself. The Highlanders are insensitive to the relationship. Scott himself, however, feels something which it is possible that Osbaldistone does not feel. The latter's civilised sentimentalism is transcended by his creator's sense of the scene as a whole, in which all the actors, including Nature itself, share a unity which violence outrages but cannot destroy. This is in fact the element in Scott's work which encouraged contemporaries to compare him with Shakespeare, and which we can see as something which he shares with Cervantes, in spite of the latter's complete lack of awareness of the individual existence as an end in itself. Over the intervening centuries Scott and Cervantes meet in their ability to see human life as a sum total of conflicting tendencies, pressures, energies, and as something more. In Cervantes' case this vision was the result of his ability to occupy more than one standpoint at the same time, to see mankind from the viewpoint of the medieval realist, the picaresque satirist of human pretensions, and yet to preserve the fundamental respect for man which was embodied in the idealist literature of the Renaissance. The elements of Scott's position were quite different, but its basis the same. He combined the reductive realism of the Enlightenment writers with the values developed through the literature of sentimentalism. For him the meaning of life had to be validated through individual experience; it could not be an abstract thing as it was for Cervantes. Yet at the same time he could see the individual and the general as part of a total unity; he could reconcile sentimentalism and reductive realism and achieve a completeness of view which was itself an enormous contribution to the literature of European romanticism and the basis of the work of generations of later novelists. The novel of the nineteenth century rests on foundations which he laid. In terms of the novel they were no more than foundations. Scott's vision depended on the mediation of history and was inapplicable to immediate reality. He seems only to have been able to attain it by the contemplation of different aspects of historical reality imposing themselves on each other, and as he came closer to his own time the ability to do this weakened and ceased, but this at least he could do, and its greatness was well understood by those who followed him, from Stendhal to George Eliot and Pérez Galdós.

The theoretical equivalent of Scott's highly practical vision can be found in the rather pedestrian fiction of a French writer much admired by Balzac and Matthew Arnold but almost ignored in his own day. This is the *Obermann* (1804), of Etienne Pivert de Senancour, who is among the earliest of writers to use the novel as a form to extend sentimentalism into a system of thought which takes account of man as an objective entity as well as a feeling subject. Senancour's hero explains to his correspondent:

> Si l'homme sent dans tout ce qui est animé, les biens et les maux de ce qui l'environne sont aussi réels pour lui que ses affections personnelles; il faut à son bonheur le bonheur de ce qu'il connait; il est lié à tout ce qui sent, il vit dans le monde organisé.
>
> L'enchaînement de rapports dont il est le centre, et qui ne peuvent finir entièrement qu'aux bornes du monde, le constitue partie de cet univers, unité numérique dans le nombre de la nature. Le lien que forment ces liens personnels est l'ordre du monde, et la force qui perpétue son harmonie est la loi naturelle. . . .
>
> Un être isolé n'est jamais parfait: son existence est incomplète; il n'est ni vraiment heureux ni vraiment bon. Le complément de chaque chose fut placé hors d'elle, mais il est réciproque.

If man sympathises with all that lives the weal and woe of his surroundings are as real to him as his personal emotions; the happiness of everything known to him is essential to his own; he is bound up with all that feels, he lives in this organic whole of the world.

The network of relations of which he is the centre, and which are only bounded by the limits of the world, constitute him a part of that Universe, a unit in nature's number. The bond formed by those personal links is the order of the world, and the force which perpetuates its harmony is natural law. . . .

An isolated being is never perfect; his existence is incomplete; he is neither truly happy nor truly good. The complement of each particular object has been placed outside itself, but the need is mutual.

Obermann, Lettre LXIII (1804); ed. G. Michaut (1912), pp. 74, 75

The essential thing here is the idea of life as an *organic* whole, and man as a creature essentially connected with the rest of animate nature by virtue of his emotions. This idea is the very centre of Romantic theory and also at the basis of later realist fiction which explored the organic connections between man and his total environment. We can find equivalent passages, of course, in the work of Wordsworth, in *The Prelude*, the Lucy poems or in *Tintern Abbey*; in Shelley, Keats and Byron. It is the basic frame in which Coleridge elaborated his idea of the imagination in *Biographia Literaria* (1817). According to Coleridge's discussion man shares the nature of God through the primary imagination or consciousness, in so far as this is a faculty which both perceives and defines. In human consciousness the perceiving self and the object perceived are held in relation to each other even at the same time as they are understood as separate entities. This is 'a repetition in the finite mind of the eternal act of creation' because it reflects the instantaneous self-consciousness and creativity of God. The secondary imagination Coleridge describes as an 'echo' of this, under the control of the conscious will but sharing its dual nature: 'It dissolves, diffuses, dissipates, in order to recreate; or where this process is rendered impossible, yet still, at all events, it struggles to idealize and to unify.'[60] According to Coleridge the imagination of the artist is a primary mode of apprehending truth, essentially beyond the reach of the analysing intellect precisely because it is organic, whole and integral. And the work of art which is itself organic, expressing its statement in its own terms and not referring to any group of ideas or elements which are not

[60] *Biographia Literaria; or Biographical Sketches.* . . . (1817). Scolar Press ed. (1971), p. 296.

validated within it, is the embodiment of that truth.

This idea of life as an organic unity does not originate with Rousseau or any other single writer, but it is reasonable to see Rousseau's work, and especially his novel, *La Nouvelle Héloise*, as marking the decisive step beyond existing attitudes which was to lead inevitably to the development of the central Romantic idea. For Rousseau projected a view of reality in which all values should be ascertainable by subjective criteria, by the emotions of the individual rather than any objective tests. What followed, and is clearly documented throughout the literature of the later decades of the eighteenth century, particularly in lyric poetry and drama, though not particularly in France, was a shift in the self-consciousness of writers at least, an increase of subjectivity which was painful and productive of stress. Subjectivity became, as Goethe described it, a form of sickness, which ultimately destroyed the emotions of the individual and his capacity to respond to experience of any kind. To see life as Obermann saw it was to go beyond this stage, to devise a method of containing subjectivism without retreating to outdated attitudes or rejecting the new values which came with it.

This new view of life developed steadily throughout Europe in the decades which followed 1760, but most quickly and thoroughly in Germany. Explicit in the work of Kant, the organic idea was further elaborated in the work of Fichte, Schelling and Hegel. As a political concept it was also more clearly developed in Germany, in the reaction which followed French invasions under Napoleon. There is an amusing and instructive passage in the memoirs of Goethe which shows us what power it had to bring together men of different and even conflicting tendencies and interests. Goethe had avoided meeting Schiller for some time because he disapproved of the idealistic tendency of his work and of his emotionalism, but he met him by chance at a scientific lecture in 1794 and left in his company. He describes what followed:

He appeared to interest himself in the lecture we had heard, but with sharp understanding and insight, and to my great pleasure observed, how such a dismembered way of treating nature was not calculated to engage the outsider who would willingly take part in such studies.

To this I replied, that perhaps even to the initiated it was not attractive, and that undoubtedly there was another way of going to work, presenting nature not sundered and detached, but operative and alive, striving with sure determination out of a whole into parts. He desired further light on this subject, but did not conceal his doubts; he could not admit that such a view of nature was, as I maintained, the presentation of experience.

We reached his house, the conversation allured me in; I set forth in a lively manner the metamorphosis of plants, and with many characteristic strokes of the pen caused a symbolic plant to arise before his eyes. He perceived and observed it all with great interest, with a decided power of comprehension; but when I finished he shook his head and said, 'That is no observation, that is an idea.' I was startled, chagrined in a certain measure; for the line dividing us was by this expression most palpably indicated.

The Autobiography of Goethe . . . Together with his Annals II, tr.
J. Oxenford (1894), pp. 210–11

Fortunately for them both, and for literature, Goethe overcame his annoyance, succumbed to the charm of Schiller's personality and the friendship developed. 'And so,' Goethe concludes, 'by means of a dispute between object and subject, the most fundamental of all disputes —one indeed, perhaps never to be wholly composed—we sealed an alliance, which has lasted without interruption. . . .'[61]

It is doubtful if any similar encounter could have taken place in England and France at the same time. The subject was understood more clearly in Germany in philosophical terms. In France discussions of this kind would not have been heard at all before Madame de Stael published her *De l'Allemagne* in England in 1813 after the first French edition had been seized by Napoleon's police. In England Coleridge was almost unique in his acquaintance with the work of German philosophers, let alone in his understanding of them. English literature of the period makes it quite clear, of course, that it was not necessary to understand the subject in terms borrowed from Kant. Wordsworth and Scott together developed the central ideas of Romanticism at least as far as Goethe or Schiller in purely practical terms. In France, on the other hand, perhaps mainly because of the Revolution of 1789 and the military adventures of the Empire, the impulse to unify rather than to resolve conflicting pressures in individual and social experience was much weaker. French poetry and drama does not reflect the preoccupations of English and German writers until after the turn of the century.

So conditions in the period after 1760 in England, France and Germany were very different and yet can be seen from the same point of view. In the decades after Rousseau there is widespread throughout

[61]P. 211.

Europe an increasing sense of tension between different aspects of personal and social experience and particularly an increasing need to resolve the discrepancy between systems of value which were based on the novel view of the individual human being as the final unit of meaning and social and political systems which embodied different, older, assumptions. The results for the novel were not beneficial. The transition from the eighteenth century to the nineteenth, or perhaps we should rather say, the early decades of the nineteenth century, were marked by the processes according to which Romantic ideology came to be assimilated into social forms. Only when this had happened could a novel emerge which could present the reconciliation between individual and social experience in its own terms. Until there are ways by which the individual may transmute his personal aspirations through social forms, the novel as we know it in the nineteenth century cannot exist; and even then it does so primarily as a critical if not a satiric form. In the late eighteenth century the tension between values derived from individual experience and social institutions which are antagonistic to them is so acute that the novelist is hard put to it to continue his work at all.

BETWEEN TWO WORLDS; THE NOVEL IN FRANCE AFTER 1757

The Revolution of 1789 was an event of great cultural as well as political significance and as such had immeasurable effect on the long-term development of the novel. In the short term, however, the years preceding and immediately following the Revolution make up a period when the novel as a whole found it difficult to flourish, although in certain directions its development was abnormally pronounced. The influence of the *libertins* on the novel in France had always been important, from the time when Théophile and Sorel interested themselves in the Comic Romance, till Crébillon fils, in *Les Egarements du coeur et de l'esprit* (1736) used sexual intrigue as a medium for the presentation and analysis of character. Through the middle years of the century this influence had grown, as Enlightenment authors, Voltaire at their head, used various forms of fiction—*nouvelle, conte de fées*, fantasy and imaginary travels—as means of attacking orthodox conceptions of character and human behaviour. In the century's last decades the *libertin* influence reached such proportions that it could be thought of as a cause contributing as much to the Revolution as the *Encyclopédie* of Diderot and d'Alembert, the greatest monument to the achievement of the *philosophes*. As the record of the immorality of a decadent aristocracy, the contemporary novels added fuel to the diatribes of popular orators. At the same time, they are part of the Revolution themselves, reflecting a sensibility at once libertine and idealist, which took to licentious fiction with an energy and excitement which it was quite unable to control and direct.

The clearest example of this sensibility is provided by Jean-Baptist Louvet de Couvray (1760–97) who was both a revolutionary politician and a novelist. From 1789 Louvret de Couvray was prominent in the National Assembly, in the ranks of the Girondins; proscribed in 1792, he fled from Paris and went into hiding; after the fall of Robespierre he returned, became President of the Assembly and had just been appointed Consul to Palermo by the Directoire when he died. In 1789, the year of the Revolution itself, Louvet de Couvray published the first part of *Les Amours du Chevalier de Faublas*, which he followed in successive years with two continuations. The novel covers ground which Gautier later covered more economically but not more licentiously in his *Mademoiselle de Maupin* (1835), describing the transvestite adventures of the youthful hero. It is light-hearted debauchery, but by no means soul-less. The Chevalier loves and wishes to marry the sister of a friend, Sophie, his courtship of whom does not interrupt his numerous affairs but is made much more difficult by them. Towards the end of the first volume he succeeds in marrying Sophie, but immediately loses her in mysterious circumstances and is only eventually reunited with her when he has been driven mad by remorse for the death of another mistress. *Les Amours . . . de Faublas* is a strange book, not without considerable charm in its way, combining erotic adventure with melodramatic moralising within the frame provided by a story of honest love. What is especially interesting about it is the presence of these elements together and the failure to relate them coherently. In itself it is a comment on the political career of its creator, engaged in direct political action under the impetus of strong revolutionary fervour, at the same time drawn strongly to represent in fiction a character completely at the mercy of sexual circumstances and quite unable to do this without recourse to manipulation and absurd machinery.

This one example suggests an interpretation of the period around 1789 that is borne out by other cases. In a time of great intellectual excitement, when orthodox morality had broken down completely under the pressure of Enlightenment criticism, writers sought to explore the libertine idea of mankind in the interests of a new morality. They failed, in the short term, for the same reasons that brought about the failure of the Revolution itself. Behind the intellectual advance, there was inadequate social or cultural pressure. Social and cultural forms, held back by the centralising orthodoxy of the *ancien régime*, disintegrated rather than developed. It is significant that when the end of the Revolution came, with the rise of Napoleon Bonaparte, there was a return to established cultural patterns. One of the first beneficiaries of the Revolution had been the notorious Marquis de Sade, incarcerated in 1772 by order of the Parlement, guardian of morality in pre-Revolutionary Paris, and freed in 1789. During the Revolution de Sade published his works, including *Justine ou les malheurs de la vertu*, but under the Consulate he found himself in prison again — this time as a lunatic!

It is striking that French fiction of this period shows very little originality in terms of action or social setting. It continues narrow in social range, reflecting a continual preoccupation with the master-servant relationship and it also reflects an incapacity to reconcile conflicting attitudes to human character. On the one hand the material-ism of the Enlightenment critics of orthodoxy stressed the sexual impulses so as to overturn conventional ideas about the function of the will. On the other hand the sentimentalism which had been strongly developing throughout the middle years of the century, often in the writings of the *philosophes* themselves, emphasised the importance of the emotions and the tender affections of love and benevolence as the basis of value and meaning in human life. Louvet de Couvray is a victim of this situation, but he was by no means alone. More substantial writers suffered similarly in their work as novelists, failing to project an image of contemporary life as a coherent whole because this could not be done in terms of the values which most concerned them.

One of the factors contributing to the Revolution was the deliberate attempt by some contemporary authors to cast scorn on the social classifications of the *ancien régime* by depicting noblemen as inferior to their servants. The most famous example is Beaumarchais' *Le Mariage de Figaro*, which created an enormous effect in Paris in the years before its publication in 1784, in spite of royal censorship. This was preceded in date of composition by Diderot's *Jacques le Fataliste et son Maître*, which was not published until after the author's death, in 1796. Diderot's novel is revolutionary in itself, if only in its humour. Leaning heavily on Laurence Sterne's *Tristram Shandy* (1759–67), Diderot flouts all the neo-classic ideas about unity of narration, composition, unity of time and place. Focusing his narrative on a particular journey undertaken by the master and valet, a journey to and from places unspecified, he creates a bewildering pattern of narratives which intersect and interrupt each other and begin again and again without finishing, and yet maintains a fundamental unity and coherence of tone. Diderot also introduces an element of social democracy greater than the French novel had seen before. The personal relationship between Jacques and his master transcends the relationship between servant and master, partly because of Jacques' greater readiness, courage and general ability, but mainly because the emotional bond between the two men makes it irrelevant. The scene in which the master, piqued by Jacques' assertion of their equality as lovers, tries to reassert his authority over the servant, is a brilliantly comical demolition of social pretentiousness.

However, it is interesting that Diderot remains within the framework of comedy, just as he maintains the master-servant relationship which Le Sage too had been unable to dispense with, without being able to expand his characters to the dimensions attained by Don Quixote and Sancho, where social classifications become irrelevant. And it is interesting to notice that Diderot remains dependent on the techniques of the novel of the seventeenth century. His use of the *nouvelle* and inserted *conte* in *Jacques le Fataliste* is brilliant, but fundamentally similar to that of Scarron in *Le Romant comique*. From this point of view Diderot's novel represents a regression from the work of Marivaux. If we compare the latter's *Le Paysan parvenu* (1735–36), especially, with *Jacques le Fataliste*, we notice immediately that although Diderot is insisting continually that what he is giving us is an historical account of contemporary reality, he is quite unable to present a single context in which the different social levels represented by his central characters can be coherently related. It would not be fair to say that he also fails to present a coherent idea of human character as a whole, because he does this through the cleverly interpolated *nouvelle* about the Marquis des Arcis and Mme de La Pommeraye, but it is true to say that it is very much left to the reader himself to make the relationship between the view of character offered here and what he learns about human beings through studying the narratives and the relationship of Jacques and his master. As far as they are concerned, and we must suspect, as far as Diderot himself was concerned, the dichotomy we noticed in Louvet de Couvray's work, between sexual impulses and sentimental affection, remains, and looks as if it is one of the main factors in governing the humoristic mode of the novel.

One of the most powerful forces at work in France at the time was the work of Rousseau, which greatly added to the strength of those who were working to undermine the ethos of the *ancien régime*, but Rousseau himself was aware of the destructive and impoverishing effects of some aspects of Enlightenment thought. Consequently he tried to reconcile the views of the *philosophes* with those of the orthodox upholders of the moral view of mankind. Ironically, he made the situation much worse, because *La Nouvelle Héloise*, which was designed to effect this reconciliation, annoyed both sides by its outrageous idealism. The effect on contemporary sensibility was in a way disastrous because his novel gave such an enormous boost to sentimentalism itself in a world not socially capable of receiving it, creating needs and expectations which could not possibly be satisfied. The Revolution could sweep away the political forms and institutions of the *ancien régime* but it could not in one lifetime initiate social reforms which would lead to the development of a society based on Rousseau-an ideals. Even Rousseau himself suffered. To say nothing of his biography, but considering him merely as a novelist, we cannot read *La Nouvelle Héloise* without noticing how much he had to pay in terms of absurdity and strain as the price of the great effort of idealism which underlay his vision of human character.

The composition of *La Nouvelle Héloise* followed Rousseau's withdrawal from Paris to the countryside and his decision to live a more natural life, and it is mixed up with his partly Platonic passion for the mistress of his friend Saint-Lambert, Mme Sophie Houdenot. In a state of acute emotional excitement Rousseau invented characters who would satisfy desires in their creator which were incapable of being satisfied in the real world: 'The impossibility of attaining the real persons precipitated me into the land of chimeras; and seeing nothing that existed worthy of my exalted feelings, I fostered them in an ideal world which my creative imagination soon peopled with beings after my own heart.'[62] He began by imagining two woman friends and inventing a lover for one of them—'to whom the other was a tender friend and even something more'[63]—and endowing the lover with his own virtues and his own faults. Through the scheme of education

---

[62] 'L'impossibilité d'atteindre aux réels me jeta dans le pays des chimères; et ne voyant rien d'existant qui fût digne de mon delire, je le nourris dans un monde idéal, que mon imagination créatrice eut bientôt peuplé d'êtres selon mon coeur.' *Les Confessions*, ix; ed. Ad. Van Bever (1926), II, p. 274.

[63] '. . . dont l'autre fut la tendre amie, et même quelque chose de plus.' *Op. cit.*, p. 278.

projected by her lover for Julie he expresses the fundamentally idealist view of human nature which underlies the whole work. The number of books Julie is to study are drastically reduced. Languages and history are to be abandoned for the most part, and Julie is to concentrate on eliciting the riches of her own nature:

> . . . je pense que quand on a une fois l'entendement ouvert par l'habitude de réfléchir, il vaut toujours mieux trouver de soi-même les choses qu'on trouverait dans les livres; c'est le vrai secret de les bien mouler à sa tête, et de se les approprier: au lieu qu'en les recevant telles qu'on nous les donne, c'est presque toujours sous une forme qui n'est pas la notre.

> I think that once one's understanding has been opened by the habit of reflection, it is always better to find out for oneself those things which are found in books; it is the true secret of moulding them to one's self and assimilating them; whereas in receiving them as they are given, it is almost always in a form which is not our own.
>
> *Julie ou La Nouvelle Héloise*, Letter xii (1761); ed. M. Launay (1967), p. 29

Rather than trusting to books, Julie's lover argues, we should rely on ourselves, because our own feelings will be the best guides, not only in matters of taste, but also where morality is concerned:

> Sitôt qu'on veut rentrer en soi-même, chacun sent ce qui est bien, chacun discerne ce qui est beau; nous n'avons pas besoin qu'on nous apprenne à connaître ni l'un ni l'autre, et l'on ne s'en impose là-dessus qu'autant qu'on veut s'en imposer.

> As soon as we wish to return into ourselves, each one of us feels what is good, each one discerns what is beautiful; there is no need for anyone to teach us to recognise either one or the other, and we are only imposed on in this respect to the extent that we wish to be.

A little farther on in the same letter he comes to the central tenet of his philosophy—that goodness is what the soul recognises as beautiful:

> J'ai toujours cru que le bon n'était que le beau mis en action, que l'un tenait intimement à l'autre, et qu'ils avaient tous deux une source commune dans la nature bien ordonée. Il suit de cette idée que le goût

se perfectionne par les mêmes moyens que la sagesse, et qu'une âme bien touchée des charmes de la vertu doit à proportion être aussi sensible à tous les autres genres de beautés.

I have always believed that the good is only the beautiful put into action, that the one is intimately related to the other, and that they both have a common source in the well ordered nature. It follows from this idea that taste perfects itself by the same means as wisdom, and that a soul which is really sensitive to the charms of virtue must also be proportionately sensitive to all other kinds of beauty.

This was the sentimentalism through which Rousseau hoped to reconcile the Encyclopedists with their opponents and which actually to some extent displaced them both. It represented a step more revolutionary than the critical materialism of the *philosophes* and yet at the same time did provide the basis for a later revival of religious feeling. But in the short term both rationalism and orthodoxy were undermined by the sentimentalism of Julie's St Prieux. If their story was to inculcate the sacredness of morality and marital fidelity, as Rousseau hoped, it was to be on a new basis, according to the idea that they were the highest means to the development of the individual soul and not the ends of the individual's moral conduct.

The story of *La Nouvelle Héloise* was aptly summarised by one of Rousseau's contemporary English readers in rather amusingly typical, but essentially accurate terms:

A young lady, the only and darling child of a man of rank, and proud of that rank, conceives a passionate attachment for a youth entrusted with the delicate charge of her education; a clandestine intercourse is carried on; the impossibility of union reverberates the flame, and kindles intolerable ardour; the youth is modest and reserved; the enamoured maid invites him to her bed, and rewards his passion with the last favour a virgin can bestow: an improper sympathy is suspected by the father; he proposes and presses an equal match on which he had long set his heart: she reluctantly consents; she dismisses her lover; she marries; she resumes her old correspondence with her favourite paramour; she admits him, with her husband's permission, an inmate of the house; she is indulged with opportunities of renewing with him the passionate scenes, and reviving the harrowing remembrances, of former days; and expires in this unnatural intercourse.

T. Green, *Extracts from the Diary of a Lover of Literature* (1810),
p. 74

With one or two additions, this may stand as a reasonable account of
the plot of the novel: we need to add that Julie's husband is equal in
fortune but not in age or in temperament, and that she only agrees to
marry him after her father's violence has brought about a miscarriage;
and that her husband knows all about her history before he agrees to
accept her unwilling hand. It is still worth stating it as baldly as this
because of Rousseau's success in weaving round the bones of the plot a
garment of eloquence and enthusiasm which carried many contemporary readers completely away from the harsh reality of life. In Rousseau's scheme Julie herself represents an essentially pure and elevated
soul, carried away by her own passion for St Prieux, but capable of
sublimating it and making it the means of a farther refinement of her
own nature and his. She is the counterpart to her husband's stoical
atheism and eventually the means by which he is converted to a
religious belief which stems in her case from her emotional nature. Her
lover—St Prieux in their correspondence but never given his real
name—changes because of his relationship with Julie from a creature
of his own passions to a man who can control them. In the first instance
he is swept away by the passion which Rousseau represents as the debt
which a noble nature pays to beauty and virtue co-existing in the
heroine. Later he purifies this feeling until virtue itself becomes the
object of his highest desire and the demands of his physical nature
subside. This happens only as a result of Julie's patient guidance, the
helpful friendship of the calm-natured Englishman, Lord Edward
Bomstock, and the cautious oversight of Julie's husband himself, M.
Wolmar.

If we compare the actual situation with the interpretation which
Rousseau gives it, the weakness of his scheme is immediately apparent.
Julie's death itself is a condemnation of what Green aptly called the
'unnatural intercourse' in which she was engaged. As far as Rousseau
was concerned it was the completion of his plan, the final vindication of
human nature in its most elevated form, showing the power of natural
religion in the pure soul. But to the modern reader it is likely to appear
as the one natural thing in Julie's conduct after her marriage, a triumph
of her human nature, in all its complexity, over the super-ego. For Julie
dies from nothing more than a wetting which she gets when one of her
children falls into the water. Her deathbed was obviously suggested by

that of Clarissa, indeed her whole character, but whereas Richardson showed the will dominating over instinct, Rousseau actually shows the reverse.

There is a good deal that is hectic or perverse about all the characters in *La Nouvelle Héloise* from one time to another. Claire's response to Julie's death is wildly enthusiastic and worthy of Rousseau himself. M. Wolmar, in his decision to marry Julie in spite of her indifference to him, is never fully excused. Lord Edward is incredibly enthusiastic and tactless. St Prieux is negative to the point of being completely uninteresting. The novel as a whole, in fact, is kept alive and indeed intriguing by Rousseau himself, writing through the pens of his various correspondents. In striking contrast to those in *Clarissa Harlowe*, his letters maintain a consistent tone regardless of characterisation and address the reader directly. His whole novel, in fact, succeeds as an essay rather than a fiction. As a novel, indeed—that is, as a fiction which genuinely attempted to present human nature in terms of its contemporary manifestations—it could not have succeeded, because the characters Rousseau created existed nowhere in contemporary France or Switzerland. Or at least, had they existed, their actual story would have related to the one that Rousseau wrote in the same way that Fielding's *Shamela* related to *Pamela, or Virtue Rewarded*.

The enormous success of *La Nouvelle Héloise* increased the problems that Rousseau himself had faced and failed to overcome. By giving concrete shape and clear direction to the forces which showed themselves in eighteenth-century sentimentalism, he made it harder for other novelists who felt the influence of his work to locate their own fictions in contemporary reality. Consequently anything like complete success in the novel in France in the period after Rousseau is rare indeed. Indeed, Choderlos de Laclos seems to stand almost quite alone. Laclos confirms Rousseau at every point. *Les Liaisons dangereuses* takes an action from a world which is fundamentally awry precisely because it does not recognise the validity of Rousseau's ideas about human beings. The characters in Laclos' novel all respond naturally to the nature of the world in which they find themselves and find their way to disaster because of the disharmony between their own nature and the conditions in which they have to live.

It is often felt that Laclos himself lacked confidence in his own scheme. It is significant that the novel should have been most severely attacked in the periods of greater formality—it was condemned as dangerous under the Restoration, for example, though left alone during the Revolutionary period. Laclos felt obliged to pander to a contemporary idea of the morality of fiction in making his heroine suffer at the end of the novel from a disfigurement—the loss of an eye—as well as loss of her fortune, but this is a superficial matter. The important thing is that the damage—her exposure, and the consequent loss of social status and the power to manipulate others—has already taken place. The subsequent loss of her fortune and her beauty are relatively unimportant matters. The closing of the action is not really important either; the action is effectively ended by the breakdown of the relationship which it relates, that between Mme de Merteuil and M. de Valmont. The fact that they are evil does not impair the important fact that they are also the hero and the heroine, that their evil is seen as an instinctive response to the world in which they find themselves and that they are destroyed ultimately by their inability to deal with their own human nature. The alliance between them is an aggressive one against other people, but perhaps just as much a defensive one, in which they try to protect themselves from their knowledge of each other. Its breaking down reduces them to the weakness of their own victims, and inevitably destroys them. The world reasserts itself at the end of the novel, victorious over human nature.

Mme de Merteuil and Valmont conspire in an unholy alliance to manipulate other people, primarily through their sexuality, for no discernible motive other than the satisfaction of their own vanity and love of power. Accordingly, while Valmont woos the virtuous Mme de Tourvel, he also, in consultation with Mme de Merteuil, a friend and relative of Mme de Volanges, incites and forwards an intrigue between her daughter and the Chevalier de Danceny and seduces her himself. It is fascinating to study the way in which all these characters are drawn into the net of intrigue by methods which are subtly varied according to their different natures and situations. To Mme La Présidente de Tourvel Valmont pleads tenderness of feeling:

> Par où, dites-moi, ai-je mérité cette rigueur désolante? Je ne crains pas de vous prendre pour juge: qu'ai-je donc fait? que céder à un sentiment involontaire, inspiré par la beauté et justifié par la vertu; toujours contenu par le respect, et dont l'innocent aveu fut l'effet de la confiance et non de l'espoir. . . .

> How, tell me, have I deserved to be treated with this crushing severity? I am not afraid to let you be my judge: what, then, have I done? but yield to an involuntary feeling, inspired by beauty, sanctioned by virtue: always kept within the bounds of respect, the

innocent avowal of which was the effect not of hope but of trust?
Les Liaisons dangereuses, Lettre XXIV; *Oeuvres Complètes*, ed.
M. Allen (1951), pp. 55–6

To such appeals Mme de Tourvel has eventually no answer to make.
Valmont's case is quite unanswerable when urged by a man who is
tender, handsome, affectionate to a woman whose own nature seems to
echo his own.

With the almost idiotically naïve Cécile de Volanges Valmont's
methods are totally different and quite diabolical in their coolness and
effrontery. He relies entirely on naïveté, on Cécile's mixture of fear,
ignorance of what is being done, and her instinctive physical response.
The letter describing her seduction, after she has given him a key to her
room under the impression that it will forward the intrigue with
Danceny, whom she genuinely loves, is a masterpiece, drawing on the
long tradition established by Challes, and developed in their different
ways by Crébillon and Richardson. Mme de Merteuil's seduction of
Danceny is equally instructive, the method in this case depending on a
subtle mixture of sentiment and sensuality, employed in her role as
consultress regarding the ironically slow-moving affair with Cécile.

In neither one of these three instances does the victim have any
adequate defence to make. Cécile's case is the most obvious. Brought
up in the convent in complete ignorance of the nature of the world, of
contemporary society, and of her own body, she is quite unable to deal
with a man of Valmont's experience. Her ineffective defence is followed
by actual corruption. She becomes, in effect, common, deceitful and
depraved, all the time under Valmont's expert tuition. Her case has
been taken to imply the author's cynical view of human nature, and at
first sight it might seem an attack on Rousseauean ideas about the
simplicity of uncorrupted youth. But in fact Cécile has been prepared
by her upbringing for what happens to her. Far from being natural, her
ignorance is highly unnatural; and far from being her natural protec-
tress, even her mother plays into Valmont's hands. Firstly she frus-
trates the natural development of the affair with Danceny, determined
to marry her daughter to an older man whom she has never met, for the
sake of her 'happiness'. For all her virtue and decency Cécil's mother
has the most formal and superficial ideas, entirely reflecting her social
situation, and the fact that she allows herself to be manipulated by
Mme de Merteuil into actually persecuting Cécile is only the natural
consequence of the fact that her whole attitude to her daughter is based
on a mistrust of her nature and a determination to make her fit in with a

preconceived, and shallowly conceived, idea of human nature and happiness.

Danceny is also an easy target because he has nothing to fall back on in his relationship with Mme de Merteuil and Valmont but commonplace ideas of virtue and honour which belong to his class. The case of M. de Préval, whom Mme de Merteuil manoeuvres into a situation where he loses social status, rank and even freedom and honour, indicates the tenuous nature of the gentleman's hold on all these sources of moral stability. Danceny's case is illuminated by this. When he is undeceived as to the whole sordid affair in which he has played so ignominious a part his response is quite pointless. He withdraws like Cécile from society, but withdraws into the order of the Knights of Malta, abandoning a world which he cannot make the effort to understand.

Mme de Tourvel's case is more pathetic precisely because she has a depth of nature which makes her abandonment of virtue an act of real importance. Mme de Tourvel is a virtuous woman, a woman who has taken fully to heart the moral precepts of her day, who has withdrawn from the world of vanity and does her best to follow the precepts of religion. Her abandonment of them in responding to Valmont after his intense wooing, is an implicit criticism of them. She can never afterwards fully regret her love, even after her terrible disillusionment. And though Valmont proves unworthy of it, she still prays for him on her deathbed. The happiness she has known, the level of experience her love has opened to her, make it impossible for her to continue living at all. Her death, entirely natural and so much more convincingly rendered than that of Rousseau's Julie, stems from a similar failure on the part of nature to adjust to what is quite unacceptable.

This moving death scene is in effect a condemnation of the whole range of ideas which are meant to suffice for the characters in the society which the novel depicts. But we are not left only with the point as Mme de Tourvel's death gives it us. Her fate, after all, comes to us only as an incident in the development of the relationship between Valmont and Mme de Merteuil, and the important thing is that their fate brings home exactly the same point. They are characters, in fact, who have realised the shallowness of contemporary ideas of virtue and decency, who understand the inevitable discrepancy between profession and action in a society which organises itself on purely formal principles. Understanding this, they attempt to exploit their own intelligence so as to control their environment and allow their nature full scope for its expression. The problem for them is two-fold. Firstly, they suffer from an inability to admit the demands of emotion—love, for them—in the Chevalier's case at least, an all important motive—does not exist as a serious force. And consequently he is drawn on by Mme de Merteuil to deny his affection for Mme de Tourvel and inflict the cruellest of injuries on her. Beyond this, however, lies another factor, which eventually destroys them. In judging human nature in general from the society in which they found themselves, they had implicitly judged their own nature. Human beings they saw as creatures either exploited and manipulated by their own desires or by other people's, and they attempt to free themselves from their situation by systematising their own desires and attaining mastery over them. Their friendship is an attempt to extend their own freedom and their sphere of action. Ironically it leads to their downfall precisely because they cannot admit of any link but that of self-interest. And self-interest is not as strong as the instinct, purely irrational as it is, towards power. Both these quintessential villains, manipulators of others, fail to control themselves. Both are drawn on, inevitably, through the manipulations that are permitted within the alliance, eventually to deny the alliance. The novel's splendid climax is contained in the letter with which Mme de Merteuil replies to Valmont's assertion that their relationship is such that they must either love or hate: 'Very well: war.'[64]

In that declaration, their eventual destruction is contained, as they both had previously admitted. It comes with complete inevitability, and that is the factor which triumphantly justifies Laclos's choice of hero, heroine and plot. Through their relationship he finds an action which permits him to make an astonishingly deep analysis of the possibilities of response to the society he depicts. It is one in which relations based on affection are impossible. And yet, as his characterisation of Mme de Merteuil and Valmont brilliantly implies, relationships which are not so based are eventually self-destructive. The implication is directly in support of Rousseau, and directly, too, in support of our thesis concerning the development of the novel. Only a novel written in this manner, in a mirror, could succeed in this transitional period. To live in society and to live satisfactorily in 1782, Laclos suggests, is impossible, just as Rousseau had asserted the same thing in 1758. The friendship between his two central characters is a distorting mirror which yet leaves this central point completely clear.

[64]'Hé bien! la guerre.' P. 362.

THE LIFE AND OPINIONS OF TRISTRAM SHANDY; SENSE AND SENSIBILITY FROM 1758

We can look at the period from 1758 to 1800 in England as preceding the appearance of the novels of Jane Austen, or following the publication of *Tristram Shandy* (1759–67). Either way, it is not of great intrinsic interest. It would be unfair to associate this too closely with the accession to the throne of George III—the loss of America is enough to hold against him, without taking the decline of the novel into account—but the beginning of his reign does mark a change in manners which affected the nation as a whole. The decency of the Royal Family under George III, strikingly new in its time, became increasingly typical of the upper classes as a whole in the years leading up to the century's end. Typical too was the pride which George took in his title of the Patriot King, in being and speaking English, rather than the German of his Hanoverian predecessors. This is the period too of the Pitts, father and son, who shared the patriotism of the monarch and who prepared for expansion overseas and naval supremacy by introducing greater efficiency in government and impartiality in statesmanship than the eighteenth century had previously seen. This is the period when Catholicism ceased to be a political threat, when Jacobitism and Toryism were finally separated, leaving Dr Johnson free to make his purely cultural tour of the Scottish Highlands and even to indulge the sentiment of nostalgia for a vanished society. An increasing self-consciousness and confidence, greatly accentuated by the events following the French Revolution, is the keynote of the period, and with it went a conservatism in cultural matters which operated very strongly on the novel. In these years any form of subversive thought was strongly suspect and strongly discouraged. Sentimentalism, the strongest current in eighteenth-century thinking, was lumped together with free-thinking and political radicalism and deliberately channelled within the conduits provided by an anxious orthodoxy. The novel itself was labelled a dangerous form and a host of essayists and lady writers laboured hard to refashion it into an expression of the national moral interest.

This conservatism was by no means wholly a negative movement, but reflected a feeling that sentimentalism and other progressive tendencies threatened moral and cultural values which were inextricably connected with various institutions. It is worth noting the conclusion of the English critic of Rousseau already mentioned, who appealed to a typically practical and modified sentimentalism in his condemnation of *La Nouvelle Héloise*:

> We see by an intuitive glance, we feel by an instinctive thrill, all the pestilent disorders which would flow in upon us, from our encouragement, from our toleration, of such practices; from our not driving them, as we do, by common consent, from society, with shame and scorn and detestation. It requires no logic to convince us, that if the settled restrictions on these subjects were once removed, and nothing substituted but loose personal discretion, swayed by every gust of appetite and passion, that all domestic security and comfort, all parental care, all filial duty, all pure and hallowed affection, all conjugal confidence and endearment, would be overwhelmed under a flood of gross adulterous lust and corrupted sentiment.
>
> T. Green, *Extracts from the Diary of a Lover of Literature* (1810),
> p. 75

A bit highly-coloured, we may have the benefit of thinking, now that the dreadful event has finally come about, but substantially a reasonable objection. What Green feared was that sentimentalism would actually destroy emotional life because that itself depended on relationships which were necessarily institutionalised, and his fear is closely related to the factors which combined to affect the development of English Romanticism in this period as a movement which reflected a strong sense of place and appreciation of man's relationship with nature and a concern for the integrity of human experience and character as a whole. At the same time writers like Green took care to maintain the importance of sensibility as the basis of practical charity and personal relationships. As the Reverend Vicessimus Knox, one of the most popular and highly respected of contemporary essayists, explained:

> Sensibility, with all its inconveniences, is to be cherished by those who understand and wish to maintain the dignity of their nature. To feel for others disposes us to exercise the amiable virtue of charity, which our religion indispensably requires. It constitutes that enlarged benevolence which philosophy inculcates, and which is indeed comprehended in Christian charity. It is the privilege and ornament of man; and the pain which it causes is abundantly recompensed by that sweet sensation which ever accompanies the exercise of benefi-

cence.
'On True Patience, As Distinguished from Insensibility,' *Essays, moral and Literary*, No. 163 (1782); *The British Essayists, University Edition* V (1828), p. 265

We might be hearing here the narrator of Diderot's subversive *Le Neveu de Rameau*, assuring his wretched companion that it is impossible to be unhappy with two good deeds to one's credit. The difference is, of course, a matter of degree. In the Englishman's case sensibility and social orthodoxy were capable of being reconciled if 'the arms of reason and religion' were kept on hand and freely used.

What this meant in practice, as far as the novel was concerned, was that sentiment should always be shown as an important constituent of character in conjunction with a respect for propriety. In the first instance this insured a predominance of female heroines in the novels of the period. Secondly it condemned them to insipidity and prevented the development of sensible plotting. The heroine of the period was not merely sensitive. She had to show that she was sensitive towards the connection between personal restraint and social form on the one hand and moral values and emotional fulfilment on the other. It was on this connection that the weight of a thousand essays and novels of the period fell. And indeed it is true to say that the novel itself was consciously re-shaped in order to direct the reader's attention to it. Around *Clarissa Harlowe*, some aspects of which were delicately veiled, stood a whole ring of commentators, like Vicessimus Knox, Dr Hawkesworth and Samuel Johnson, all conscious of the novel's potential danger for youthful readers and females of all ages and classes and all determined that it should be forced out of the paths fashioned for it by writers like Fielding, Smollett and Rousseau. The effects were disastrous!

These can be clearly seen in the career of a writer like Fanny Burney, who is exceptional only because she showed quite such a high degree of promise as a novelist and underwent such a positive decline. Fanny Burney's first novel, *Evelina* (1778), met with a deservedly enthusiastic reception and was highly praised by the highest authorities, including Johnson himself. *Evelina* showed wit, spirit, sharp social observation and contained a sensitive treatment of the emotions of its young heroine. Two factors might have been disturbing at the time, though they would have been forgiven such a young authoress. These were her dependence on Marivaux's *La Vie de Marianne* as a model and her tendency to coarsen the issues raised by the situation of her heroine, sensitive beyond her apparent status in society. Evelina never develops as a strong character as Marianne does, so the question of social status never becomes one of identity. She is a passive character and most of the action derives from the interplay of other characters who represent different social groups.

In *Evelina*, in fact, there is very little for the heroine to do, except demonstrate her sensitivity and await the development of the plot, which is completely mechanical and without any intrinsic interest. In *Cecilia* (1782) the same characteristics are more prominent. The heroine is again quite passive and indeed, so helpless in dealing with experience that she finally runs mad in a pawnbroker's shop. The novel is supposed to direct our attention to the dangers of 'PRIDE AND PREJUDICE', which, we are told at the end by an authoritative doctor, has been the cause of it all. But the only real importance in this is that it served Jane Austen as the title for her own novel. *Cecilia* actually focuses on the dilemma of the heroine who is constantly threatened with social displacement as a result of her passion for the hero and her acute sense of propriety. When we come to *Camilla* (1796), the picture is bleaker still. By this time Fanny Burney had run out of ways of concentrating attention on the female sensibility under strain. The action of *Camilla* is grotesquely unconvincing and the novel absurdly boring. It could have been marginally more interesting if the author had let her heroine actually starve to death instead of rescuing her at the last moment, but even that would not have made much difference.

Fanny Burney wrote one novel after *Camilla—The Wanderer; or, Female Difficulties* (1814), but we can safely pass it by in silence, not only because it is so much worse even than *Camilla* but because Jane Austen had already transformed the scene by the publication of her novels. In Jane Austen's development Fanny Burney's fiction had been an important element. Their background is very similar and their values almost interchangeable. The difference between them derives from the shift of emphasis which Jane Austen was able to achieve, as a result of which she could work out her moral preoccupations in terms of situations which reflected the conditions of actual social life. Her technique as a novelist, working through directly represented scenes and conversations, is dependent on the type of situation she chooses and the kind of action she develops from it. Her choice of this type of situation cannot be attributed simply to personality but may be seen in connection with the fact that she is so much of a *practical* moralist as distinct from so many other female writers who had preceded her. Among these Fanny Burney stands out precisely because she might have been expected to develop towards the type of action that Jane

Austen achieved and yet she so signally failed. The failure was inevitable, resulting from the fact that she thought of the function of the novel as being much more abstract than Jane Austen did. She was concerned not so much primarily to study contemporary forms of sensibility and behaviour as to project them against the pattern personalities of her heroines. Life for these poor creatures was a series of tests, all proceeding to the same conclusion. This was the demonstration of the various ways that true sensibility poured itself into the moulds provided by social propriety and orthodox morality. Jane Austen fortunately had a touch of irreverence about her, in spite of her seriousness, and she put the novel back on the path marked out for it by the work of Fielding and Richardson together.

Laurence Sterne might be said to be at the opposite extreme to Jane Austen. Whereas she found it possible to reconcile sense and sensibility by representing the forms of contemporary social life, he found it impossible to reconcile them at all. In his work they are held in uneasy balance through the medium of humour. Like Jane Austen, Sterne was socially and culturally a conservative, accepting the religious and philosophical orthodoxies of his day. In Yorick's sermon in *Tristram Shandy* he shows himself a faithful supporter of the Establishment in Church and State, reflecting in his view of man a mixture of caution and common sense which is directly attributable to the influence of John Locke. Neither self-knowledge nor self-consciousness will help against evil disposition or self-interest, argues Yorick's sermon, read out to the approving Shandy brothers by Corporal Trim. If the individual has no will to virtue in the first place, then conscience is powerless, no more, as Locke put it, than 'Our own opinion of our own actions'.[65] And even if he does possess a will to virtue, he still needs the support of morality and religion. Yorick is a true Lockean and a true supporter of social orthodoxy in his day. His idea of virtue is identical with that of Locke, whose opinion being that God 'by an inseparable connection, joined virtue and public happiness together, and made the practice thereof necessary to the preservation of society, and visibly beneficial to all', inevitably came to emphasise the human faculties which encouraged conformity.[66] Yorick's idea of virtue involves being 'an honest man, an useful citizen, a faithful subject to your king, or a good servant to your God' and depends on a rather confusing combination of 'the law of God', 'calm reason' and the 'unchangeable obligations of justice and

[65] *An Essay concerning Human Understanding* (1690); ed. A. C. Fraser (1894), I, p. 71.
[66] *Op. cit.*, I, p. 70.

truth'.[67] In his mind rationalism and authoritarianism are in an uneasy balance.

Locke's philosophy was a sharp weapon in the hands of Anglican divines such as Yorick and Laurence Sterne, to be used against the Catholic Church, but it was not their only weapon. Catholicism was still felt to be a pressing danger in 1758. Anglican thinking, and indeed, English thought in general, had been formed for more than two generations under the political and religious threat of Jacobitism and Jesuit intrigue. Dr Slop's Catholicism in *Tristram Shandy* lacks a political dimension, reflecting the political defeat of Jacobitism following the 1745 rebellion, in the repression of which Sterne's own uncle had played such a prominent part. But it is interesting that in the absence of an immediate political threat what Yorick's sermon does, performing the reflex of Anglican polemic, is turn to the Inquisition in its operation in Catholic countries and present this as a threat to humanity in general. *Tristram Shandy* contains a running attack on Catholicism in general on the grounds of intolerance and inhumanity. The great curse of Ernulphus is one part of this. Sterne also tends to criticise the French government and way of life for a similar lack of humanity, and reasonableness, deriving from over-centralisation and officiousness. The ground of his attack in both cases is sentiment, which is brought out strongly throughout the novel.

One of the classic moments in *Tristram Shandy*, summarising the spirit of the whole book, and indeed, a whole literary movement, is when Uncle Toby catches the fly:

> —Go—says he, one day at dinner, to an over-grown one which had buzzed about his nose, and tormented him cruelly all dinner-time, —and which after infinite attempts, he had caught at last, as it flew by him; —I'll not hurt thee, says my uncle *Toby*, rising from his chair, and going across the room, with the fly in his hand, —I'll not hurt a hair of thy head: —Go, says he, lifting up the sash, and opening his hand as he spoke, to let it escape; go, poor devil, get thee gone, why should I hurt thee?—This world surely is wide enough to hold both thee and me.
>
> *The Life and Opinions of Tristram Shandy* II, xii; ed. G. Saintsbury (1912), p. 82

This is no more than the most extravagant and touching manifestation

[67] *The Life and Opinions of Tristram Shandy, Gentleman* (1760–67), II, xiv; ed. G. Saintsbury (1912), p. 96.

of the benevolence which informs Toby's whole character and which plays an important part in the character of the narrator as well. During the sermon-reading it comes prominently into play, asserting itself as a principle of human nature capable of overcoming even religious prejudice but strongest where prejudice is replaced by reason. Yorick's sermon argues that where human sympathy is absent religion itself will be undermined, and presents a harrowing picture of the suffering of a prisoner of the Inquisition. Corporal Trim, reading the sermon, is moved by the thought that his own brother is in the hands of the Inquisition in Portugal and although his response is irrational and attracts the scorn of Dr Slop, it strikes a sympathetic chord in the hearts of all his listeners:

> 'Behold *Religion*, with *Mercy* and *Justice* chained down under her feet, — there sitting ghastly upon a black tribunal, propped up with racks and instruments of torment. Hark! — hark! what a piteous groan!' — [Here *Trim's* face turned as pale as ashes.] — 'See the melancholy wretch who uttered it' — [Here the tears began to trickle down.] — 'just brought forth to undergo the anguish of a mock trial, and endure the utmost pains that a studied system of cruelty has been able to invent.' — [D-n them all, quoth *Trim*, his color returning into his face as red as blood.] — 'Behold this helpless victim delivered up to his tormentors, his body so wasted with sorrow and confinement!' — [Oh! 'tis my brother, cried poor *Trim* in a most passionate exclamation, dropping the sermon upon the ground, and clapping his hands together, — I fear 'tis poor *Tom*. — My father's and my uncle *Toby's* heart yearned with sympathy for the poor fellow's distress; even *Slop* himself acknowledged pity for him. . . .]
> *The Life and Opinions of Tristram Shandy* II, xvii, p. 101

The consolation that Walter Shandy offers Trim is quite ineffective. It matters not in the least, after all, that Trim is reading an imaginary description rather than an historical account. As we know ourselves, reading the scene in much the same spirit that Trim is reading the sermon, the pain lies in the contemplation of such evils as actually existing and not in the thought that they have existed in historical time. Thereby Yorick's theological point is strongly made.

In his sentimentalism Sterne represents a strong English tradition which goes back to the work of Steele and Addison and Lord Shaftesbury, through the work of Fielding. Sterne shows no immediate influence from French writers and no tendency to develop sentimentalism as Rousseau had, as an instrument of revolutionary change in morals and manners. In England the history of sentimentalism is closely connected with the development of a tradition of humorous writing which culminates in the nineteenth century, in George Eliot. The humorist arouses sentiment in his reader by presenting characters whose peculiarities of manner and behaviour are amusing but legitimate responses of human nature to situations which prevent its balanced development. In spite of his oddities the humorist is essentially an integral human being capable of provoking a human response from the reader. Humour had its political dimension because eighteenth-century writers often attributed England's richness in humorous characters to its political and social freedom. As we have seen in the representation of Corporal Trim reading the sermon, it is also capable of being used in a religious context. Consequently we may think of it as a useful weapon in the armoury of the Protestant divine and the conservative essayist.

To interpret Sterne's sentimentalism in only this way, however, would be to misunderstand it. Although he refuses to develop his own mode of thinking to its logical conclusion, he is aware of certain tensions and inconsistencies in his view of the world. And indeed, *Tristram Shandy* amounts to an attempt to explore those tensions and perhaps to reconcile them. Primarily it amounts to a thorough-going critique of common-sense materialism, as represented by Locke's *Essay*. It could not have been a question for Sterne of abandoning Locke, whose thought was too intimately associated with all aspects of his own thinking. Rather it was a matter of a persistent but inconsistent review of Lockeanism. Or, in other words, a *humorous* revaluation of Locke.

Sterne makes it quite explicit that he is unable to accept Locke's mechanistic analysis of human nature. So in his Author's Preface, designed as an attack on those who criticised the integrity of his fiction on the grounds that it possessed wit but not judgement, he employs an absurd elaboration of a Lockean argument to assert that wit and judgement are different forms of an integral faculty of the mind rather than separable qualities. Justifying himself by an appeal to simplicity and clarity not dissimilar to the many Locke makes in his *Essay*, Sterne introduces a figurative analogy which Locke would definitely not have been prepared to accept. He is sitting, he tells the reader, upon a cane chair:

Will you give me leave to illustrate this affair of wit and judgement by the two knobs on the top of the back of it?—they are fastened on, you see, with two pegs stuck slightly into two gimlet-holes, and will place what I have to say in so clear a light, as to let you see through the drift and meaning of my whole preface, as plainly as if every point and particle of it was made up of sun-beams.

I now enter directly upon the point.

—Here stands *wit*—and there stands *judgement*, close beside it. . . .

—You see, they are the highest and most ornamental parts of its *frame*—as wit and judgement are of *ours*—and like them too, indubitably both made and fitted to go together, in order, as we say in all such cases of duplicated embellishments—*to answer one another.*

Tristram Shandy III, xx, p. 144

A similar method is used very frequently in *Tristram Shandy*. In fact, it could be said that this is the method of the whole book, affecting the whole conception of characterisation and the mode of narration. Uncle Toby is introduced to us by means of his hobby-horse. Sterne tells us that he is doing this because no more direct method exists, in the absence of Momus's glass from the human breast. Absurdly he argues that the heated parts of the rider, coming into constant contact with the hobby-horse, the body is eventually filled with 'HOBBY HORSICAL matter . . . so that, if you are able to give but a clear description of the nature of the one, you may form a pretty exact notion of the genius and character of the other'.[68] This humorous explanation is actually the reverse of the truth, of course, because the hobby-horse's value as an indication of character consists in the fact that it manifests the integral character of the individual, which cannot be examined by more analytical methods. In all this Sterne sticks fast to his Lockeanism, which provides him with a means of explaining why Uncle Toby began to imitate contemporary military operations on his bowling green. Uncle Toby, he explains, after another long passage in which the terms of Lockean analysis are distorted in fanciful elaboration, has been confused by words. Trying to explain where and how he obtained the wound which has confined him to bed, Toby arrives at a state of confusion from which the only issue is through practical demonstration. Toby proceeds from words, to maps, and eventually to deeds, abandoning the attempt at communication and retiring farther into his own world, which is a bizarre parody of the real one within the compass

[68] I, xxiv, p. 56.

of a bowling green.

Both Toby and his brother Walter Shandy, Tristram's father, are humorous characters who combine various defects of the understanding with a powerful capacity to attract and retain the love of those around them and the fascinated attention of the readers. Whereas Toby withdraws from the attempt to understand the world farther and farther into his own innocence and so remains unaffected by it, Walter, more active and intellectual, struggles with it in vain. Walter Shandy is enquiring and active in things of the mind. Understanding clearly the capacity of experience to form the character, he attempts to control the important circumstances of Tristram's introduction into the world. But the history of his attempt shows nothing more clearly than his total failure to control even the workings of his own mind. His external failure, which begins even at the moment of conception, continues through delivery, baptism and circumcision, and is paralleled by an internal disaster which consists in the fact that he is carried away beyond reason into absurd elaborations of the principle of determinism.

Walter Shandy's life as we know it is an unending series of frustrations, and life in general as his son presents it to us takes on the same perspective. Mankind in Tristram's view is condemned to frustration and absurdity, unable to control itself, its impulses or its circumstances. Many of his monstrous digressions point in the same direction. The Abbess of Andouillets and her novice, abandoned on the road by their bibulous driver, are forced to swear at their mules or to remain where they are. Their hopeless attempts at equivocation end in a comic admission of their inability to maintain an appropriate demeanour in a difficult situation: '"They do not understand us," cried Margarita. . . . "But the Devil does," said the Abbess of Andouillets.'[69] Slawkenbergius' tale shows a whole city affected to distraction by curiosity regarding the authenticity of an enormous nose. The story about the court of the Queen of Navarre which ends with the young Sieur de Croix having to leave the kingdom for lack of whiskers indicates the power of association which carries the weight of a sexual innuendo.

All these stories, of course, have a pronounced element of *double entendre*, which runs throughout the commentary of Tristram himself, who is not averse even to implying his own at least temporary impotence, revealed in one of his many conversations aside with Jenny.[70] This has attracted the disapproval of generations of more or less sombre-minded critics who have rightly sensed that the traditional

[69] VII, i; p. 372.
[70] VII, i, p. 378.

defence of straightforward open speaking fails to apply. Tristram's prurience is in fact an important part in the process by which he embeds his own Lockeanism in a humorously inappropriate medium. Tristram's method is one which ensures the reader's own collaboration, resulting in a two-way process by which his implications about the problematic nature of the lower instincts are made uncomfortably explicit in our understanding of them.

Tristram's method of narration has the same effect. It would not be unfair to say that in Lockean terms the whole book is a species of madness, for association of ideas in anything but a reasonable way, according to 'natural correspondence', is treated in the Essay as a universal disease attributable to the same cause as madness. What Locke meant by 'natural correspondence' here was that certain ideas are naturally linked as the things which they represent are linked in Nature. It is the office of the reason to follow out these correspondences and ignore those of chance and circumstance.[71] Sterne, however, presents the human mind as dominated by associations of chance and circumstance, as indeed it must be while men receive their ideas primarily through sense impressions. As a narrator Tristram confesses his confusion and concern at the fact that the way his story comes to him in his own reflections brings with it certain problems of order and proportion which are simply insoluble. He comments on his father's absurd failure to prepare his programme of education quickly enough to keep pace with Tristram's growth to the effect that 'the wisest of us all . . . outwit ourselves, and eternally forego our purposes in the intemperate act of pursuing them'.[72] And this is substantially true of himself.

Tristram's basic difficulty is one of order. So he must either stop in the process of narrating the events of his birth night to explain the basis of Corporal Trim and his father's misunderstanding regarding bridges, or take the risk of confusing the reader. Either way, he fears, he is likely to spoil one story, so he appeals to the powers presiding over his work in comic helplessness:

O ye powers! (for powers ye are, and great ones too)—which enable mortal man to tell a story worth the hearing—that kindly shew him, where he is to begin it—and where he is to end it—what he is to put into it—and what he is to leave out—how much of it he is to cast into a shade—and whereabouts he is to throw his light!—Ye,

[71] An Essay concerning Human Understanding, I, pp. 528–30.
[72] V, xvi, p. 276.

who preside over this vast empire of biographical freebooters, and see how many scrapes and plunges your subjects hourly fall into; — will you do one thing?

I beg and beseech you ... that wherever in any part of your dominions it so falls out that three several roads meet in one point, as they have done just here, — that at least you set up a guide-post in the centre of them, in mere charity, to direct an uncertain devil which of the three he is to take.

Tristram Shandy III, xxiii, p. 149

This is only the basic difficulty, however. Because he is narrating his own life-story according to his own version of the process of natural association of ideas, he finds himself in situations of grotesque absurdity in which the reader's sense of time is deliberately confused. So in Chapter xxviii of Book VI he pauses to draw our attention to the fact that he has created a situation in which he is doing three different things at the same time. That is, according to the time of the narrative, he is crossing the square of Auxerre with his father and Uncle Toby during his grand tour; according to his narration of the later journey through France which frames his reference to the grand tour, he is entering Lyons, having left Auxerre behind him; and according to his present time he is sitting in a handsome pavilion on the banks of the Garonne, contemplating his own difficulties.

Tristram laments at one point that he is in the same dilemma as his father and is outgrowing his own narration just as he outgrew Walter's system of education.[73] So it is impossible for him to finish his *Life and Opinions* or even to advance with them. Of course, this is true of all autobiographers, as Gines de Pasamonte knew, a long time before, but it has a special significance for Tristram. The humour and comedy of Tristram's mode of narration spring naturally from Sterne's awareness that he would have been unable on any conditions to finish Tristram's story. Sterne could not, in fact, bring Tristram's life into the present, or focus on any dimension of Tristram's experience except the continuous present of the time of narration. *Tristram Shandy* is not actually a biography, or a history of life and opinions; it is an historical novel, an exercise in historical imagination, reporting events which occurred either before or shortly after the birth of the supposed hero and at various times after that, but never centring on the consciousness of the hero as anything other than a narrator of his own story. *Tristram Shandy* entirely avoids the dimension of ordinary experience as far as

[73]IV, xiii, pp. 207–8.

the hero is concerned and also avoids the dimension of contemporary reality. It is very striking that the only two important characters who are not humorists die broken-hearted. Yorick is bruised by the world's savage reaction to his innocent wit; Le Fevre submits in the unequal battle between a hard and unfeeling universe and a soft-natured individual. Both these stories are narrated off-centre, through digression, and it is difficult to see how Sterne could have managed them in any other way. The world as they encountered it is cold and unresponsive, society lacking in honesty and charity. A direct presentation of their lives would inevitably have led to a questioning of several of Sterne's most firmly held values.

A direct presentation of Tristram's experience would have required something else which is lacking from Tristram—that is, a serious treatment of the sexual passions or affections. Sex is present in plenty in *Tristram Shandy*, of course, but we never learn the precise nature of the narrator's relationship with Jenny, nor see him making a relationship with anyone else. This is another area of experience which would have been problematic for Sterne, the area which Rousseau had developed most fully and which it would have been impossible to treat directly without representing the clash between social forms and the interests of the passions. It is the area which we most frequently associate with the novelist's art, of course, and that makes its absence from Sterne's work the more notable. Jane Austen never treats passion directly and it occurs in her work only as an aberration, but she is able to concentrate on the relations between the sexes as the sphere in which what is problematic in contemporary experience is likely to reveal itself most sharply. But of course in Jane Austen humorous characters are very much off-centre. Those who hold the centre of the stage in *Tristram Shandy*—Toby, Walter and Tristram himself—suggest a view of the world in which a normal balance of functions and faculties is impossible: that is, a world which is defective but which Sterne himself is unable to confront as such. His humorous vision is the result of his response to the world in which he lived and his humorous technique the only means by which the various potentially conflicting parts of his own sensibility could be allowed to develop without conflict. The unique balance between these elements, and particularly between sentimentalism on the one hand and Lockean philosophy on the other, was a product of his personality and at the same time a result of the period in which he lived. In the years after his death, and even immediately before, growing conservatism made even the degree of challenge he offered unacceptable. His successors consequently are his

inferiors—the gentler Goldsmith and the languorous Henry Mackenzie. After Sterne and until Jane Austen the English novel flagged. To
see how the novel could develop in these years we must look elsewhere.

THE ACHIEVEMENT OF GOETHE

In Germany in the later half of the eighteenth century the reputation of
recent English fiction stood particularly high. Not only Richardson but
Sterne and Goldsmith, on account of his *Vicar of Wakefield*, and
Fielding and Fanny Burney for different reasons, were widely read and
enthusiastically praised. But though German writers appreciated the
concrete achievement of the English novelists, their skill at treating
relationships and social scenes, their own achievement, completely
complemented that of the English novel. In Germany, to a far greater
extent than in any other European country, the central ideas of Romanticism were consciously and elaborately developed. The philosophy of
the period, in the suddenness of its rise and the breadth of its achievement, can only be compared to the change that took place so rapidly in
the English novel in the 1840s. After Kant, complementing and amend-
ing his work, but always working out their thoughts in relationship to
the same central problem, came Fichte, Schelling and Hegel, in all of
whom the organic idea is expanded and developed as a central part of
doctrine.

Against this background the achievement of German writers in the
novel is relatively slight, but the two fields throw clear light upon each
other. In the first instance the name of Christoph Wieland deserves far
more attention in the history of the novel than it has received outside
Germany. Wieland is the father of the German novel and strikes out
lines of development which Goethe developed. Starting with his satirical *Don Silvio de Rosalva* (1763), he shows himself to be firmly in the
Enlightenment tradition of using the novel as a means of asserting
judgement against fancy. He is as far from the real tradition of
Cervantes as any of the Spaniard's French imitators had ever been, and
indeed depends largely on the combination of fancifulness and indecency in the French fairy story which his novel is supposed to attack.
Wieland's solid achievement comes in his later, lengthy novel, *Agathon*
(1766–7 and 1794), which can fairly claim to be the first European
novel constructed around a process of development in the central
character, tracing the intellectual and spiritual education of its young
hero. But Wieland's achievement in *Agathon* is mainly a theoretical

one. His novel is backward-looking in form, and practically unread-able. Set in Greece in the late classical period, it adopts the techniques of the Heliodoran romance. Structurally it is more like a satirical romance of the seventeenth century than a precursor of *Wilhelm Meister*.

Wieland's failure in this respect is hardly surprising, but the more significant for that. In his early youth a religious enthusiast, in his maturity a representative of the Enlightenment in Germany, and a leading figure at the ducal court of Weimar, Wieland was effectively isolated from his own early development and from society at large. Indeed, it would be difficult to maintain that in the Germany of the period there *was* a society at large. Two factors dominated German life of the period, responsible at once for the great achievements in litera-ture and culture and for its peculiar limitations. In the first instance, it is notable, in contrast to the society of England and France, that Germany, through its system of small courts and independent rulers, all of whom had some degree of patronage, and its free towns which had a tradition of culture and independence, gave opportunities for indi-viduals to rise from the ranks and to acquire intellectual independence. At the same time, as a result of the influence of the Pietistic movements in religious thought and the activity of groups like the Moravian communities which figure in *Wilhelm Meister*, a greater degree of self-consciousness and a deeper concern for completion of the individu-al was fostered than existed in England or France. One typical result of these forces working together and pulling sometimes together and sometimes apart may be seen in the autobiography of Goethe's friend, Jung-Stilling, who grew up from a peasant background to be a univer-sity professor, but who passed through dreadful trials and overcame enormous social and intellectual difficulties during the process. What is notable about Jung-Stilling is the extent to which his sensibility was formed and indeed, misformed, in the process, so that he grew to intellectual maturity unable to relate to any social group and unable to outgrow the conception of a special Providence which gives a grotesque shape to the touching story of his life and work.

Perhaps the clearest illustration of wht the situation was like in Germany in the years between 1756 and 1793 is provided by the account which another friend of Goethe, Karl Moritz, provided in the fictional autobiography which he published between 1785 and 1790, leaving it unfinished at his death three years later. Moritz is particularly impor-tant because he was a significant figure in the development of the organic idea in so far as it affects literature and was elaborated by the Schlegel brothers as a central Romantic doctrine. But Moritz's life

shows no sign of such an idea in terms of concrete achievement, though
the whole consciousness he depicts obviously demands such an idea.
Without it, or without the possibility of its realisation, the life of his
hero, and even his hero's character, remains incomplete and incoherent. The most prominent elements in his hero's life are the elements of
Pietism which he imbibes from his father, whose melancholy and
apparently obsessive religious feelings seem to prevent the development of any proper paternal relation and even destroy his marriage.
Second is Anton's ambition and elevation of soul, which is constantly
forcing him onwards and bringing him into sharp conflict with circumstances and his own social and intellectual inadequacies. Even success
brings him humiliation in a world where achievement must be regis-
tered in terms of approved forms and where every action is open to
comment, every motive to interpretation. The small city, its charity, its
institutions, are a living hell for the sensitive hero.

The theatre impinges on his over-heated imagination as another
world. Suffering bitter self-scorn and self-humiliation, Reiser is unable
to adjust to any situation. The combination of a loveless childhood with
his Pietistic training had at once stunted and over-developed his
personality so that he is quite unable to make use of kindness and
tranquillity. At work on a poem on the Creation, he is tormented by the
task of depicting Chaos, to which his morbid imagination returns again
and again:

He imagined Chaos upheld by a false deceptive structure, which in a
moment turned to dream and illusion; a structure which was far more
beautiful than reality but for that reason unsubstantial and unendur-
ing. A mock sun rose on the horizon and announced a brilliant day.
Under this deceptive influence the bottomless morass became covered with a crust, on which flowers blossomed and springs mur-
mured: suddenly the contending forces worked up from the depths,
the storm roared from the abyss, darkness with all its terrors burst
from its hidden ambush and swallowed up the new-born day in an
awesome grave. . . . With such vast images Reiser's fancy over-
wrought itself in the hours when his mind was a chaos, with no beam
of tranquil light to light it, when the faculties of his mind had lost
their balance and darkness overshadowed his spirit, when the charm
of the actual disappeared and dream and illusion were more prized
than ever, light and truth. . . . Painful struggle and unrest dogged
him at every step. It was this which drove him from the society of
men to garrets and attics, where he often spent his pleasantest hours

in fantastic dreams, and it was this too which inspired in him his irresistible bent for the romantic and theatrical.

In any other country such a state of mind would have been identified as madness. Moritz's lack of ability to relate to himself or to other people consistently can be compared in some respects to the terrible state of mind of Rousseau in his later years, suffering a disorder which has its roots in a life-long inability to reconcile his inner character with his actions, his aspirations with his course of action. But of course, in Germany, Reiser's story was the story of a whole generation, whose psyche finds partial expression in the Storm and Stress movement, to whom the publication of Goethe's *The Sorrows of Young Werther* (1774) was such an important event. Out of this background the new ideas were developed, and developed with almost magical rapidity under enormous psychological and social pressure. What Reiser wanted, and his generation with him, was a world in which the intensely over-excited self-consciousness could find means of fulfilment or could be set at rest.

This is Goethe's achievement in *Werther*. Of course *Werther's* impact in Europe as a whole was as a novel which advocated sensibility rather than attacked it, but the actual weight of the novel comes down against the sentimentalism and morbid self-preoccupation which drives the hero to a pointless and sordid act of suicide. Contemporaries in Germany recognised that *Werther* spoke to them—its appearance was one of the most important events in Anton Reiser's spiritual development. In *Werther* Goethe depicted step by step the development of the consciousness, the hero's clashes with the outside world, his gradual involvement in a futile love relationship, and finally his descent into a mood of complete fatalism and futility. Strictly speaking Werther has no motive for suicide; but at the same time, he has no motive for living. Experience for him has become entirely internalised; even love sends him back on himself, and what he finds there is a frightening hollowness from which self-destruction is the only escape.

Goethe's disapproval of Werther is clear in the conclusion of the novel, but contemporaries might well have been excused for thinking it advocated suicide rather than attacked sentimentalism, for it is written throughout with a degree of understanding and even enthusiasm which seems to belie the severe ending. During the next twenty years Goethe changed greatly until he left his early sentimentalism completely behind. And in this period he worked steadily at a new novel which was to give complete expression to his new attitude, which recorded his own abandonment of Wertherism and pointed the way forward. This was *Wilhelm Meister's Apprenticeship* (1785–96), which not only depicts a new sensibility but presents a new fictional structure, in which the treatment of internal experience can be reconciled with a representation of external reality. This one novel, in fact, is a revolution in itself, not wholly successful, it is true, but certainly a revolution complete.

The originality of *Wilhelm Meister* consists in the fact that it is the first novel successfully constructed around a process of development in a central character. The importance of this as a pattern is indicated not only in the fact that it is the first of a series of *Bildungsromane* but also that the balance of internal action and external event that Goethe struck out here is basically that which dominates the fiction of the following century. The central action of the novel relates to a series of quasi-picaresque adventures in which the hero is engaged. Wilhelm falls in love, is apparently betrayed and disappointed in Book I. At the same time he conveniently relates his earlier history for the benefit of his actress-mistress. In subsequent Books Wilhelm sets out to travel in the interests of his father's business, falls in with a troop of actors and fulfils his youthful ambition of acting, directing and writing for the theatre, firstly at the castle of a count, later with the company of his friend Serlo. Later he comes to know the nobleman Lothario and the various important characters who live with him, particularly Jarno and the Abbé, and learns that they have previously affected his fate at important moments. He learns that they all belong to a secret society which interests itself in supervising the development of promising youths, that they have not only guided his progress so far but have entered into negotiations with his family firm for the purchase of large estates which he will supervise. The novel ends with his betrothal to Natalie, who has haunted his imagination as the ideal woman since an earlier chance meeting and who now is revealed as sister to Lothario, sister-in-law to the Count, and to the mysterious Felix whose path has often crossed Wilhelm's during his time with the theatre company.

This bare framework is filled out in an astonishingly skilful manner by reference to Wilhelm's intellectual development and by the series of complex and semi-allegorical relationships with a wide range of characters. The idea of the theatre is of great importance and the plays of Shakespeare, and particularly *Hamlet*, are of prime importance in the middle sections. Wilhelm's attraction to the theatre stems from the fact that it provides him with a second dimension of existence in which the central difficulty of his life can be solved. This derives from the fact that as a son of a burgher, aspiring to the kind of all-round, personal development that can only be acquired in the public life of the aristocracy, he is doomed to frustration. The desire for self-development is the central spring of Wilhelm's character and what governs his interest as the novel's hero. The stage represents a dimension in which he can resolve his frustration and a means of acquiring culture for the society of Germany as a whole. Shakespeare is important because his works represent another world, more clearly illuminated but as complex as the real one, into which Wilhelm is constantly tempted to withdraw himself. Hamlet preoccupies him because according to his own analysis, he is out of step with his surroundings, unable to respond as they require, cursed with an over-excited self-consciousness which prevents action, and yet dragged on towards involvement by a tragic Fate.

Wilhelm learns eventually, under the tutelage of Jarno and the Abbé, that his fixation with the theatre has been a passing phase and that he has no lasting or substantial attraction to and talent for the theatre. His sphere of action will lie rather with the real world, in which he will be able to act wholly, achieving coherent expression of his complete character in action, unlike his friend and relation by marriage, the burgher Werner, who is drawn more and more into the one-sided world of commerce. Other characters help to fill out our understanding of this central action of Wilhelm's development rather than being of importance in their own right. In the first instance Mariane, Wilhelm's early love, is important, who dies as a result of his mis-informed desertion and leaves him a son. The actress Philine, to whom he is later attracted, seems to represent the unstable state of his mind rather than being of importance in herself. The masculine Aurelie, dying for love of Lothario, Serlo's sister, the over-efficient Therese, whom Wilhelm almost marries but who actually marries her earlier lover Lothario, the Countess, and even Natalie herself, represent different kinds of character in response to love situations and to the circumstances of social life. Detached from the action altogether are the adventures of Natalie's aunt, which are narrated in the inset, 'Confessions of a Fair Saint'. Here Goethe presents us with the course of development which he rightly might have suggested lay behind the development of his own work, but which functions as an alternative, the Pietistic withdrawal from social living. The presence of this as an inserted tale has been criticised, and yet, even in a novel supposedly structured around Wilhelm's development, it has a strong relevance. It is present as an alternative, strong in contemporary society itself but essentially in opposition to the ideas presented in the novel.

Characters who function in a different way are Mignon and the Harper, who are important to some extent in that they affect Wilhelm in his development, rather more in so far as they tell us what his state of mind is at any given time, but also because they are the protagonist and the product of an incestuous union contracted in a society dominated by superstition. Goethe's judgement of the forms of human nature in such situations is expressed in his representation of the Harper and Mignon and in their fate. The madness of the one, the hectic, perverse development of the other, represent almost allegorically his judgement on the society which produced them.

Mignon and the Harper consort, in fact, rather oddly with some of the other characters in the novel, and the manner in which Goethe conceives and develops them is similarly disjointed — *Wilhelm Meister* is by no means as successful in aesthetic terms as it is complete as an intellectual statement. Wilhelm himself, in argument with Serlo, strongly proposes the organic view of art in opposition to the mechanical view associated with the eighteenth century. And clearly this idea informs the novel. But unfortunately it does not penetrate the novel's structure. Its composition is in large part purely mechanical. Generations of readers have objected to the manipulation of action and especially to the idea of the Fellowship which itself is given no adequate psychological or social motivation. Throughout the novel there is a debate concerning the dominance of fate or chance in the world. Goethe would presumably wish to substitute for either the idea of development, and yet he seems able to rest short of the logical conclusion of this idea and settle for a strong element of chance. The secret society has actually been dominating Wilhelm's fate ever since the early days when his father sold his grandfather's collection of pictures, but cannot be related to any process taking place within the hero. The same mechanical quality is apparent in the way in which the action is developed. Schiller complained about the elimination of Mariane, which is clearly necessary on grounds of the plot, but arbitrary. Mignon's extinction is abrupt, and she leaves little trace behind her on the permanent emotions of the characters. Aurelie likewise fades out with the good wishes of Lothario and Wilhelm. Wilhelm himself swops with amazing lack of grace from Therese to Natalie. The change itself is adequately motivated, though rather ungracious, but the whole section at the end of the novel, where couples pair off in different relations is strangely cold. Worrying episodes include the incident of the affair between the Countess, Natalie's sister, arranged by the Baroness and Jarno. What is Jarno's motivation here?

Does it form part of the plan?

The unified plan of *Wilhelm Meister* is unassailable, but its effectiveness in fictional terms is not. Yet this seems to have been an inevitable consequence of two factors, from neither of which Goethe could have escaped. Firstly, there is the fact that in identifying culture with the formal culture achieved by the aristocracy in the eighteenth century he is very much affected by the period in which he lived and by his own character and position at Weimar. But behind this lies the fact that the classes were actually so opposed in the Germany of his day, and that there was no social dimension other than that of the small court or the large estate which would have been the scene of a development such as he had in mind. A second equally important factor was that in the process of development from the state of mind, or sensibility in rebellion that we get in *Werther* Goethe himself had jettisoned important elements which he could not replace. *The Sorrows of Young Werther* has a larger dimension than the simply human. The novel is informed with a romantic assumption that the stuff of human nature is essentially similar to the stuff of the universe, that they are at the deepest level in sympathy and that human society should reflect this reality. In *Wilhelm Meister* Goethe seems to have abandoned this idea. He asserts that the concern of man is not with Nature but with man himself, a view prevalent in the eighteenth century and an important part of the Enlightenment attitudes which Rousseau himself had attacked. Werther's central problem was that he was driven by the disorder in his own feelings to reflect on the disorder in the universe and that when he reacted from this to find security in himself, he found instead that hollowness and insecurity which drove him to suicide. Wilhelm has no such problem. Self-consciousness in his case does not go beyond the degree experienced by Hamlet, who never extends his complaints about the state of society and the state of man to question the nature of reality itself.

In abandoning this idea Goethe deprived himself of one of the most important fictional ideas of Romantic literature, which was dominant in the fiction of the nineteenth century and essential for the development of the *Bildungsroman*. He presents the device of the secret society instead of allowing the full authority to natural processes. It is not the law of nature that governs Wilhelm's development but purely casual, human circumstances. What is the problem here is not merely that they are unconvincing, but that they are inadequate even if convincing, because they inhibit the development of the question concerning the nature of experience as a whole. Because of his machinery Goethe's novel withdraws from universality; it becomes merely a means of putting a series of arguments about life rather than an investigation of life in its innermost processes. Consequently it falls short of the achievement of the novel in the period that follows. And yet, without *Wilhelm Meister*, it is difficult to imagine how that development would have taken place. Sir Walter Scott, in this central matter, was farther advanced than Goethe, and was able to inflame the imaginations of a whole generation of novelists and poets in Europe, in a way that Goethe could not. And yet when novelists of the 1830s and 1840s faced the central task which Scott had failed in—the adaptation of the Romantic vision of man to contemporary reality—then they looked back to Goethe, who to a very great extent had solved the problem of the nineteenth century before it began.

Bibliography

This select bibliography consists of a series of lists of primary texts relating to the contents of each chapter, followed by a general list of secondary material. It is not directed to the specialist but aims to suggest further reading within the framework of argument contained in the text.

I

Abravanel, J. (Leone Ebreo), *The Philosophy of Love*, tr. F. Fredeberg-Seeley and J. A. Barnes (1937)
Alemán, M., *Guzmán de Alfarache* (1599–1604)
Anon, *Amadis de Gaula* (1508)
   Lazarillo de Tormes (1554)
   La Tragicomedia de Calisto y Melibea (1499 and 1502)
Ariosto, L., *Orlando furioso* (1516)
Avellaneda, A. F. de, *Segundo Tomo del Ingenioso Hidalgo Don Quixote* (1614)
Boiardo, M. M., *Orlando innamorato* (1487)
Cervantes, Miguel de, *Don Quixote* (1605 and 1615)
   La Galatea (1585)
   Novelas Ejemplares (1613)
   Persiles y Sigismunda (1617)
Delicado, F., *La Lozaña andaluza* (1528)
D'Urfé, H. de, *L'Astrée* (1607–27)
Espinel, V., *Vida de Marcos de Obregon* (1618)
Galba, M. J. dé and Joanot Martorell, *Tirante lo Blanc* (1490)
Gil Polo, G., *Diana enamoranda* (1564)

Grimmelshausen, J. J. C., von, *The Adventurous Simplicissimus* (1669); tr. H. Weissenborn and L. Macdonald (1963)

Heliodorus, *The Aethiopian Romance* (3rd C. A.d.)

La Salle, A. de, *Le Petit Jehan de Saintré* (1456)

Martorell, J., and Martin, Joan de Galba, *Tirante lo Blanc* (1490)

Montemayor, J. de, *Los siete libros de la Diana* (1559)

Quevedo y Villegas, F. G. de, *La historia de la vida del Buscón* (1626)

Segura, J. de, *Proceso de cartas de amores* (1548)

Sidney, Sir P., *Arcadia* (1590)

Tasso, T., *Discourses on the Heroic Poem*, tr. M. Cavalchini and I. Samuel (1873)

    Gerusalemme liberata (1575)

Villega, A. de, 'Historia del Abencerraje y la hermosa Jarifa', in *Inventario* (1565)

Yañez, J. A., *Alonso, mozo des muchos amos* (1624 and 1626)

II

Barclay, J., *Argenis* (1621)

    Euphormionis Satyricon (1603–7)

Calprenède, G. de C. de la, *Cassandre* (1644–50)

    Cléopatre (1647–56)

    Pharamond (1661–70)

Descartes, R., *Discours de la Méthode* (1637)

    Traité des passions de l'âme (1649)

Lannel, J. de, *Le Roman Satyrique* (1624)

Le Petit, C., *L'Heure du berger . . .* (1662)

Le Roy, M., Sieur de Gomberville, *Discours des Vertus de l'Histoire* (1620)

    Polexandre (1637)

Préchac, J. de, *Desordres de la bassette* (1682)

Scarron, P., *Nouvelles tragi-comiques* (1655)

    Le Romant comique (1651)

Scudéry, M. de, *Clélie* (1654–60)

    Ibrahim (1641)

    Le Grand Cyrus (1649–53)

Sorel, C., *Le Berger Extravagant* (1627)

    La Bibliothèque française (1664)

    La Connoissance des bons livres (1671)

Sorel, C. (*cont.*)
   L'Histoire comique de Francion (1623)
   Polyandre (1643)
Vergne, G. J. de la, *Lettres Portugaises* (1669)
Viau, T. de, *Fragments d'un roman comique* (*c.* 1620)

III

Asse, E. (ed.), *Lettres de la Présidente Ferrand au Baron de Breteuil*
   (1880)
Bunyan, J., *Grace Abounding* (1666)
   The Holy War (1682)
   The Life and Death of Mr. Badman (1680)
   The Pilgrim's Progress (1678)
Challes, R., *L'Histoire de l'admirable Don Quichotte*, VI (1711)
   Les Illustres francoises (1713)
Courtilz de Sandras, G. de, *Mémoires de M. de d'Artagnan* (1700)
Charnes, J.-A., Abbé de, *Conversations sur la Critique de la Princesse
   de Clèves* (1679)
Fénelon, F. de S. de la Mothe-, *Télémaque* (1699)
Furetière, A., *Roman bourgeois* (1666)
Hamilton, A., *Mémoires du Comte de Grammont* (1673)
Lafayette, M-M., Comtesse de, *La Princesse de Clèves* (1678)
   La Princesse de Montpensier (1662)
   Zaïde (1670)
L'Hermite, T., *Le Page Disgracie* (1643 and 1664)
Le Sage, A. R., *Le Diable boiteux* (1707)
   L'Histoire de Gil Blas (1715, 1724 and 1735)
   Nouvelles avantures de Don Quichotte (1704)
Perrault, P., *Critique du livre Don Quichotte* (1679)
Saint-Martin, F. de, *L'Histoire de l'admirable Don Quichotte*, tr. in
   four vols (1677–8)
   Continuation, Vol V to the above (1697)
Segrais, J. R. de, *Les Nouvelles Francoises* (1657)
Valincour, J.-H. du Trousset de, *Lettres . . . sur . . . la Princesse de
   Clèves* (1678)
Vischard, C. Abbé de Saint-Réal, *De l'Usage de l'histoire* (1671)
   Dom Carlos (1672)
   La Conjuration . . . contre . . . Venise (1674)

IV

Crébillon, C. P. J. de, *Les Egarements du coeur et de l'esprit* (1736)
    Le Sopha (1745)
Defoe, D., *Captain Singleton* (1720)
    Colonel Jack (1722)
    Moll Flanders (1720)
    Robinson Crusoe (1719)
    Roxana (1724)
Duclos, C. P., *Les Confessions de Comte de* *** (1742)
    Histoire de Madame de Luz (1741)
Fielding, H., *Adventures of Joseph Andrews* (1742)
    Amelia (1751)
    Jonathan Wild the Great (1743)
    Journal of a Voyage to Lisbon (1755)
    Shamela (1741)
    Tom Jones (1749)
Haywood, E., *Betsy Thoughtless* (1751)
    The History of Jemmy and Jenny Jessamy (1753)
Manley, M., *New Atlantis* (1709)
Marivaux, P. C. de Chamblain de, *Les Aventures de* *** (1713)
    Le Paysan Parvenu (1735–6)
    Pharsamon (1737)
    La Vie de Marianne (1731–41)
    La Voiture embourbée (1714)
    Le Télémaque travesti (1736)
Mézières, M.-J. Laboras de, dame de Riccoboni, *Lettres de Mistriss Fanni Butlerd* (1757)
Prévost, d'Exiles, A. F., *Le Doyen de Killerine* (1735–40)
    Le Philosophe anglais ou l'histoire de M. Cleveland (1732–9)
    Mémoires d'un homme de qualité (1728–3)
Richardson, S., *Clarissa Harlowe* (1747–8)
    Pamela (1740 and 1741)
    Sir Charles Grandison (1754)
Smollett, T., *Ferdinand Count Fathom* (1753)
    Humphrey Clinker (1771)
    Peregrine Pickle (1751)
    Roderick Random (1748)
    Sir Lancelot Greaves (1760–62)
Swift, J., *A Tale of a Tub* (1704)
    Gulliver's Travels (1726)

Tencin, C.-A. de, *Mémoires du comte de Comminge* (1735)

V

Austen, J., *Emma* (1815)
   Mansfield Park (1814)
   Northanger Abbey (1818)
   Persuasion (1818)
   Pride and Prejudice (1813)
   Sense and Sensibility 1811)
Bretonne, R. de la, *Le Paysan Perverti* (1775)
Burney, F., *Camilla* (1796)
   Cecilla (1782)
   Evelina (1778)
   The Wanderer (1814)
Diderot, D., *Eloge de Richardson* (1761)
   Jacques le fataliste (1771–73)
   Le Neveu de Rameau (1761–72)
   La Religieuse (1760)
Chateaubriand, F.-R. de, *Atala* (1801)
   René (1805)
Coleridge, S. T. *Biographia Literaria* (1817)
Constant, de Rebecque, H.-B., *Adolphe* (1816)
Goethe, J. W. von, *Elective Affinities* (1809)
   The Sorrows of Werter (1774)
   Wilhelm Meister (1795–6)
Goldsmith, O., *The Vicar of Wakefield* (1766)
Johnson, S., *Rasselas* (1759)
Laclos, C. de, *Les Liaisons dangereuses* (1782)
Louvet de Couvray, J.-B., *Les Amours du Chevalier de Faublas* (1789–90)
Mackenzie, H., *Julia de Roubigné* (1777)
   The Man of Feeling (1771)
   The Man of the World (1773)
Richter, J.-P., *Flower, Fruit and Thorn Pieces* (1796–7)
   Hesperus (1795)
   Titan (1800–3)
Rousseau, J.-P., *Emile* (1762)
   La Nouvelle Héloise (1761)

Schiller, F., *Don Carlos* (1787)
    Wallenstein (1798–9)
Schlegel, K. W. F. von, *Lucinde* (1799)
    Dialogues on Poetry and Literary Aphorisms, tr. E. Behler and R. Struc (1968)
Senancour, E. P., de, *Obermann* (1804)
Sterne, L., *Sentimental Journey* (1768)
    Tristram Shandy (1760–67)
Voltaire, F.-M. A., *Candide* (1759)
    L'Ingénu (1767)
    La Princesse de Babylone (1768)
Wieland, C. M., *The Adventures of Don Sylvio de Rosalva* (1763)
    Agathon (1766–7 and 1794)
Wordsworth, W., *The Prelude* (1805)

GENERAL

Adam, A., *Histoire de la Litterature Française du xviie Siècle* (1949–56)
Allen, W., *The English Novel* (1954)
Alter, R., *Rogue's Progress* (1964)
Auerbach, E., *Mimesis*, tr. W. P. Trask (1953)
Avalle-Arce, J. B. and E. C. Riley, *Suma Cervantina* (1973)
Baker, E. A. *The History of the English Novel* (1929)
Bardon, M., *'Don Quichotte' en France au xviie et au xviiie siècle* (1931)
Bray, R., *La Formation de la doctrine classique en France* (1931)
Bruel, A., *Romans Français du Moyen Age* (1934)
Brunetière, F., *Etudes critiques sur l'histoire de la littérature francaise* (1891)
Champfleury (Jules Husson), *La Réalisme* (1857)
Chandler, F. W., *The Literature of Roguery* (1907)
Church, R., *Growth of the English Novel* (1951)
Coulet, H., *Le Roman jusqu'à la Révolution* (1968)
Dallas, D. F., *Le Roman Français de 1600 à 1680* (1932)
Deloffre, F., *La nouvelle en France à l'Age classique* (1967)
Godenne, R., *Histoire de la Nouvelle Française au xviie et xviiie siècle* (1970)
Goldman, L., *Le Dieu caché*
    Pour une sociologie du roman (1964)
    Recherches dialectiques (1958)

Hainsworth, G., *Les 'Novelas Ejemplares' de Cervantes en France au xviie siècle* (1933)

Hazard, P., *The European Mind 1680—1715*, tr. L. May

Kahler, E., *The Inward Turn of Narrative* (1970)

Kettle, A., *An Introduction to the English Novel* (1951)

Kellog, R. and R. Scholes, *The Nature of Narrative* (1966)

Le Breton, A., *Le Roman Français au xviie siècle au xviiie siècle* (1912)

Lukács, G., *Goethe and his Age*, tr. R. Anchor (1968)

    The Historical Novel, tr. H. and S. Mitchell (1962)

    Studies in European Realism (Universal Library, 1964)

    The Theory of the Novel, tr. A. Bostock (1971)

    Writer and Critic, tr. A. Kahn (1970)

Magendie, M., *Le Roman Français au xviie siècle* (1932)

May, G. *Le Dilemme du Roman au xviiie siècle* (1963)

Menendez Pelayo, *Origenes de la Novela* (Espaso-Calpe, 1946)

Miller, S., *The Picaresque Novel* (1967)

Morillot, P., *Le Roman en France depuis 1610 jusqu'à nos jours* (1892)

Mornet, D., Introduction to *La Nouvelle Héloise* (1925)

Mylne, V., *The Eighteenth Century French Novel* (1965)

Parker, A. A. *Literature and the Delinquent . . . 1599—1753* (1967)

Paulson, R., *Satire and the Novel in Eighteenth Century England* (1967)

Ratner, M., *Theory and Criticism of the Novel in France from L'Astrée to 1750* (1938)

Reynier, G., *Le Roman Réaliste au xviie siècle* (1914)

    Le Roman Sentimental Avant L'Astrée (1908)

    Les Origines du roman réaliste (1912)

Richetti, J. R., *Popular Fiction Before Richardson* (1969)

Riley, E. C. and J. B. Avalle-Arce, *Suma Cervantina* (1973)

Scholes, R. and R. Kellog, *The Nature of Narrative* (1966)

Showalter, E., *The Evolution of the French Novel 1641—1782* (1972)

Stemmler, T., *English Theories of the Novel* (1970)

Stevenson, L, *The English Novel* (1960)

Tomkins, J. M. S., *The Popular Novel in England, 1700—1800* (1932)

Vinaver, E., *The Rise of Romance* (1971)

Warren, A., and R. Wellek, *Theory of Literature* (1949)

Watt, I., *The Rise of the Novel* (1957)

Wellek, R. and A. Warren, *Theory of Literature* (1949)

Wellek, R., *Concepts of Criticism* (1963)

    Discriminations (1970)

Williams, I. M., *Novel and Romance, a documentary record, 1700–1800* (1970)

The Realist Novel in England (1974)

Sir Walter Scott on novelists and fiction (1968)

Wilmotte, M., *Les Origenes du roman en France* (1940)

Index of Names

Index of Titles